CRITICAL RESPONSE TO BRAM STOK
ER

SENF, CAROL A

PR6037.T61726 1993

THE
CRITICAL RESPONSE
TO BRAM STOKER

Recent Titles in
Critical Responses in Arts and Letters

THE
CRITICAL RESPONSE
TO BRAM STOKER

Edited by
CAROL A. SENF

Critical Responses in Arts and Letters, Number 9
Cameron Northouse, Series Adviser

GREENWOOD PRESS
Westport, Connecticut • London

Library of Congress Cataloging-in-Publication Data

The Critical response to Bram Stoker / edited by Carol A. Senf.
p. cm.—(Critical responses in arts and letters, ISSN
1057-0993 ; no. 9)
Includes bibliographical references and index.
ISBN 0-313-28527-6 (alk. paper)
1. Stoker, Bram, 1847-1912—Criticism and interpretation.
2. Horror tales, English—History and criticism. 3. Dracula, Count
(Fictitious character). 4. Vampires in literature. I. Senf, Carol
A. II. Series.
PR6037.T617Z6 1994
823'.8—dc20   93-28055

British Library Cataloguing in Publication Data is available.

Library of Congress Catalog Card Number: 93-28055
ISBN: 0-313-28527-6
ISSN: 1057-0993

First published in 1993

Greenwood Press, 88 Post Road West, Westport, CT 06881
An imprint of Greenwood Publishing Group, Inc.

Printed in the United States of America

The paper used in this book complies with the
Permanent Paper Standard issued by the National
Information Standards Organization (Z39.48-1984).

10 9 8 7 6 5 4 3

Copyright Acknowledgments

The editor and publisher gratefully acknowledge permission for use of the following material:

William Patrick Day, *In the Circles of Fear and Desire: A Study of Gothic Fantasy*. Chicago: The University of Chicago Press, 1985, 143-49. Copyright (c) 1985 by The University of Chicago Press.

Howard Phillips Lovecraft, *Supernatural Horror in Literature*. 1932; rpt. New York: Dover, 1973, p. 78.

Joseph S. Bierman, "*Dracula*: Prolonged Childhood Illness and the Oral Triad," *American Imago* 29 (1972), 186-98.

Stephen D. Arata, "The Occidental Tourist: *Dracula* and the Anxiety of Reverse Colonization," *Victorian Studies* 33 (1990), 621-45. Reprinted from *Victorian Studies* by permission of the Indiana University Board of Trustees.

Reprinted by permission of the publishers from *Woman and the Demon: The Life of a Victorian Myth* by Nina Auerbach, Cambridge, Mass.: Harvard University Press, Copyright (c) 1982 by the President and Fellows of Harvard College.

Daniel Pick, "'Terrors of the Night': *Dracula* and 'degeneration' in the late nineteenth century," *The Critical Quarterly* 30 (1988), 83-85.

Carol A. Senf, "*The Lady of the Shroud*: Stoker's Successor to *Dracula*," *Essays in Arts and Sciences* (1990), 82-96.

Daniel Farson, *The Man Who Wrote Dracula: A Biography of Bram Stoker*. New York: St. Martin's Press, 1975, 217-24.

Gregory A. Waller, *The Living and the Undead: From Stoker's Dracula to Romero's Dawn of the Dead*. Chicago, Ill.: University of Illinois Press, Copyright (c) 1986 by the Board of Trustees of the University of Illinois.

Material on *The Jewel of Seven Stars* and *The Man*: Reprinted with permission of Twayne Publishers, an imprint of Macmillan Publishing Company,

Contents

Contents

Series Foreword

Critical Responses in Arts and Letters is designed to present a documentary history of highlights in the critical reception to the body of work of writers and artists and to individual works that are generally considered to be of major importance. The focus of each volume in this series is basically historical. The introductions to each volume are themselves brief histories of the critical response an author, artist, or individual work has received. This response is then further illustrated by reprinting a strong representation of the major critical reviews and articles that have collectively produced the author's, artist's, or work's critical reputation.

The scope of *Critical Responses in Arts and Letters* knows no chronological or geographical boundaries. Volumes under preparation include studies of individuals from around the world and in both contemporary and historical periods.

Each volume is the work of an individual editor, who surveys the entire body of criticism on a single author, artist, or work. The editor then selects the best material to depict the critical response received by an author or artist over his/her entire career. Documents produced by the author or artist may also be included when the editor finds that they are necessary to a full understanding of the materials at hand. In circumstances where previous, isolated volumes of criticism on a particular individual or work exist, the editor carefully selects material that better reflects the nature and directions of the critical response over time.

In addition to the introduction and the documentary section, the editor of each volume is free to solicit new essays on areas that may not have been adequately dealt with in previous criticism. Also, for volumes on living writers and artists, new interviews may be included, again at the discretion of the volume's editor. The volumes also provide a supplementary bibliography and are fully indexed.

While each volume in *Critical Responses to Arts and Letters* is unique, it is also hoped that in combination they form a useful, documentary history of the critical response to the arts, and one that can easily and profitably employed by students and scholars.

Cameron Northouse

Acknowledgments

This book, which has occupied my thoughts and my word processor for the past year and a half, would not have been possible without the help of numerous people to whom I can now express my appreciation.

First of all, I am grateful to the numerous other people who have studied Stoker. I owe a particular debt of gratitude to the following people: Margaret Carter and Clive Leatherdale for their work with *Dracula*; to Richard Dalby for his bibliographic study of Stoker's works; to Phyllis A. Roth, whose critical study is the only one to examine everything Stoker wrote; and also to Harry Ludlam and Daniel Farson for their biographies of Bram Stoker. Your excellent pioneering works inspired me to take Stoker seriously. If Stoker and his works remain elusive to readers, these writers cannot be held responsible.

To the many other contemporary scholars and critics--those whose works are reprinted here as well as all those others whose serious treatment of Stoker's works may have influenced me at one time and encouraged my own thinking on Stoker--I am also extremely thankful. Your works have provided both information and inspiration.

Thanks are also due to my colleagues and students at the Georgia Institute of Technology, who offered me support and encouragement on this project. Special thanks are due to Ken Knoespel, Director of the School of Literature, Communication, and Culture, who freed me of many committee responsibilities; to Ione Sibley, Assistant to the Director, who cheerfully did more than she was asked; and to the staff in Information Exchange at the Georgia Tech Library. They were willing to track down obscure references, to check dates and figures, and to locate materials from all around the country. Without the cheerful cooperation of Kathy Tomajko, Nancy Drury, Katharine Calhoun, and Ann Campbell, this project would probably have never gotten off my desk.

While the help of professional colleagues is easy to discern in the finished work, the help of other individuals may not be so obvious. Thanks also go to my friends and family and to numerous other people who have no connection to scholary activities but who were nonetheless understanding when I declined to help with Cub Scouts or PTA because of a publication deadline. The most special thanks go to my husband Jay and my sons Jeremy and Andy. They tolerated spaghetti on numerous evenings when they might have preferred more variety in their diet; they were willing to play second fiddle to Bram Stoker on numerous occasions; they walked the dog on rainy mornings; and they also accepted my preoccupation with Stoker as well as my impatience when things didn't fall right into place.

I am also grateful to the advice and support of series advisor, Cameron Northouse, who offered guidance and more than a little moral support one December day when a publication deadline and jury duty had me near hysteria, and to Greenwood Press, who gave me the opportunity to put all this material on Stoker together. Whatever errors or omissions a reader may find in the following volume are certainly not the fault of any of the people I have mentioned or anyone else that I may have failed to name.

Chronology of Stoker's Life 1847-1912

1847

Abraham Stoker is born on November 24 in Dublin, the third of seven children of Abraham Stoker (a clerk in the Civil Service, employed at Dublin Castle) and his wife Charlotte. Known throughout his life as Bram, he will spend the next seven years of his life as an invalid.

1849

A brother Tom is born in August when Bram is twenty-one months old.

1854

Bram's youngest brother George is born on July 20. Bram leaves his bed and walks for the first time. Whatever condition led to his invalidism will not return, and Bram will be blessed with robust health for most of his life.

1864

Stoker enters Trinity College, Dublin.

1866

Stoker becomes University Athlete and sees Henry Irving perform at the Theatre Royal, Dublin. (The twenty-nine year-old actor, a member of Miss Louisa Herbert's company, plays Captain Absolute in Sheridan's *The Rivals*.)

1868

Stoker graduates Trinity with honors in science and enters civil service at Dublin Castle.

1871

Stoker becomes drama critic for the *Dublin Mail*. His first review (unsigned) appears in November. His parents and sisters move to the Continent where they hope to live cheaply and pay off debts.

1872

Stoker delivers an address, "The Necessity for Political Honesty," at Trinity College; the work, which was published in Dublin by James Charles & Son, is Stoker's first signed work.

1874

Stoker visits Paris and takes notes that he will later use in "The Burial of the Rats."

1875

Stoker's first horror story, "The Chain of Destiny" appears as a four-part serial in the weekly magazine, *Shamrock*.

1876

Stoker's father dies in Naples at age seventy-seven. Stoker first meets Henry Irving and goes into hysterics on hearing Irving recite Thomas Hood's poem, "The Dream of Eugene Aram."

1877

Stoker resigns as drama critic to work on book for the clerks of the Petty Sessions.

1878

Stoker marries Florence Balcombe, third daughter of Lieutenant-Colonel James Balcombe. Florence, who was known for her beauty, had been courted by Oscar Wilde. Stoker assumes duties as acting manager of the Lyceum Theatre and helps his younger brother George prepare *With the Unspeakables* about his experiences as a doctor in the Turkish army during the Russo-Turkish War. Stoker will later incorporate the atrocious conditions that George witnessed first-hand into the novels that feature Turkey or Turkish subjects.

1879

Stoker's first book, *The Duties of Clerks of Petty Sessions in Ireland,* is published in Dublin by J. Falconer. His only child, a son named Noel Thornley Stoker, is born.

1882

Stoker's first work of fiction, a collection of short stories called *Under the Sunset* is published in London by Sampson Low, Marston, Searle, and Ribington and is dedicated to his son. Stoker receives the Bronze Medal of the Royal Humane Society for his attempted rescue of a suicide.

1883

Stoker organizes the first American tour of Irving's company. During his visit, he studies American customs, research that he will later use in a number of novels that feature American characters, American settings, or both.

1885

Stoker delivers lecture on the United States at London Institution.

1886

Stoker's lecture on the United States is published in London as *A Glimpse of America* by Sampson Low, Marston & Co.

1887

Stoker returns to United States to plan tour.

1889

The Snake's Pass is serialized in the *People.*

1890

Stoker's first novel, *The Snake's Pass* is published in London by Sampson Low, Marston & Co.

1893

Stoker spends Cruden Bay holiday working on *Dracula.*

1894

The Watter's Mou', one of the many works to feature Stoker's beloved Cruden Bay, is published in Westminster by Archibald Constable.

1895

The Shoulder of Shasta, one of the novels that features both American characters and American setting, is published in Westminster by Archibald Constable. Henry Irving and William Thornley Stoker, Bram Stoker's oldest brother, are knighted by Queen Victoria. The Lyceum Theatre Company tours the United States.

1896

Stoker continues to work on *Dracula* while on vacation at Cruden Bay.

1897

Stoker's best-known work, *Dracula*, is published in Westminster by Archibald Constable. In May, a dramatic version is acted at the Lyceum to establish copyright and protect the drama from piracy.

1898

Stoker's only historical novel, *Miss Betty,* is published in London by C. Arthur Pearson Limited. *Miss Betty* is dramatized on January 31. A fire in the Lyceum storage area destroys scenes from forty-four plays.

1899

A collection of short stories, *Snowbound: The Record of a Theatrical Touring Party*, is published in London by Collier.

1900

Irving signs the Lyceum over to syndicate.

1901

Charlotte Stoker dies at age eighty-three. The Lyceum Theatre Company tours the United States.

1902

The Mystery of the Sea is published in London by William Heinemann. The dramatic version is presented at Lyceum on March 17. The Lyceum closes its doors.

1903

The Jewel of Seven Stars is published in London by William Heinemann. Ellen Terry leaves Irving's company.

1904

Irving's company embarks on its last tour of the United States.

1905

The Man is published in London by William Heinemann. Henry Irving dies on October 13 while on provincial tour.

1906

Personal Reminiscences of Henry Irving is published in London by William Heinemann.

1908

Lady Athlyne is published in London by William Heinemann. A slightly abridged version of *The Man* is published in New York by Cupples and Leon under the title *The Gates of Life*.

1909

The Lady of the Shroud is published in London by William Heinemann.

1910

Famous Impostors is published in London by Sidgwick and Jackson.

1911

Bram Stoker's oldest brother, William Thornley Stoker, is made a baronet. *The Lair of the White Worm* is published in London by William Rider and Son, Ltd.

1912

Bram Stoker dies on April 20. The death certificate lists cause of death as exhaustion.[1]

1914

Florence Stoker edits the stories her husband was preparing when he died and includes a previously unpublished story known as "Dracula's Guest." The collection, *Dracula's Guest--And Other Weird Stories* is published in London by George Routledge & Sons, Ltd.

NOTE

[1] One of his biographers, along with other critics, suggests that Stoker's death may have resulted from tertiary syphilis, the result of a sexual encounter with a prostitute. Daniel Farson. *The Man Who Wrote Dracula: A biography of Bram Stoker.* (London: Michael Joseph), 234.

Introduction

Bram Stoker and I share an interest in the monstrous, especially where the monstrous intersects with what is perfectly normal and ordinary; a concern with gender, race, and ethnicity (though Stoker was horrified by the increasing power of groups that had previously been marginalized); a love of theater; and a preoccupation with narration, especially the different ways that stories are told.

I first "met" Stoker in 1970 when I was a young high school teacher. After I had discussed different methods of narration, a student asked me whether I had ever read *Dracula*, which he characterized correctly as a variation on the epistolary novel. Later, when I returned to graduate school and was thinking of a thesis topic, I again turned to *Dracula*, though the thesis (revised and later published by Bowling Green as *The Vampire in Nineteenth-Century Fiction* [1] examined a number of works besides Stoker's best-known novel.

During the research phase of this project and several related shorter projects, I discovered quite a bit about Bram Stoker. Although he has come to be identified as the writer of *Dracula* (the entry on *Dracula* in *The Oxford Companion to English Literature* is three times longer than the entry on its creator),[2] Stoker wrote eighteen books--novels, romances, and works of nonfiction--plus numerous articles and short stories.

Dracula has received more attention than Stoker's other works for several reasons. Recent criticism explores the way it touches on turn-of-the-century anxieties about the British imperial presence as well as on anxieties about gender relationships and questions of identity. In addition, Stoker appears to have spent more time on *Dracula* than he did on many other works. Joseph S. Bierman, who studied Stoker's notes for the novel, which are held in the Collection of the Philip H. & A.S.W. Rosenbach Foundation in Philadelphia, observes that the "earliest date on any manuscript is 8 March 1890"[3] seven years before *Dracula* was published. Although some of Stoker's other works--including *The Snake's Pass, The Jewel of Seven Stars, The Mystery of the Sea*, and *Famous Impostors*-- also show the evidence of factual research, many others appear to have been tossed off during vacations from his rigorous work with

Henry Irving's Lyceum Theatre or in his later years when Stoker was suffering from exhaustion or from what another biographer (and Stoker's grand-nephew), Daniel Farson, describes as tertiary syphilis.[4]

While I share the critical consensus--summarized by Kenneth W. Fair, Jr., who observes that the other novels do not equal "*Dracula* in their imaginative force"[5]--I also believe that many of Stoker's other works deserve critical attention either because they help us to understand *Dracula* or because they are interesting in their own right. In fact, although Stoker's style and characterization has frequently received negative criticism, most of what he wrote deserves further study. My particular favorites are the ones that Phyllis A. Roth characterizes as tales of horror. (Her excellent psychoanalytic study, which was published by Twayne in 1982, is the only critical study of the entire Stoker canon.) These tales include--in addition to *Dracula* (1897)--*The Jewel of Seven Stars* (1903), *The Lady of the Shroud* (1909), *The Lair of the White Worm* (1911), as well as numerous short stories. Of the romances--*The Snake's Pass* (1891), *The Watter's Mou'* (1894), *The Shoulder of Shasta* (1895), *Miss Betty* (1898), *The Man* (1905), and *Lady Athlyne* (1908), which were generally admired by Stoker's contemporaries, I find only *The Man* and *Lady Athlyne* genuinely interesting. In fact, I share Roth's critical appraisal that *The Man* is his "most leisurely and sophisticated romance" and that "with regard to characterization, it is his most painstaking and satisfying novel."[6]

Furthermore, understanding Stoker provides insights into his own time. His fascination with technological development as well as his concern that the traditional powers of civilized Northern European men were being eroded and his fear that morality was being destroyed are characteristic of his age. In addition, although Stoker's concern with gender, race, and ethnicity is important to our understanding of English culture at the turn of the century, these topics are--perhaps even more importantly--subjects that continue to concern us a century later as we wend our way toward the twenty-first century.

My objectives in putting together the accompanying anthology of criticism are threefold--to provide readers with easy access to criticism of Stoker's work (often a difficult and frustrating task since much of the commentary by Stoker's contemporaries is located in late nineteenth and early twentieth-century journals and magazines); to put *Dracula* into the context of Stoker's other works; and to interest both readers and scholars in Stoker's other works (another difficult task since many of these works are no longer in print or are available only in truncated paperback editions). Finally, since so much of what Stoker wrote is currently out of print, the following brief introduction provides plot summaries of his novels.

The critical reception to Stoker has been mixed--as the following materials indicate. While *Dracula* has consistently received more enthusiastic response than Stoker's other works, the period between Stoker's death in 1912 and 1972 saw little interest even in *Dracula*. There were, of course, film versions of the novel including F.W. Murnau's *Nosferatu, the Vampire* (1922); Tod Browning's *Dracula*, starring Bela Lugosi (1931), and literally hundreds of others that are loosely based on the novel.[7] However, these films were regarded as popular and received relatively little critical or scholarly attention.

Furthermore, critics in the last quarter of the twentieth century tend to have a different view of Stoker than did his contemporaries, who saw him primarily in his capacity as business manager for Henry Irving's Lyceum Theatre rather than as a novelist. Therefore, to provide a critical response to Bram Stoker, the following book includes a number of contemporary reviews of *Personal Reminiscences of Henry Irving* (1906) as well as critical responses to *Famous Impostors* (1910), which was also widely reviewed--albeit not especially favorably--by Stoker's contemporaries even though modern readers and critics will probably be less interested in these works than they are in his novels. *Personal Reminiscences*--as Stoker's contemporaries indicate--suffers from the same inability to cull extraneous details as *Dracula* and is too anecdotal to provide a thorough understanding of Irving (and for our purposes not personal enough to reveal much about the relationship between Stoker and Irving). *Famous Impostors*, on the other hand, is interesting primarily because of the light it sheds on Stoker's ongoing interest in questions of identity, a topic that appears in his best fiction.

This book is arranged chronologically by title to enable readers to gain a historical perspective of criticism of each work. As the title indicates, this book examines the critical response to Bram Stoker. Therefore, it ignores a major part of what Stoker wrote--including his early unsigned drama reviews for the *Dublin Mail*, periodical material, and his first full-length published work, *The Duties of Clerks of Petty Sessions in Ireland*, because these works were not reviewed. It also ignores the book that he wrote with his brother George, *With the Unspeakables* (1878), which recounts George's experiences as a doctor with the Turkish army during the Russo-Turkish war.

Moreover, while my goal has been to look at the entirety of Stoker's work, I also include excerpts from several recent articles on *Dracula* though I have deliberately avoided duplicating works found in Margaret L. Carter's excellent anthology of recent criticism, *Dracula: The Vampire and the Critics*, [8] because that work is still readily available. (Other critical material on *Dracula* and on Stoker can be found in Clive Leatherdale's study,[9] which summarizes a number of works on *Dracula* and puts these works into critical perspectives, including social and political, psychoanalytic, and feminist.) Readers who want to know about Stoker's life can find material in two biographical studies by Harry Ludlam and Daniel Farson.[10] In addition, since much of the recent criticism has focused on psychoanalytic material, one can find material on Stoker's life in various critical studies. Finally, information on the various editions of Stoker's work can be found in Richard Dalby's *Bram Stoker: A Bibliography of First Editions*.[11]

UNDER THE SUNSET (1881)

Stoker's first book, *The Duties of Clerks of Petty Sessions in Ireland* (Dublin: J. Falconer, 1879), was not reviewed though Dalby observes that it was for many years "recognized as the standard reference work" (7) for clerks in the Irish civil service. Dalby also cites Stoker's introduction to the work, which refers to the numerous works that he had to consult:

This book has been compiled from all the sources of information at my disposal--Statutes, General Orders, Circulars, Law Opinions, Files of Papers, Registry Books, Returns, etc. The collation of the enormous mass of such, accumulating since 1851 and following the slow growth of the splendid systems now in practice, has been a work of excessive labour. Thousands of documents--entries, briefs, etc.--have been consulted. (Cited by Dalby, 7)

In the introduction, Stoker alludes to his work as a researcher, skills he will continue to use to prepare his fictional works.

His second book, *Under the Sunset* (London: Sampson Low, Marston & Co., 1882), includes the following short stories: "Under the Sunset," "The Rose Prince," "The Invisible Giant," "The Shadow Builder," "How 7 Went Mad," "Lies and Lilies," "The Castle of the King," and "The Wondrous Child." "The Invisible Giant" is modeled on one of Charlotte Stoker's experiences as a girl during the cholera outbreak in Sligo in 1832. She had shared this story with her son while he was still an invalid. Although cholera had claimed thousands of lives in Ireland, the story concludes when "innocence and devotion save the land;"[12] and the other stories often combine horrifying episodes with a dreamlike quality.

All the stories take place in a beautiful country under the sunset that people see only in dreams, and all the stories seem designed to reinforce the behaviors that Stoker saw as admirable. For example, "Lies and Lilies" concludes happily only when Claribel, the youthful protagonist, confesses to her teacher that she had been daydreaming the day before instead of doing her work. "The Rose Prince," which resembles the story of David and Goliath, shows that a brave child can overcome a cruel persecutor. "The Shadow Builder" celebrates a mother's love.

As Douglas Menville notes in his introduction to the 1978 reissue of this book, it "was not an easy book to review: its mood of dreamlike unease was set by the title story" (vi). He concludes his introduction by observing that none of Stoker's other books contain the "eerie, poetic mixture of innocence and evil of *Under the Sunset*" (vii).

Clive Leatherdale describes the collection in the following grim way:

Although each of the constituent tales is self-contained, they all concern themselves with repeated motifs: familial love; the division of the world into Good and Evil; the horrendous punishments meted out to those who sin; the inevitable triumph of Good; and the mysterious boundary between life and death. The oppressive moralizing that pervades them all was a feature common to many nineteenth-century fairy tales, and even the barbarous cruelty that Stoker gratuitously describes was not out of keeping with the mainstream of the genre. (63)

Thus Leatherdale places Stoker's collection of fairy tales firmly into late nineteenth-century culture, and the *Spectator* review, which places the collection in the context of other Victorian fantasy tales, also reminds us of the extent to which Stoker is a man of his time.

More important for our perspective, Leatherdale also suggests a direction that Stoker's other works will take. For example, Stoker will continue to celebrate family love especially in *The Watter's Mou'*, *Miss Betty*, *The Lady of the Shroud*, and *The Lair of the White Worm*. He will also continue to examine the issue of Good and Evil in his future novels. Many of these novels--including *The Snake's Pass*, *The Mystery of the Sea*, and *The Lady of the Shroud*--will address purely human evil while others--including *Dracula*, *The Jewel of Seven Stars*, and *The Lair of the White Worm*--will examine a larger supernatural Evil. Finally, Stoker will continue to be interested in the mysterious boundary between life and death, a boundary that he will examine in *Dracula*, *The Jewel of Seven Stars*, and *The Lair of the White Worm*.

The anthology, which was dedicated to his two-year old son Noel "whose angel doth behold the face of the king" and illustrated by W.V. Cockburn and one of Stoker's former Trinity schoolmates, William Fitzgerald, was reviewed in *Punch*, the *Spectator*, and the *Academy*. For a work by a first-time author, *Under the Sunset* was reasonably well reviewed. *Punch*, which had already established its reputation as the most famous of Victorian comic newspapers, will continue to review Stoker's works including those that include nothing that might be considered comic.

The *Punch* review characterizes the collection as "rather too goody-goody"[13] but is otherwise positive. The response in the late twentieth century is more critical and indicates how the critical reception to the book has changed over the past century. Stoker's contemporaries were inclined to be charmed by the fantasy elements in *Under the Sunset*. However, the response by the physician Joseph S. Bierman, which examines several of the stories along psychoanalytic lines, is more typical of the critical response in the late twentieth century. Bierman looks at two stories--"How 7 Went Mad" and "The Wondrous Child"--as evidence of Stoker's resentment for his younger brothers and his own son.[14] Equally eager to probe the hidden context of these stories for children is Douglas Menville, who wrote an introduction when Newcastle Forgotten Fantasy Library reissued *Under the Sunset* in 1978 and who points out mythological and Christian symbolism as well as occult references in the stories.

A GLIMPSE OF AMERICA (1886)

Based on the impressions that Stoker gained on tour with Irving's company and delivered as a lecture at the London Institution on December 28, 1885, this discussion of American life was later published by Sampson Low, Marston and Company. It was not reviewed though Dalby cites the observation of H.M. Stanley, the explorer, who found in it "more information about America than any other book that had ever been written" (13).

THE SNAKE'S PASS (1890)

This work, which first appeared as a serial story in the *People* and several provincial papers late in 1889, was published the following year in book form. Stoker's first novel is a romantic adventure story with a single narrator, Arthur Severn. A wealthy man, Arthur hears of a fabulous treasure that had been buried by French soldiers in the Snake's Pass, an opening in the mountain that leads down to the sea. The story combines the quest for this treasure with Arthur's love for Norah Joyce, daughter of an Irish farmer. Moreover, it demonstrates Stoker's ability to integrate mythic material with modern characters and interests and his ability to create an interesting landscape (an ability that often goes unnoticed); and it also introduces two distinctly Irish characters: the folksy Andy Sullivan (a horse-car driver and gossip, who provides much of the humor in the story) and the gombeen man (a kind of usurious money lender) Black Murdock. A minor character explains to Arthur (and the reader) what a gombeen man is:

He's a man that linds you a few shillin's or a few pounds whin ye want it bad, and then niver laves ye till he has tuk all ye've got--yer land an' yer shanty an' yer holdin' an' yer money an' yer craps; an' he would take the blood out of yer body if he could sell it or use it anyhow![15]

This brief excerpt provides evidence of the dialect that so many of Stoker's contemporaries observed in this novel, a practice that Stoker will continue to use in many of his later works, including the often criticized Dutch accent of Dr. Van Helsing in *Dracula*. Moreover, it reveals Stoker's skills as a local colorist as well as a creator of landscape and suspense.

More important, the gombeen man reveals Stoker's interest in personifications of evil and in the conflict between an evil force and the unified good of the community, a conflict that will appear again in *Dracula, The Mystery of the Sea, The Lady of the Shroud, The Lair of the White Worm,* and in somewhat different fashion in *The Jewel of Seven Stars.* Unlike many of the personifications of evil in Stoker's other novels, Murdock (as well as the kidnappers in *The Mystery of the Sea*) is decidedly of this world rather than a supernatural figure of evil.

This short novel also introduces a topic that will remain significant in many of Stoker's other novels--the belief that science and technology provide hope for the future. (Of his novels, only *The Jewel of Seven Stars* seems to suggest that the modern faith in science is misplaced. On the other hand, science and technology are irrelevant to *The Watter's Mou'* and *Miss Betty*.) In this novel, Arthur's old school friend Dick Sutherland is an engineer and geologist hired by Murdock to explore the bog on his property and on Farmer Joyce's property in hopes of recovering the treasure. Contemptuous of Murdock's greed, Sutherland nonetheless warns him that his house is in danger of being overtaken by the shifting bog. Murdock, who refuses to listen to the warning of the scientist, is eventually drowned.

The novel also includes a subject that later appears in *Dracula* and many of Stoker's other novels--two young men in love with the same woman--and gives Stoker an opportunity to illustrate heroic renunciation and masculine strength. In fact, Arthur and Dick anticipate the brave young men in Stoker's future novels, including Rafe Otwell (in *Miss Betty*), Harold An Wolf (in *The Man*), and the group of brave young men who take on a centuries-old evil being in *Dracula*. On the other hand, the beautiful and passive Norah Joyce anticipates many of Stoker's virtuous heroines though she does not have the spirit of Mina Harker (in *Dracula*), Marjory Drake (in *Mystery of the Sea*), Teuta Vissarion (in *The Lady of the Shroud*), or Stephen Norman (in *The Man*), however.

Although *The Snake's Pass* was recently reissued and is certainly deserving of analysis if only for the light it would shed on *Dracula*, it has received almost no critical attention in the twentieth century. A single exception is Charles Osborne, who includes the third chapter, "The Gombeen Man," in *The Bram Stoker Bedside Companion*.

It was reasonably well reviewed by Stoker's contemporaries--including the comic *Punch* and the *Athenaeum*, which was the most influential of the Victorian literary reviews--even though he had published only one book seven years ago. These contemporary reviewers were most interested in the vivid description and the local color aspects of the novel, though they were as impatient with the unflinching virtue of his good characters as a late twentieth-century reader is likely to be. *Punch* characterizes it as a "simple love story" [16] and praises it for its charming local color, but the *Atheneum* is far less charitable, calling it "so long, so good, and so dull" [17] and commenting on Stoker's characterization or lack thereof, a problem that will continue to affect his future novels. The reviewer does seem to enjoy some of the minor characters, however. The *Punch* review also notes Stoker's awareness of science, a characteristic of Stoker's novels that continues to interest critics in the late twentieth century.

In addition to reviews, Ludlam refers to several personal compliments that Stoker received. For example, Hallam Tennyson wrote, "My father asks me to say that he read your *Snake's Pass* with pleasure. . . " Prime Minister Gladstone made his comments in person when he next visited the theatre. According to Ludlam, he "surprised Bram with his quotations from *The Snake's Pass*, his remarks on the gombeen man and other characters showing that he had read it very carefully. 'That scene at Mrs Kelligan's is fine--very fine indeed!'" (88)

THE WATTER'S MOU' (1895)

One of several works that reveals Stoker's love for Cruden Bay, a remote fishing village on the Aberdeenshire coast where he spent his available holidays and where he did much of his writing, this long story of young love, divided loyalty, and early death tells of William Barrow's love for Maggie MacWhirter and what happens when her father and brothers become involved in smuggling. Willy

Barrow is the kind of noble and self-sacrificing man that Stoker so admired and
often featured in his works, as the following quotation demonstrates:

> William Barrow, popularly known as Sailor Willy, was a very young man to be a
> chief boatman in the preventive service, albeit that this station was one of the
> smallest on the coast. He had been allowed, as a reward for saving the life of his
> lieutenant, to join the coast service, and had been promoted to chief boatman as a
> further reward for a clever capture of smugglers, wherein he had shown not only great
> bravery, but much ability and power of rapid organisation. [18]

Maggie is equally noble and self-sacrificing. The conflict emerges when her
impoverished father and brothers become involved in smuggling. Maggie, who
sails out to warn her family that Willy will arrest them if they are discovered
with contraband goods, is drowned in a storm. The distraught Willy then drowns
attempting to rescue Maggie's body. The conclusion, which is so full of the
pathos that Stoker liked to evoke, appealed more to Stoker's contemporaries than
it will to readers in the late twentieth century:

> There, on the very spot whence the boat had set sail on its warning errand, lay its
> wreckage, and tangled in it the body of the noble girl who had steered it--her brown
> hair floating wide and twined round the neck of Sailor Willy, who held her tight in his
> dead arms. The requiem of the twain was the roar of the breaking waves and the
> screams of the white birds that circled round the Watter's Mou'. (223-24)

Although Charles Osborne reprinted *The Watter's Mou'* in *The Bram
Stoker Bedside Companion*, it has been largely ignored by other critics in this
century; and even Osborne admits that Stoker's "sentimental style . . . was less
effective and individual than his way with the macabre and the supernatural" (12).
However, the novel was well received by both *Punch* and the *Athenaeum* whose
reviewers admired its excitement and descriptive writing. The reviewer in the
Nation, on the other hand, makes several observations that will be often repeated
by readers of Stoker's other novels--that his use of dialect is too broad and too
obtrusive and that his treatment of character is too stagey and artificial.

THE SHOULDER OF SHASTA   (1895)

This romantic novel, which is hardly ever mentioned by twentieth-century
critics, is interesting for its American setting. Stoker is known for his interest in
the United States, and he came to know this country through his travels with the
Lyceum Theatre Company. In fact, Americans and American settings will appear
in several of Stoker's other novels including *Lady Athlyne*, which features both
an American family and some American settings; *The Mystery of the Sea,*
which has an American heroine; and *Dracula*, which includes among the band of
men who follow Dracula home to Transylvania the Texan Quincy Morris, the
only person killed in the battle.

Set in California, the romance features American characters: a spirited young woman, Esse Elstree, whose physician has advised mountain air and other natural tonics to cure her anaemic condition, her mother and their servants, and a mountain man named Grizzly Dick. As a result of the doctor's prescription, her mother has purchased a cabin in the mountains and has taken her daughter and an entire entourage of retainers and servants there.

While they are in the mountains, Esse regains her health and becomes infatuated with Dick who has been employed to provide game for the group. Esse saves his life when he is attacked by a grizzly bear and nurses him back to health. During this period, she believes that she has fallen in love with him although the narrative is adamant about Esse's youth and naivete. Young and romantically inclined, she is ready to fall in love with love; and the glorious mountain scenery and the absence of young people make Dick a likely candidate.

Esse and her family return to San Francisco, and a mutual acquaintance tells Dick of Esse's infatuation. However, when Dick visits her home in San Francisco, she discovers that his rough behavior, outlandish clothing, and crude humor do not translate very well to sophisticated San Francisco; and she is briefly embarrassed until she comes to realize Dick's native dignity. The story ends happily when Esse renews her friendship with Dick and introduces him to her fiance Reginald Hampden, a man who combines Dick's strength of character with sophisticated manners.

The mountainous setting in the early chapters gives Stoker an opportunity to describe the natural setting at length and later to contrast it with San Francisco at the turn of the century. Moreover, the movement between cultures and the presence of both the rough mountain man and a tribe of native Americans at the mountain retreat give Stoker an opportunity to contrast different cultures and ultimately to praise Anglo-American culture and to celebrate the superiority of civilization over primitive cultures, a subject that often appealed to him and one that would appear in *Dracula*, *The Mystery of the Sea*, and *The Lair of the White Worm*.

In addition, Stoker introduces several other characters primarily for their comic relief. Miss Gimp, formerly Esse's governess, believes that Dick is in love with her because she discovers gifts of game outside her room. In reality, the Indians are bringing the gifts to her parrot, which they regard as a god. In addition, Mr. Le Maistre, Mrs. Elstree's ironically named "male factotum, steward, butler, agent, handy-man, engineer and courier," [19] serves as a contrast to the more masculine men in the novel.

The Shoulder of Shasta has received little attention from scholars and critics in the late twentieth century. Ludlam, usually full of high praise for anything Stoker did, describes it as "hastily written and its characters scarcely credible" (106). He mentions, however, strengths in its "descriptive passages, so real that one could almost breathe the raw mountain air and smell the smoke fires" (106).

Stoker's contemporaries, according to Leatherdale, were less generous:

This time the critics were merciless: The *Athenaeun*, for instance, castigated the book for its lack of maturity, its haste, poor humour, weakness of plot, and lack of characterization. Nothing Stoker had previously written had been so maligned. (68)

On the other hand, the *Spectator's* brief review is enthusiastic about characterization, especially about Dick, a kind of mountain man who, like Quincy Morris, has the kind of natural nobility that Stoker admires in his male characters.

Virtually ignored since its publication, *The Shoulder of Shasta* is nonetheless important because it was written while Stoker was working on Dracula and because it examines many of the same issues of gender and culture as that work. (Dick has the same masculine nobility as many of Stoker's young heroes while Esse very much resembles Lucy Westenra in her lack of maturity and her as-yet-unawakened eroticism.) Moreover, the descriptive passages clearly reveal Stoker's relationship to romanticism. Finally, its concern with American culture, which Stoker had researched thoroughly by reading everything he could read about the United States, will continue to appear in *Dracula* (The martyred Quincy Morris can be seen as a more polished version of Grizzly Dick), *The Mystery of the Sea*, and *Lady Athlyne*. For all these reasons, it deserves further exploration.

DRACULA   (1897)

Stoker's best-known fictional work, *Dracula* is so well known to twentieth-century readers that it seems almost redundant to summarize it--though it sometimes turns out that one remembers a film or comic-book version rather than Stoker's novel. In fact, this novel has never been out of print since it was first published almost a century ago; it has been translated into at least a dozen foreign languages; and it has inspired more movies, television shows, and other popular culture characters than any other single work.

The novel opens as Jonathan Harker, a young English solicitor, travels to Transylvania at the request of Count Dracula. Already unnerved by the primitive people around him and by their unusual customs, Harker is initially worried by Dracula's barbaric behavior and ultimately horrified to discover himself a prisoner in the castle, which houses Dracula and three equally bloodthirsty women followers. One scene, which is often noted by critics in the late twentieth century, shows a supine Harker surrounded by the three women. Horrified equally by their aggressive and unfeminine behavior as well as by his desire *for* them, Harker is literally paralyzed. It is a scene that calls into question much of what the nineteenth century believed about the relationships of men and women:

The fair girl went on her knees, and bent over me, fairly gloating. There was a de-liberate voluptuousness which was both thrilling and repulsive, and as she arched her neck she actually licked her lips like an animal, till I could see in the moonlight the moisture shining on the scarlet lips and on the red tongue as it lapped the white sharp teeth. . . . I could feel the soft, shivering touch of the lips on the supersensitive skin of my throat, and the hard dents of two sharp teeth, just touching and pausing there. I closed my eyes in a languorous ecstasy and waited--waited with beating heart. [20]

Only Dracula's return rescues Harker from being "devoured" by the three predatory women.

Back in England, the reader meets Harker's fiancee Mina Murray and her friend Lucy Westenra, who is beloved by three men: Quincy Morris, an American adventurer; Dr. John Seward, a psychiatrist; and Arthur Holmwood, a young aristocrat who later inherits his father's title, Lord Godalming. As so many critics have observed, the group seems to represent the strengths of England in the nineteenth century. Unfortunately, aristocratic wealth, science, and entrepreneurial skills are inadequate to prevent Lucy from succumbing to Dracula's advances; and, upon dying, she becomes as voluptuous (one of Stoker's favorite words to describe women vampires) as Dracula's Transylvanian followers had been. However, aided by Dr. Van Helsing, Seward's old friend and teacher, the young men band together and manage to destroy Lucy before she can harm them and before her desire for blood can damn her soul for all eternity.

The second half of the novel revolves around the group--now joined by the Harkers--and its efforts to prevent Mina Harker from falling prey to Dracula and all the temptations that he the vampiric life represents. Ultimately tracking Dracula to his castle, the group is confident that it has managed to destroy him and his three women companions though several film versions focus on Stoker's ambiguous conclusion and suggest that Dracula is not really destroyed at the end of the novel:

It was like a miracle; but before our very eyes, and almost in the drawing of a breath, the whole body crumbled into dust and passed from our sight. (330)

Notable among the several film adaptations that focus on this apparently open ending is John Badham's 1979 version, which stars Frank Langella as Count Dracula and Kate Nelligan as Mina. Badham's conclusion has Dracula appear to float away and suggests that he will return to reclaim Mina, who has decided that a passionate and immortal lover is to be preferred to a rather pedestrian mortal one.

Stoker's powerful story reveals the conflict between the forces of light and the forces of darkness, technology and superstition, the past and the present, the urban and the primitive. As such, it has become a metaphor of a modern crisis. Dracula, the king vampire, is both a supernatural figure and a Renaissance nobleman from a primitive region who comes into conflict with the emissaries of modern law and medicine who fight him with with the latest technological weapons (a pattern that will also appear in *The Mystery of the Sea*, *The Lady of the Shroud*, and *The Lair of the White Worm*). Stoker's story has struck such a responsive chord that it has never been out of print. Furthermore, it has been translated into more than a dozen foreign languages as well as into other media-- drama, film, television, and comic books.

From its first publication, *Dracula* was well received by the critics though the *Spectator* objected to the "up-to-dateness of the book," [21] a characteristic more likely to be admired by twentieth-century critics. His contemporaries recognized that *Dracula* was a more powerful novel than Stoker's earlier works though they were not inclined to examine why it exerted such a hold on them. Critics at the end of the twentieth century are more likely to examine the novel's power over us. In fact, Royce MacGillivray, whose essay on the novel is excerpted in the chapter on *Dracula,* claims that only Stoker's weak characterization, a weakness in all his novels (with the possible exception of *The Man*), prevents it from being recognized as a masterpiece.

Even though it continues to explore questions that Stoker had probed in other works--the conflict between good and evil, the question of identity, the conflict between civilization and primitive culture, and the relationships between the sexes--it does so in a manner that is more successful than these other works.

Written during a decade when people were very interested in gender and when the presence of the New Woman and the novels about her called women's traditional roles into question, [22] Dracula is overtly concerned with questions of gender and the relationships between the sexes. As a result, Stoker's concern with gender has been thoroughly explored by Stephanie Demetrakopoulos, Gail B. Griffin, Marjorie Howes, Alan Johnson, Judith Roth, Carol Senf, Judith Weissman, and Leonard Wolf. Moreover, the question of gender has often been linked with questions of sexual behavior among twentieth-century commentators.

In addition, because Dracula focuses on the conflict between Dracula, a Renaissance warlord, and residents of turn-of-the century London, it provides an opportunity to see Stoker as typical of his day in that he hoped that science and technology would ultimately enable human beings to solve their problems. This optimism does not mean that he was totally blind to the problems in the science and technology of his own day. John L. Greenway and Rosemary Jann are two of the late-twentieth-century critics who have examined Stoker's treatment of science and technology, but even Stoker's contemporaries sometimes noted that he linked Gothic horror with details taken from modern life.

Furthermore, Stoker's interest in science and technology is linked to his celebration of the behaviors and values of civilized peoples; and Stoker's treatment of cultural issues is explored by Stephen D. Arata (who also looks at the relationship between England and the United States at the time Stoker wrote the novel), Ernest Fontana, Burton Hatlen, Mark Hennelly, Daniel Pick and Richard Wasson, whose 1966 essay is one of the first scholarly explorations of the novel.

In addition to these broad thematic concerns, scholars and critics have examined Stoker's narrative strategy and his work as a mythmaker. Of all Stoker's works, *Dracula* has received the most attention from scholars and critics--both his contemporaries and ours--as is evident from the materials collected in the chapter on *Dracula.*

MISS BETTY (1898)

A period piece set in the first years of the eighteenth century, *Miss Betty* has been virtually ignored during the twentieth century. The only one of Stoker's novels to be dedicated to his wife as well as the only one of his novels to be set in the distant past rather than his own time, *Miss Betty* is a historical romance that features Rafe Otwell, a poor gentleman and a distant kinsman of Robert Walpole; Betty Pole, a wealthy heiress who inherits a fortune from her grandfather; and Walpole himself.

Like so many of Stoker's other romances, *Miss Betty* tells of love and sacrifice. The title character, a wealthy heiress, is saved from drowning by a poor man, Rafe Otwell, the kind of brave young man that Stoker loved to write about (though Rafe's decision to turn highwayman adds a dimension of moral ambiguity not generally found in Stoker's one dimensional good characters). He first meets Betty when she falls into the river, a situation from Stoker's own life that recurs again and again in his novels including this one, *The Mystery of the Sea*, and *The Man*. The two immediately fall in love, and the reader is permitted a glimpse of their blushing courtship.

In debt and in fear of debtors' prison and choosing neither to marry Lady Mary, an older woman whom Sir Robert has chosen for him (though Stoker never reveals why the marriage is so important to Walpole) nor accept money from Betty, Rafe turns highwayman.

Suspecting that Rafe has gotten money on the highway, Betty sets herself up as a victim and confronts him. Rafe, who is ashamed of himself and aware that Betty could have been killed by a less scrupulous highwayman, goes off to regain his honor. In the meantime, Betty chooses to wait patiently for her lover's return. She is thus a fairly typical Stoker heroine, for she is capable of self assertion when it will help her lover. Otherwise, she is dutifully passive and submissive.

The chastened Rafe finally returns to England five years later and marries Betty after he has proved his bravery in warfare; and Stoker emphasizes the strength of his character by detailing his attempt to repay his debts:

. . . quite a number of persons who had been robbed near London in the early half of 1717 had had full restitution made to them. The matter was the subject of comment in the coffeehouses, and many were the surmises as to the cause or means of so unusual a set of circumstances. [23]

Revealing himself to Betty, Rafe tells what had happened while he was away. He had discovered himself while a prisoner on a Turkish galley. (The Turks for Stoker apparently represent cruelty here as they do in *The Lady of the Shroud* though *Miss Betty* does not develop this cultural conflict.):

These scars shall be warnings to me for all my life; till at the last, if it may be in God's good time, the hands that bear them shall lie folded over a peaceful heart. (153)

There are similarities to other novels, for once again Stoker found inspiration in place (this time Cheyne Walk, Chelsea, one of the most fashionable streets in London, where Bram and Florence lived). Not only did they entertain guests there, but it was also the house to which Stoker had brought the body of the suicide he had attempted to rescue.

Like most good romances, the novel concludes with the marriage of hero and heroine. Furthermore, like many romances, *Miss Betty* spends very little time analyzing character. As a result, the characters are one-dimensional figures rather than fully developed characters; and their marriage represents the union of strong male figure with loving female, a pattern that Stoker delighted to explore.

More tolerant of sentimentality, Stoker's contemporaries were enthusiastic about this love and self-sacrifice. Both the *Athenaeum* and the *Bookman* openly prefer it to *Dracula* while *Punch* praises its ability to capture "something of the literary style of the age." [24] The enthusiasm of Stoker's contemporaries for this rather slight work is perhaps the clearest indication of how attitudes to his novels have changed in the past century.

SNOWBOUND: THE RECORD OF A THEATRICAL TOURING PARTY (1899)

Although *Snowbound* is almost never discussed today, it raises a number of important questions for scholars and critics. In fact, there is some doubt about the date of the first edition. Both Leatherdale and Dalby cite the 1908 date and link the collection to *Lady Athlyne*. However, the copyright date on the University Microfilms facsimile edition clearly lists 1899, and the material seems to fit in with Stoker's active days with Irving's company. The work includes a frame tale about a theatrical touring company whose train is snowbound somewhere between Aberdeen and Perth and fourteen short stories told by members of the company. The stories are not among Stoker's best though they do reveal the range of his literary abilities and feature a broad range of styles from almost slapstick comedy to very serious. Noticeably absent are the tales of supernatural horror that most twentieth-century readers have come to associate with the writer of *Dracula*, and even tales of adventure and romance are in the minority. The works are rarely anthologized or even discussed, but Osborne reprints one of the best ones, "A Star Trap," in *The Bram Stoker Bedside Companion*.

Because *Snowbound* is both difficult to find and is rarely discussed by critics, this introduction provides a very brief synopsis of the stories in the book.[25]

The Manager, a man who resembles Stoker in some ways, tells a humorous story about babies, dogs, and boa constrictors. Titled "A Lesson in Pets," the story also warns about what happens when members of the company bring too many pets along, for the manager then brings along his "pets," a crate of boa constrictors.

The second story, "Coggin's Property," is told by the Leading Lady and illustrates class differences that cause problems between the well-bred leading lady and a Cockney property master. Like *The Snake's Pass*, this story reveals Stoker's currently appreciated ability to reproduce dialogue and also suggests the degree to which his ideas about characterization may have stemmed from his experience with Irving's company. Reading Stoker's works often leads me to suspect that he associated characterization with vocal response, dialect, and tone of voice.

Story three, "The Slim Syrens," by the Sewing Woman tells about a young woman who believes that the show must go on even if she has to be sewn into her costume. She is thus a minor version of Stoker's determined women characters, including Mina Harker, Marjory Drake, and Stephen Norman.

"A New Departure in Art" by the Low Comedian tells of a wake that he attended while "Mick the Devil" by the Prompter is a suspense tale of a flood and a train going over a bridge.

"In Fear of Death" relates the confessions of the Second Low Comedian. "At Last" by the Young Man picks up a strand mentioned by the Sewing Woman about a dead baby and relates a sentimental story of a mother returning to her estranged husband to nurse their sick child. "Chin Music" by the Second Heavies tells about a crying baby on a train. Although the story initially appears to be a comedy, Stoker provides a serious twist by revealing that the baby is crying because its mother had just died.

"A Deputy Waiter" by the singing Chambermaid tells a real story of having to sing at gunpoint for a deranged convict while "Work'us" by the Tragedian, apparently a real story about a writer who had grown up in the workhouse, is a cruel story about a cruel practical joke.

"A Corner in Dwarfs" by the Super-Master tells of using small women in a pantomime instead of children. "A Criminal Star" by the Advance Agent reveals what he had done as a press agent to interest people in his client. "A Star Trap" by the Master Machinist is a story of revenge that stems from a love triangle between the master carpenter (the machinist's old master), the Harlequin, and the wife of the master carpenter. "A Moon-Light Effect" by the Scene Painter, also a tale of revenge, reveals how several people manage to "put one over" on a greedy landlord.

The stories reveal Stoker's versatility and his ability to work in a variety of forms and might also be interesting to people who want to explore Stoker's relationship to the theatrical community of his day. Osborne, who includes "A Star Trap" in *The Bram Stoker Bedside Companion*, observes that "the stories were based on Bram Stoker's own experiences on tour with the Irving company," [26] and Stoker's accounts of situations in *Personal Reminiscences* suggests that he had indeed taken material from his own life and experiences. (Material from Volume 2 reveals that the Irving company had been trapped on a snowbound train during one of their American tours while "Mick the Devil" was also based on an experience that the Irving company had near New Orleans during a period of flood, and all the stories celebrate the courage and ingenuity of the theatrical community, traits that Stoker will continue to praise in his *Reminiscences*.)

The collection received virtually no attention from Stoker's contemporaries and has received even less from scholars and critics in the late twentieth century, who haven't yet explored Stoker's relationship with the theater. Ludlam does little more than mention it; Dalby says only that it was "perishable and certainly not made to last" (unpaged preface); and Leatherdale merely describes it and *Lady Athlyne* as "rushed, hack works that could not raise his fallen literary reputation" (72).

THE MYSTERY OF THE SEA   (1902)

One of the novels that Stoker set in his beloved Cruden Bay, this novel, like *The Snake's Pass*, combines a romantic interest between Archibald Hunter, the narrator, and Marjory Anita Drake with a buried treasure--this time gold left during the time of the Spanish Armada. However, although the plots are similar, the characterization in this novel is more rich and diverse, and the mysteries surrounding the search for the lost treasure and the kidnapping of the heiress are more fully developed. In addition, Hunter's experiences with second sight (a preternatural ability that Stoker will explore again in *The Lady of the Shroud*) and the presence of the old witch woman Gormala MacNiel allow Stoker to explore strange and mysterious events even though this novel is a romantic adventure story rather than a tale of supernatural horror.

Stoker handles the suspenseful sections of the novel capably and manages to maintain the suspense until the very end; and the main characters are more fully developed than is often the case. However, readers at the end of the twentieth century will probably be more interested in the fact that this novel explores the same subjects as many of Stoker's other novels. For example, Stoker reveals his interest in gender and disguise by having Marjory free to come and go only when she is disguised as a footman, an interest in cross dressing and gender identity that he will later explore more fully in *Famous Impostors*. Moreover, the romance interest provides Stoker with ample opportunity to comment on gender roles, mostly in terms of blushing femininity and heroic masculine endeavors. Like so many of Stoker's heroes, including Lord Athlyne and Rafe Otwell in *Miss Betty*, Archie first meets Marjory when he rescues her and her companion Mrs. Jack from drowning; and he later rescues Marjory from the kidnappers. On the other hand, Marjory is more complex than many of Stoker's passive heroines. She has the same kind of intellectual strength as Mina Harker, Teuta Vissarion, and Joy Ogilvie: she is the one to suggest that Archie work with the biliteral cipher; she manages to leave a trail for Archie to follow so that he can rescue her; and she is certainly capable of arguing her point with her assailants.

In addition, *The Mystery of the Sea* reveals numerous thematic links with Stoker's other novels. Like *The Lady of the Shroud*, it reveals an interest in politics and in the hand that technological development will have on politics. And, like *The Snake's Pass, The Lady of the Shroud, The Lair of the White Worm*, and even *Dracula*, it reveals the potential power of science and technology over all aspects of human life. As usual, those who understand science and technology are presented favorably in the social-Darwinian sense of being most capable of surviving.

This late nineteenth-century pride in the accomplishments of Northern Europeans--a pride found also in *Dracula, The Shoulder of Shasta*, and *The Lady of the Shroud*--is reinforced by the names of some of the major characters, names that suggest patriotic identity. For example, the patriotic Marjory is a direct descendant of Sir Francis Drake, who helped to defeat the Spanish Armada when it sailed against England in 1588. Following in her famous ancestor's footsteps, she gives a battleship to the American government to help Cuba gain independence from Spain. (Stoker explores the same idea of freedom from political oppression in *The Lady of the Shroud*.) The American diplomat Samuel Adams who warns Archie of the plan to kidnap Marjory also bears a patriotic American name; and Archibald Hunter, whose name rings no historical bells, incorporates the kind of intellectual acumen that Stoker associates with Northern Europeans: He is the best hunter who breaks the biliteral cypher and uses it to find the lost treasure.

The Mystery of the Sea--like *Dracula* and *The Shoulder of Shasta*--also reveals a markedly unattractive aspect of Stoker's late-nineteenth century consciousness--blatant racism. Although Archie will later decide that Don Bernardino is a gentleman, his racism is apparent in the following description:

As he spoke, the canine teeth began to show. . . . Somehow at that moment the racial instinct manifested itself. Spain was once the possession of the Moors, and the noblest of the old families had some black blood in them. In Spain such is not, as the West, a taint. The old diabolism, whence sprung fantee and hoodoo, seemed to gleam out in the grim smile of incarnate, rebellious purpose.[27]

The following scene is likely to disgust readers at the end of the twentieth century even more though Archie's anger in this particular scene may be somewhat justified by his knowledge that the black man plans to kill the woman Archie loves:

Never before did I understand the pleasure of killing a man. Since then, it makes me shudder when I think of how so potent a passion, or so keen a pleasure, can rest latent in the heart of a righteous man. It may have been that between the man and myself was all the antagonism that came from race, and fear, and wrongdoing; but the act of his killing was to me a joy unspeakable. It will rest with me as a wild pleasure till I die. (277-78)

As in *The Lair of the White Worm*, where another African is killed by the primeval serpent and dragged to its underground lair, the black man is treated as a sub-human species, whose death doesn't bother the white characters.

Finally, *The Mystery of the Sea* reveals Stoker's interest in Egypt and Egyptology. Exploring the caves under his house, Archie is reminded of

Belzoni's explorations in the Pyramids (163), an interest more fully explored in *The Jewel of Seven Stars*.

As with its predecessor, Stoker's contemporaries were enthusiastic about this adventure novel that includes a gaunt old witch woman, ancient manuscripts in cypher, hidden treasures, secret agents, a Gaelic rune of how to solve the mystery of the sea, a castle with secret passages, shipwrecks, a futuristic gun battle, a blushing American heiress as heroine, and a noble hero who has experiences of second sight. In fact, the *Punch* reviewer compares it to a number of well-known adventure novels while the reviewer in the *Bookman*, which describes it as "a thrilling and absorbing romance, ingeniously constructed and exceedingly well written," [28] indicates that Stoker is without peer for this kind of adventure novel. In addition to published reviews, Stoker received praise from Conan Doyle:

> "My dear Bram--I found the story admirable. It has not the fearsomeness of 'Dracula' but it is beautifully handled and the girl very admirable indeed. . . . " And the creator of the baffling Sherlock Holmes mysteries added the modest postscript, "I've done a bit in cryptograms myself, but that knocks me out!"
>
> Conan Doyle's praise was for a fascinating piece of 'secret writing'. . . which Bram had based on a cipher described by Francis Bacon. (Ludlam, 138)

It has been virtually ignored since then. In fact, recent scholars seem most interested in the fact that Stoker set this novel in one of his favorite locations, Cruden Bay and that his hero, Archie Hunter, shares his enthusiasm for the region. Leatherdale observes Stoker's attention to adventurous elements and bemoans its predictable romantic elements:

> *The Mystery of the Sea* (1902) features Gaelic runes, ancient manuscripts in cryptic writing, hidden treasures, secret agents, castles with hidden passageways, shipwrecks on the Cruden shores, and even a futuristic naval gun battle. As always, there would be the predictable romantic element: blushing heroines and the importance of male valour. (71)

Ludlam's commentary on *The Mystery of the Sea* also stresses its predictability and emphasizes its reliance on suspense.

THE JEWEL OF SEVEN STARS   (1903)

Of all Stoker's novels, this one is the most difficult to categorize, for it seems to move in an altogether different direction from any of his other works. Although it examines many of the same themes (gender relationships, the link between the past and the present, the conflict between the primitive world and the civilized, the battle between Good and Evil, and issues of basic identity) and reveals Stoker's ability as a maker of myth, it is distinctly different in a number of important ways: Not only does the novel end in disaster for the civilized main characters, but Stoker reveals that masculine strength and modern technology are powerless against the feminine embodiment of ancient Egyptian civilization.

Like *The Lady of the Shroud*, *The Man*, and *The Lair of the White Worm*, this novel also exists in several different versions though the reason for the differences in *The Jewel of Seven Stars* was apparently not simply the desire to produce a less expensive edition. In fact, according to Harry Ludlam, the final scene in which Malcolm Ross, the narrator, finds the horror struck bodies of his fiancee, her father, and several other companions "was so disturbing that Bram was asked by the publishers to rewrite it for later editions, so as to provide a happier denouement" (143-44). Ironically, the revised version with its happy ending and the marriage of hero and heroine makes *The Jewel of Seven Stars* more consistent with Stoker's other works rather than the anomaly that it clearly is.

This work has greater appeal for people in the latter part of the twentieth century than it did for Stoker's contemporaries. (It was, however, favorably reviewed by James MacArthur in *Harper's Magazine*.) Largely ignored in Stoker's day, it has been made into two movies--*Blood from the Mummy's Tomb* (1971) and *The Awakening* (1980) and has also elicited the commentary of both scholars and critics. Furthermore, it has been reprinted several times in the twentieth century though Dalby notes that the work exists in several versions. British editions published by Rider, Jarrolds, and Arrow use the second, happier ending and omit the original chapters XVI, "Powers--Old and New." Two recent editions printed in the United States (Scholastic Book Services, 1972, and Fantasy House, 1974) have returned to Stoker's original ending though they abridge the original novel in other ways.

The novel, which combines horror and romance, opens when a young lawyer, Malcolm Ross, receives a midnight summons to the home of Margaret Trelawny, a young woman he has just met. Her father, who is an amateur Egyptologist, had been attacked by something and is now in a coma.

Eventually Trelawny recovers though not before Malcolm and several other characters experience the same power that had put Trelawny into a coma. Listening to Trelawny and several of his associates, Malcolm and the reader then learn of Trelawny's explorations in Egypt and his discovery of the tomb of Queen Tera, whose mummy he brings with him to England. Simultaneously Ross and Margaret fall in love.

Trelawny's interest in Egyptology and the subtle links between Margaret and Tera (Margaret resembles pictures of the great queen and ultimately seems to be possessed by her spirit) enable Stoker to weave together the past and the present. In fact, it seems that Tera has possessed Margaret and is using her body to return to the world of the living. Thus, *The Jewel of Seven Stars*, like *Dracula*, deals directly with questions of identity and with questions of power. Furthermore, like *Dracula*, it brings remote horrors from a primitive past to London.

Moreover, the romance of Malcolm and Margaret enables him to comment on gender, as does the following information about Queen Tera:

The signs of sovereignty were given with a truly feminine profusion of adornment. The united Crowns of Upper and Lower Egypt were . . . cut with exquisite precision. It was new to us both to find the Hejet and the Desher--the White and the Red crowns of Upper and Lower Egypt--on the Stele of a queen; for it was a rule . . . that in ancient Egypt either crown was worn only by a king; though they are to be found on goddesses. [29]

The observation indicates that Tera had somehow transcended gender and humanity. Moreover, Tera was clearly an exceptional ruler; and the plot revolves around her plan to be resurrected into the present, a plan that enables many of the characters to contrast the ancient past with the London of Stoker's day. (This plot twist is very close to Dracula's plan to leave Transylvania and assimilate himself into modern London though Tera at least in the first edition is more successful than Dracula.) Trelawny, for example, is convinced that the modern age can learn from the ancient:

There is here much ground for conjecture and for experiment. . . .We know as yet so little of natural forces, that imagination need set no bounds to its flights in considering the possibilities of the future. Within but a few years we have made such discoveries as two centuries ago would have sent the discoverers to the flames. The liquefaction of oxygen; the existence of radium, of helium, of polonium, of argon; the different powers of Rontgen and Cathode and Becquerel rays. (247)

Ross, on the other hand, is less convinced of the amicable relationship between past and present. He thinks of the numerous deaths that had been somehow connected to Queen Tera's mummy and worries about the potential dangers in the experiment, as the following passage reveals:

The more I thought over the coming experiment, the more strange it all seemed; and the more foolish were we who were deliberately entering upon it. It was all so stupendous, so mysterious, so unnecessary! The issues were so vast; the danger so strange, so unknown. Even if it should be successful, what new difficulties would it not raise. What changes might happen, did mem know that the portals of the House of Death were not in very truth eternally fixed; and that the Dead could come forth again! (250)

Thus Ross raises some obvious parallels with *Dracula*, and he, who is the only member of the group to survive the attempt to resurrect Queen Tera, reveals the terrors that arise when living men come in contact with the powerful past:

I found them all where they had stood. They had sunk down on the floor, and were gazing upward with fixed eyes of unspeakable terror. . . . I did what I could for my companions; but there was nothing that could avail. There, in that lonely house, far away from aid of man, naught could avail.
It was merciful that I was spared the pain of hoping. (336-37)

Here, as in *Dracula*, the past is powerful, but also evil; and the original version, which touches the present with the uncontrollable and malevolent power of the past, literally leaves the narrator speechless. In this context, Trelawny, whose interest in Egyptology is linked with his belief in scientific knowledge, is clearly a kind of "mad scientist" type; and the novel as a whole is perhaps Stoker's most ambivalent presentation of the spirit of scientific inquiry. Here there are no technological wonders. The original version has the scientist killed by the queen whom he has helped to resurrect; in the revised and rewritten version, he is somehow incapable of bringing about that resurrection at all.

Reading the critical commentary in the chapter on *The Jewel of Seven Stars* reveals how Stoker's contemporaries differ from readers at the end of the twentieth century. Note that Nina Auerbach's analysis is a response, not to the first edition and its horrifying conclusion but to a later version. Certainly, her discussion of Stoker's powerful women characters would have been reinforced by a reading of Stoker's initial conclusion.

THE MAN (1905)

Although Roth is enthusiastic about this work (which was also published in a somewhat abbreviated version in the United States as *The Gates of Life* in 1908) it has received almost no attention since it was first published. A romance, it tells the story of the young heiress with the masculine name of Stephen Norman whose father had wanted a son to inherit both his estate and his name; and it explores questions of gender when Stephen tries to be her father's son, even proposing marriage to a totally unsuitable young man, Leonard Everard. After a series of adventures, the story ends happily when Stephen learns to accept her feminine identity and marry the rugged Harold An Wolf, who is is clearly the man to whom the title refers rather than Stephen, for Stoker presents her exploration of masculine behavior as inappropriate--indeed disastrous. (Daniel Pick, whose commentary on the novel is included in the chapter on *The Man*, discusses Stephen as an example of the New Woman and suggests that Stoker's ideas on femininity had changed since he wrote *Dracula*.)

The question of gender dominates this romance from the first page, which opens with a discussion of gender differences as Stephen and Harold debate whether women can practise justice in the abstract.

Much of the plot revolves around these questions of gender and the love between Stephen and Harold. The issue of equality is mostly theoretical until Stephen attempts to test it by proposing marriage to another childhood friend, Leonard Everard. As soon as the profligate Leonard refuses her, Stephen is dejected. Although Harold attempts to come to her rescue by proposing marriage, Stephen angrily rejects his proposal; and Harold goes off to Alaska to seek his fortune.

During the period of their separation, Stoker goes to great lengths to demonstrate Harold's heroic behavior. He rescues the daughter of an American ironmaster and contractor from drowning (and it is Pearl, the little girl, who first identifies him as "The Man"), amasses a fortune in the gold fields, and saves an entire ship from disaster--though he is temporarily blinded by the latter experience. In the meantime, Stephen comes to recognize what she had lost in Harold. She also pays off Leonard's debts (making their relationship purely one of business) and inherits a fortune and the title, Lady de Lannoy.

When Harold returns from America, the ship on which he is sailing is wrecked on the shore near Stephen's new home. Although she is unaware that the heroic individual who risks his life to save the ship is her childhood friend, she recognizes his bravery. Furthermore, she is directly responsible for lighting the beacon that saves his life and for providing him with both a temporary refuge and medical attention. Attempting to provide a plot summary of *The Man* makes it appear more difficult than it is: despite the conclusion which involves Harold and Stephen's unraveling the mysteries surrounding the identity of the other, this novel--more than any of Stoker's other novels--centers around the development of a small cast of characters: Stephen, Harold, Leonard, and Stephen's aunt Laetitia Rowley (who lives with Stephen and provides her with a strong example of traditional womanhood). Moreover, the American characters on the ship provide a kind of backdrop for Harold since he earns a fortune in the Alaskan goldfields because he has a kind of frontier spirit. Nonetheless, he chooses the civilization of his boyhood when he returns to England to his (now titled) former love.

The novel concludes--as so many other romances do--with Harold and Stephen declaring their love for one another. The conclusion also wraps up Stoker's discussion of gender by reinforcing traditional gender roles:

It woke all the finer instincts of the woman. All the dross and thought of self passed away. Nature, sweet and simple and true, reigned alone. Instinctively she rose and came towards him. In the simple nobility of her *self-surrender* and her purpose, which were at one with the grandeur of nature around her, to be negative was to be false. . . . In his rapid ride he too had been finding himself. By the reading of his own soul he knew now that love needs a voice; that a man's love, to be welcomed to the full, should be *dominant and self-believing*. When the two saw each other's eyes there was no need for words. Harold came close, opening wise his arms. Stephen flew to them. In that divine moment, when their mouths met, both knew that their souls were one.[30] (emphasis added)

In spite of the emphasis on Stephen's surrender, however, she is not a duplication of her traditional aunt, who worried about Stephen's interest in world affairs and who insisted on behaving exactly as she had been taught. Nor is Harold simply a domineering man (a role played out to its most disagreeable extent in the terribly unattractive Leonard), for he ultimately learns to accept his weakness as well as his strength and comes to see Stephen as a lover and an equal.

As one can well imagine, Stoker's contemporaries were more taken with this romance than are readers at the end of the twentieth century though their comments suggest that they were also more likely to be disturbed by the question of sexual equality. The *Nation* described it as "Blatant melodrama, all the trashier for the grandiloquent moralizings,"[31] but the *Bookman* praises Stoker as a "master of the dramatic in fiction." [32]

The only two critics to examine *The Man* recently--Roth and Daniel Pick--examine the novel's subtleties. Roth is especially interested in Stoker's examination of sexual identity while Pick looks at Stoker's concern with eugenics and gender roles, both issues that had previously concerned him in *Dracula*.

PERSONAL REMINISCENCES OF HENRY IRVING (1906)

The year after Irving's death, Stoker published a two-volume memoir of the actor that covered the years from the day he met Irving to the day the actor died, a 30-year period. Moreover, it provides information about theatrical practices as well as plenty of interesting gossip about many of the public figures of the day. Initially quite popular, it went through several editions, including a less expensive one-volume edition in 1907.

Personal Reminiscences raises as many questions as it answers about Stoker, about Irving, and about their relationship. At times, however, one does glimpse something of Stoker. For example, early in Volume I, he describes a bit of the work that he did for Irving:

I had taken over all the correspondence and the letters were endless. It was the beginning of a vast experience of correspondence, for from that day on till the day of his death I seldom wrote, in working times, less than fifty letters a day. Fortunately-- for both myself and the readers, for I write an extremely bad hand--the bulk of them were short. Anyhow I think I shall be very well within the mark when I say that during my time of working with Henry Irving I have written in his name nearer half a million than a quarter million letters! [33]

Moreover, Stoker often read plays for Irving and Ellen Terry and other actors and actresses, made financial arrangements, and checked train and ship schedules. Reading *Personal Reminiscences* at least provides a partial explanation for the hurried nature of many of his novels, most of which seem to have been written during brief periods of rest.

Reading *Personal Reminiscences* also helps to explain the melodrama and romance of so many of his novels, for he spent almost every day in the theater, a theater known for its romantic excess even in an age that appreciated both romance and excess more than our own.

Moreover, one section also provides an insight into the character of Count Dracula. Although numerous critics suggest that the Count is modeled on Irving, certain passages in the *Reminiscences* suggest that Sir Richard Burton, the traveler and adventurer, whom Stoker first met on August 13, 1878, may have been a more important inspiration. Even before he knew the man's name, Stoker admits that he was fascinated:

But the man riveted my attention. He was dark, and forceful, and masterful, and ruthless. I have never seen so iron a countenance. I did not have much time to analyse the face. . . . But an instant was enough to make up my mind about him. (I: 350-51)

Their paths continue to cross, and Stoker recounts another incident--this time from 1886--when Irving had Sir Richard and Lady Burton to supper in the Beefsteak Room. Here again, Stoker is fascinated with Burton's ruthlessness and his exotic experiences:

There were passages in his life which set many people against him. I remember . . . hearing of how at a London dinner-party he told of his journey to Mecca. It was a wonderful feat, for he had to pass as a Muhammadan; the slightest breach of the multitudinous observances of that creed would call attention, and suspicion at such a time and place would be instant death. In a moment of forgetfulness, or rather inattention, he made some small breach of rule. He saw that a lad had noticed him and was quietly stealing away. He faced the situation at once, and coming after the lad in such a way as not to arouse his suspicion suddenly stuck his knife into his heart. . . . I asked him once about . . . the killing. He said it was quite true, and that it had never troubled him. . . . Said he: "The desert has its own laws, and there--supremely of all the East--to kill is a small offence. In any case what could I do? It had to be his life or mine!"
  As he spoke the upper lip rose and his canine tooth showed its full length like the gleam of a dagger. Then he went on to say that such explorations as he had undertaken were not to be entered lightly if one had qualms as to taking life. That the explorer in savage places holds, day and night, his life in his hand; and if he is not prepared for every emergency, he should not attempt such adventures. (I: 358-59)

Stoker, who began work on *Dracula* only a few years after this encounter with Burton, translates the adventurer's ruthlessness and his sharp canine tooth into his portrait of Count Dracula. Like Burton, Dracula is a stranger in a strange land who will do anything he can to survive.
  Personal Reminiscences occasionally provides insights into Stoker's fascination with science and technology and suggests that some of the adventures that he relates in his novels may have stemmed from first-hand experience. For example, the material on sea battles in *The Mystery of the Sea* may have come from an experience that happened to Stoker and Irving (August 9, 1880). Attempting to escape a mob of admirers, the two hire a boat from a deaf boatman, only to discover themselves right in the middle of a naval drill, when the boatman takes them right over a mine-bed. Stoker relates the thrill of the experience:

I think, however, that we both enjoyed the attack more that night when the actual sham battle was fought. In those days search-lights were new and rare. Both the *Glatton* and Fort Monckton were well equipped with them, and during the attack the whole sea and sky and shore were perpetually swept with the powerful rays. It was in its way a noble fight, and as then most people were ignorant of the practical working of the new scientific appliances of war, it was instructive as well as fascinating. We, who had been out in the middle of it during the day, could perhaps appreciate its possibilities better than ordinary civil folk unused to the forces and horrors of war! (II: 269)

Furthermore, the loving detail that Stoker uses to describe fires, trips by rail and by ship, reveals his interest in both technology and danger, interests that appear repeatedly in his fictional works.

Similarly, the pride with which he relates a compliment he had received from the explorer Henry M. Stanley reinforces both the pride he took in his careful research habits and his interest in the United States:

However, before we left at the conclusion of our second visit I had accumulated a lot of books--histories, works on the constitution, statistics, census, school books, books of etiquette for a number of years back, Congressional reports on various subjects--in fact all the means of reference and of more elaborate study. . . . This I published as a pamphlet in 1886, as *A Glimpse of America*. Stanley had evidently got hold of it, for one night when we were in Manchester, June 4, 1890, I had supper alone with Irving and he told me that the last time he had met him, Stanley had mentioned my little book on America as admirable. He had said that I had mistaken my vocation--that I should be a literary man! Of course such praise from such a man gave me a great pleasure. (I:368)

Both the interest and the thorough research that he had undertaken to explain the United States helps to explain the presence of so many American characters and American settings in his novels.

Since interest in Irving has waned in the period since his death, it is difficult to find much recent critical interest in this work, beyond the occasional observation of Irving's physical resemblance to Count Dracula and the occasional criticism that it reveals very little of Stoker the man and his relationship with his employer. It does, however, suggest that Stoker was influenced by the theater of his day though no critic has yet examined the possible link between Stoker's novels and his thorough knowledge of the theater.

Stoker's contemporaries, for whom the name Irving was a household word, were more interested in this work. However, possibly because they had eagerly anticipated this work, contemporaries were critical of the way he handled the subject. Often comparing Stoker to Boswell, contemporaries often commented on the fact that the work includes too much gossip and the social side of Irving's life, a criticism that the review in the *Bookman* attributes to his sensitivity to his former employer. The *Academy* observes that the book would have been much better if it omitted trivial gossip. Equally disappointed, the *Bookman* and *Blackwood's* note that Stoker doesn't help readers to know Irving. The book was also criticized for its excessive hero worship, its length, and the fact that it provided too few insights into Irving (the same lack of human detail that weakens almost all of Stoker's novels, except for *The Man* and *The Mystery of the Sea*). Stoker was also praised by contemporaries for his sensitive and touching story of Irving's last years and for his clear discussion of Irving's art. The consensus is that Stoker indulges too often in hero-worship (though this hero worship enables readers to see in Irving the kind of man that Stoker admired and featured in his novels) and that he makes no attempt to understand his subject. These flaws are also evident in his fictional works.

LADY ATHLYNE (1908)

Although *Lady Athlyne* has received relatively little critical attention either from
Stoker's contemporaries or from scholars and critics at the end of the twentieth
century, it is linked to a number of Stoker's other novels. Like *The Shoulder of
Shasta*, *The Man*, and *Dracula*, it includes American characters, this time the
Ogilvies--a Kentucky colonel, his wife and her sister Judy, and daughter Joy; like
The Shoulder of Shasta and *The Man*, it has scenes that take place in the United
States; and, like so many of Stoker's other novels, it confronts the old world
with the new when the Ogilvies take a European grand tour and Joy falls in love
with a Scottish nobleman.

The developing love Joy and Lord Athlyne and the expectations of
Colonel Ogilvie and Judy allow Stoker to examine gender issues once more.
Furthermore, like *The Snake's Pass*, *The Mystery of the Sea*, *The Lady of the
Shroud*, and *The Lair of the White Worm*, it reveals Stoker's interest in
technology--this time with the automobile.

The novel opens with an introduction to the Ogilvies, a wealthy
American family. As a joke among themselves, Aunt Judy and Joy begin to refer
to Joy as Lady Athlyne, having learned of this masculine paragon from his
former nurse.

The plot becomes more complicated when, hearing that someone is
using his name, Athlyne journeys to New York--himself under the assumed
name of Richard Hardy--to learn why. While in New York, he manages to save
Joy--whose horse has run away with her. (This scene is an obvious contrast to
the later scene in the automobile, this time when Athlyne is himself out of
control.) The two who are obviously beginning to fall in love plan to see one
another in England though their plans are complicated by Athlyne's
embarrassment over his alias and also by the fact that he is known throughout
the United Kingdom.

After some difficulty, the two meet and take an unchaperoned trip to
Scotland in Athlyne's new automobile, a "beauty. It was 100-110 h.p. and could
do sixty miles an hour easily." [34] Stoker's admiration for the automobile is clear
from his lengthy descriptions of the exhilaration that Joy and Athlyne feel, an
exhilaration that borders on the erotic. However, the "plot thickens"
appropriately when Athlyne is picked up in Scotland for speeding. In this novel
at least, technology is not presented as a savior of mankind though the contrast
between this scene and the earlier one in which Athlyne saves Joy from a
runaway horse suggests that technology may be somewhat easier for human
beings to control. So that Joy can return home safely (and without damaging her
reputation), he gives her his car to drive home. Unfortunately, she becomes lost
in the fog, and the two of them wind up staying at the same inn, a situation they
discover only moments before Colonel Ogilvie arrives on the scene to accuse
Hardy of destroying Joy's honor.

Only the efforts of a wise Scotch magistrate, who reveals that Athlyne
and Joy are married according to Scotch law, prevent the hot-headed Colonel
Ogilvie from challenging Athlyne to a duel. (According to Ludlam, Stoker had

thoroughly researched Scottish law and marriage by mutual consent to provide his neat conclusion to the novel.) This scene suggests certain cultural differences that Stoker was so fond of exploring. The American Colonel Ogilvie is reckless and impulsive (like Quincy Morris, inclined to shoot first and ask questions later) while the Scottish characters are more detached and reflective. (Athlyne, like Rupert Sent Leger in *The Lady of the Shroud,* Harold in *The Man,* and Adam Salton in *The Lair of the White Worm,* however, does seem to embody some of the individualism associated with colonial characters; and, like them, he is the master of technology in the novel, for he is able to understand the mechanics of his automobile.) However, this novel is clearly a comedy, so the cultural clash ends with cultural assimilation along with the marriage of European hero and American heroine (a union also anticipated in *The Mystery of the Sea*).

In addition to the romantic interest and the lengthy descriptions of motoring, *Lady Athlyne* provides innumerable opportunities for Stoker to discuss gender issues--most specifically heroic masculinity and blushing femininity:

Woman is, after all, more primitive than man. Her instincts are more self-centered than his. As her life moves in a narrower circle, her view is rather microscopic than telescopic; while his is the reverse. Inasmuch then as he naturally surveys a larger field, so his introspective view is wider. (257)

As in *The Man,* the problems in the novel begin when a woman usurps male power (in this case, when Joy assumes the name of a British peer and poses as the "lady" of the title). It is almost as though Stoker was becoming more adamant about rigid sex roles as he grew older. On the other hand, Joy handles the automobile better than her father; and she and Athlyne apparently see one another as potential equals.

Lady Athlyne has been virtually ignored since it was first published. Leatherdale calls it "rushed" and attributes the confusion to the fact that Stoker was ill: "he had a stroke following Irving's death, suffered from Bright's disease, and was losing his sight" (72). However, it is worth studying by people who are interested in Stoker's ideas on gender, his treatment of Americans, and his interest in technology as well as by those who are interested in early fictional reactions to the automobile. For example, the journey that Joy and Athlyne take to Scotland is plainly displaced eroticism and should be treated as such. Thus, it ties in with an entire genre of works that feature the automobile and also provides indications of how the automobile may have caused gender relationships to change even more rapidly.

THE LADY OF THE SHROUD (1909)

Although I had known for some time that most modern editions of this novel were abridged, I did not realize how much these excisions changed the original novel until I located and read a copy of the first edition. Dalby observes that modern reprints of this novel include "only two-thirds of the original novel" (58). Even more interesting is the fact that modern reprints omit the sections in which Rupert Sent Leger, the main male character, essentially becomes king of the small Balkan nation that he had rescued from political oppression.

A story of imposture in which a princess pretends to be a vampire to prevent her enemies from assassinating her includes romance between the heroic princess and a young adventurer. It is also interesting because it continues many of the issues that had preoccupied Stoker in *Dracula*--questions of narrative, an interest in science and technology, and a concern with cultural and gender differences. Like *Dracula*, *The Lady of the Shroud* is told through a variety of perspectives--an excerpt from *The Journal of Occultism*, letters and diaries written by the principle characters--Ernest Roger Halbard Melton, Rupert Sent Leger, Janet MacKelpie, Teuta Vissarian Sent Leger--letters and diaries of supporting characters, news clippings, and other sources of pertinent information. Moreover, this work continues Stoker's interest in vampirism though this time the "vampire" is really a young woman who pretends to be a preternatural figure to keep her political enemies away from her.

The Lady of the Shroud resembles several of Stoker's earlier novels. Like *Lady Athlyne*, it reveals Stoker's fascination with technological developments; like *Dracula*, it reveals that technology can help to overcome primitive forces; and like the earlier *The Mystery of the Sea*, it reveals Stoker's interest in arms and armaments though Stoker adds an air force in this novel. Written shortly after the Wright brothers' first successful flight, the novel concludes with an air battle in which the hero, Rupert St Leger, rescues the heroine's father, who has been imprisoned by the Turks. A report prepared by Christoferos, scribe of the National Council of the Land of the Blue Mountains (the small Balkan nation where most of the novel takes place) reveals the importance of armaments:

May I ask that you will come back with me in memory to the year 1890, when our struggle against Ottoman aggression, later on so successfully brought to a close, was begun. We were then in a desperate condition. Our finances had run so low that we could not purchase even the bread which we required. Nay, more, we could not procure through the National Exchequer what we wanted more than bread--arms of modern effectiveness; for men may endure hunger and yet fight well, as the glorious past of our country has proved again and again and again. But when our foes are better armed than we are, the penalty is dreadful to a nation small as our own is in number, no matter how brave their hearts. [35]

This theme continues throughout the novel, for Rupert manages to save Teuta's father because his airplane gives him the element of surprise over his opponents. However, the following exchange, which incidentally concludes the novel, recognizes that technology has not provided the answers to all problems:

The Western King said. . . "It must need some skill to drop a letter with such accuracy." . . . "It is easier to drop bombs, Your Majesty."

The flight of aeroplanes was a memorable sight. It helped to make history. Henceforth no nation with an eye for either defence or attack can hope for success without the mastery of the air. (367)

Stoker, who died before the beginning of World War I, sounds here more than a little prophetic.

His commentary on gender issues is less prophetic, for he has Teuta, who had suffered and struggled for her country, end as a traditional wife and mother. In fact, in the following passage, Teuta might well be warning a group of suffragettes about the errors of their ways:

Lords of the Council of the Blue Mountains, I am a wife of the Blue Mountains. . . . And it would ill become me . . . to take a part in changing the ancient custom which has been held in honour for all the thousand years, which is the glory of Blue Mountain womanhood. What an example such would be in an age when self-seeking women of other nations seek to forget their womanhood in the struggle to vie in equality with men! Men of the Blue Mountains, I speak for our women when I say that we hold of greatest price the glory of our men. To be their companions is our happiness; to be their wives is the completion of our lives; to be mothers of their children is our share of the glory that is theirs (319)

In addition to providing a traditional gender message, a message which is consistent with Stoker's other works, *The Lady of the Shroud* offers a traditional political message. Despite its emphasis on freedom from oppression, it ends with Rupert's being made king over the little nation. In fact, it is this section that has been excised from numerous recent editions.

The last of the six works to be published by the innovative publisher Heinemann, *The Lady of the Shroud* was not widely reviewed by Stoker's contemporaries though W.F. Purvis, the reviewer for the *Bookman*, was extremely enthusiastic, commenting on Stoker's awareness of politics and science:

He presents us with a huge prophetic melodrama of the Near East: he creates in outline at least that Balkan Federation, which may or may not be feasible, but certainly seems essential to the curbing of Austrian ambitions on the one hand and Turkish pretensions on the other. . . . But this romantic melodrama is tinged with the scientific spirit of H.G. Wells on the one side and the influence of the Psychical Research revival on the other. [36]

Thus Purvis recognizes Stoker's interest in technology as well as his interest in the supernatural.

However, the similarities with *Dracula* alone make *The Lady of the Shroud* worthy of more attention. In addition, it is likely to provide material for people who are interested in questions of narrative, to people who are interested in science (or science and technology) and literature, and for those who are interested in the relationship between political events and literary analysis.

FAMOUS IMPOSTORS   (1910)

Virtually ignored during the recent revival of interest in Stoker, *Famous Impostors* received a great deal of attention from Stoker's contemporaries although much of that attention was highly critical. In fact, this work was reviewed in most of the major journals in both England and the United States and received much more attention than his later fiction.

The case studies that Stoker discusses include numerous kinds of imposture: impersonators, pretenders, swindlers, and humbugs. While Stoker's contemporaries often observed that the histories of Perkin Warbeck, Cagliostro, Hannah Snell, Arthur Orton, and the Chevalier D'Eon were already familiar to them, they were most interested in his account of the Bisley Boy (the story that a boy was supposedly substituted for Henry VIII's daughter Elizabeth by her frightened governess when the young princess died unexpectedly and that this boy later grew up to be Queen Elizabeth I).

The book will interest contemporary students of Stoker, however, because of what it reveals about his novels. In fact, his preface even compares the methods he uses to explore historical figures with the methods novelists use to explore character. Most important, *Famous Impostors* addresses an issue that continued to fascinate Stoker--the question of identity. He had recently finished his two-volume reminiscence of Irving, a work in which he had examined Irving's art and the numerous ways in which the great actor used costume and gesture to "become" a character on stage; and the influence of the nineteenth-century stage on Stoker's novels is a subject that remains to be explored.

Furthermore, the question of identity is important in Stoker's most famous novel. (Anyone who has seen the numerous transformations of Dracula in Francis Ford Coppola's film version, *Bram Stoker's Dracula* [1992] will see that the question of identity reverberates through both the novel and the film.) For example, in *Dracula*, Jonathan Harker wonders whether the three rapacious women that he meets at Dracula's castle are ladies or ravenous beasts; Dracula wears Harker's clothes to go out hunting for fresh blood so that a young peasant woman confuses Harker with Dracula; finally, Van Helsing must persuade the young men who had once loved Lucy Westenra that she is now a bloodthirsty monster instead of an innocent upper class woman.

In *The Lady of the Shroud*, Rupert Sent Leger wonders whether the mysterious woman who appears in his bedroom is a vampire or a woman; and it turns out that she is merely using the superstition to elude potential kidnappers. *The Jewel of Seven Stars* blurs the identity of ancient Egyptian Queen Tera and Victorian heroine Margaret Trelawney, a blurring that Stoker handles differently in the first edition and in subsequent editions. Finally, Stoker's last novel, *The Lair of the White Worm*, has a character--the Lady Arabella March--who is both a beautiful aristocrat and a primeval monster.

Moreover, since Stoker's novels often consider whether his women characters are monsters or heroines, readers today will also be interested to see that so many of the cases in *Famous Impostors*--including the Bisley Boy--

involve one sex impersonating the other. Thus, this rather hurried work examines the question of gender found so often in Stoker's other works.

For example, the beginning of Chapter VII: Women as Men observes the numerous reasons that women might have disguised themselves as men:

It is not to be wondered at that such attempts are made; or that they were made more often formerly when social advancement had not enlarged the scope of work available for women. The legal and economic disabilities of the gentler sex stood then so fixedly in the way of working opportunity that women desirous of making an honest livelihood took desperate chances to achieve their object. 37

(The chapter on *The Mystery of the Sea* reveals that Stoker was certainly aware of the constraints placed on women; therefore, he offers Marjory Drake freedom from observation only when she dresses in men's clothing.) Later in *Famous Impostors*, Stoker suggests that the sheer desire for equality served as an incentive for one young woman, though he underlines that she sacrificed her femininity for equality:

It may have been the sexual equality implied by the name which gave the young woman the idea, but thenceforth she became a man in appearance; in reality, in so far as such a metamorphosis can be accomplished by courage, recklessness, hardihood, unscrupulousness, and a willing obedience to all the ideas which passion and sensuality can originate and a greed of notoriety carry into execution. (236)

Perhaps most troubling to people with ideas of distinct gender identity is the fact that the kinds of imposture described by Stoker often go undetected:

Only very lately the death of a person who had for many years occupied a worthy though humble position in London caused a post-mortem sensation by the discovery that the deceased individual, though looked on for about a quarter of a century as a man, a widower, and the father of a grown-up daughter, was in reality a woman. She was actually buried under the name of the man she had professed to be, Harry Lloyd. (227-28)

Critics at the end of the twentieth century have paid little or no attention to *Famous Impostors* except occasionally to note that the question of identity is central to Stoker's better-known fiction as well.

THE LAIR OF THE WHITE WORM (1911)

This horror novel of an ancient malevolent white serpent who can transform itself into the beautiful Lady Arabella March apparently did not interest Stoker's contemporaries though it has interested both critics and creative adaptors like the director Ken Russell in the late twentieth century. Moreover, although Phyllis A. Roth describes it correctly as "Stoker's last novel and, in every way his weakest" (80), it is likely to continue to interest readers at the end of the twentieth century because, like the earlier *Dracula*, it deals with many issues that continue to concern us today--issues of race and gender in particular, but also the relationship among various cultures and even the relationship between the civilized world and the natural world. Like many of Stoker's other novels, *Lair* demonstrates Stoker's hope that technology would enable human beings to overcome powerful remnants from the past: in *Lair* Adam Salton, the hero, uses modern explosives to destroy the primeval monster. That this work explores the relationship between an earlier non-human period suggests a slightly different direction for Stoker whose interest in the natural world had been largely descriptive in earlier works--for example, the mountainous backdrops in *The Shoulder of Shasta, Dracula,* and *The Lady of the Shroud.* In fact, only *The Snake's Pass* and *The Lair of the White Worm* ask readers to examine closely the connections between human beings and the natural world.

Like *The Man, The Jewel of Seven Stars,* and *The Lady of the Shroud,* this novel exists in several different versions including a version printed in 1925 that was, according to Dalby, severely altered and substantially abridged. Modern reprints from Jarrolds and Arrow use this abbreviated version instead of the first edition. Dalby does mention one modern edition that is faithful to the original-- *The Garden of Evil,* published by Paperback Library in 1966.[38] As a result of these textual problems, some of the questions that readers have may stem from the modern reprints. Other problems stem from the fact that Stoker was in physically frail health when he wrote *The Lair of the White Worm.* Thus, even the first edition has problems especially in consistency. For example, Stoker spends a great deal of time examining Edgar Caswall's interest in Mesmer's chest, but he drops this plot strand halfway through the novel and never picks it up again.

Furthermore, as is so typical of Stoker's novels, the characterization is weak. However, the problem of weak characterization is exacerbated in this novel by his attempt to use animal symbolism to suggest the connections between humans and the natural world. (Lady Arabella *is* the White Worm; Lilla is associated with the doves that had once lived in the monastery on which her grandfather's farm is built; Edgar resembles a hawk in both appearance and predatory behavior; and Adam Salton is associated with several different mongooses.) However, the symbolism is poorly worked out and serves only to suggest certain human character traits.

Whatever text the modern reader examines (and there are definite differences in the various editions), it is nonetheless possible to see Stoker wrestle with many of the same problems that had troubled him throughout his writing career--questions of race and gender; the relationship between past and present; the relationship between the civilized Western world and primitive forces; and the choices provided by science and technology.

In spite of these obvious similarities, *The Lair of the White Worm* stands out from most of Stoker's fiction, for it is set in the past rather than the present. However, unlike *Miss Betty,* the only Stoker novel that might be classified as an historical novel, *The Lair of the White Worm* is set in the past of Stoker's youth, 1860 to be precise. Furthermore, like *The Snake's Pass,* it manages to unite the distant past with the present because property owned by the principle characters goes back to the days of the Romans and even the Celts. Casta Regis, the family seat of the Caswall family, is now owned by the cold and hypnotic Edgar Caswall, but it was once a Roman fortification. Mercy Farm, home of Lilla and Mimi Watford and their grandfather, was once the site of a nunnery founded by Queen Bertha in the days before Saint Augustine. Diana's Grove, home of the sinister Lady Arabella March, is the site of an enormous well hold inhabited by an antediluvian monster known as the White Worm.

Moreover, as he had done with *The Snake's Pass*, Stoker manages the integrate the more remote legendary past with the present by having one of his characters relate the legend of the White Worm, an enormous serpent who is linked with Lady Arabella. In her human form, Lady Arabella merely seems cold and distant--the quintessential aristocrat--though Adam Salton notes on first meeting her that the local snakes are more afraid of her than she is of them. Before attempting to understand her connection with the White Worm, Adam is interested in the human woman:

She was certainly good to look at in herself, and her dress alone was sufficient to attract attention. She was clad in some kind of soft-white stuff, which clung close to her form, showing to the full every movement of her sinuous figure. She was tall and exceedingly thin. Her eyes appeared to be weak, for she wore large spectacles which seemed to be of green glass. Certainly in the centre they had the effect of making her naturally piercing eyes of a vivid green. She wore a close-fitting cap of some fine fur of dazzling white. Coiled round her white throat was a large necklace of emeralds, whose profusion of colour quite outshone the green of her spectacles--even when the sun shone on them. Her voice was very peculiar, very low and sweet, and so soft that the dominant note was of sibilation. Her hands, too, were peculiar--long, flexible, white, with a strange movement as of waving gently to and fro. [39]

Although Lady Arabella is occasionally presented as a temptress (she had married for money once before and hopes to use her feminine wiles to seduce Edgar Caswall), Salton's fascination is short-lived, however, for he sees her shoot a mongoose he had acquired to rid his uncle's property of snakes, charm a second mongoose, rip a third mongoose to pieces with her bare hands, and finally drag Edgar Caswall's African servant Oolanga to his death in the well hole. This last scene is graphic and designed to emphasize Lady Arabella's monstrous nature:

Lady Arabella's anger, now fully awake, was all for Oolanga. She moved forward towards him with her bare hands extended, and had just seized him, when the catch of the locked box from some movement from within flew open, and the king-cobra-killer flew at her with a venomous fury impossible to describe. As it seized her throat she caught hold of it, and, with a fury superior to its own, actually tore it in two just as if it had been a sheet of paper. The strength used for such an act must have been terrific. In an instant, it seemed to spout blood and entrails, and was hurled into the well-hole. In another instead she had seized Oolanga, and with a swift rush had drawn him, her white arms encircling him, with her down into the gaping aperture. (174)

The relation between human woman and monster is a complex one which Stoker doesn't even attempt to explain. Furthermore Mimi Watford Salton observes that most people wouldn't believe her if she told them. In fact, very much like Jonathan Harker at the conclusion to *Dracula*, she almost disbelieves her own eyes:

> The more Mimi thought over the late events, the more puzzled she was. Adam had actually seen Lady Arabella coming from her own house on the Brow, yet he--and she too--had last seen the monster in the guise in which she had occasionally appeared wallowing in the Irish Sea. What did it all mean--what could it mean? . . . On either side of her was a belief impossible of reception. Not to believe in what seemed apparent was to destroy the very foundations of belief. . . . And yet. . . and yet in old days there had been monsters on the earth, and certainly some people had believed in just such mysterious changes of identity. (245)

As in *Dracula*, however, it is not necessary for the forces of good to explain their decisions to anyone; and the novel concludes with an apocalyptic explosion that destroys both Diana's Grove and Casta Regis. Once again, the present triumphs over the past and the group over the individual, for Adam Salton, the youthful hero, places dynamite in the well hole and destroys the primeval serpent. Although Salton's fuse is lit by a fortuitous bold of lightning (the union of a healing natural force with technology perhaps), the conclusion suggests that more evolved species will triumph over the more primitive, as Sir Nathaniel suggests in the following discussion:

> In the beginning, the instincts of animals are confined to alimentation, self-protection, and the multiplication of their species. As time goes on and the needs of life become more complex, power follows need. (198)

Here--as elsewhere in Stoker's fiction (*The Jewel of Seven Stars* is the single exception), the representatives of western civilization triumph over the more primitive life. One difference should be noted, however. Although representatives of European countries generally overcome representatives of colonial groups (see Arata's discussion of *Dracula* for a full discussion of this topic), Adam Salton is an Australian and a man who prides himself on his abilities, as we see in the following discussion when he offers to repair Lady Arabella's broken carriage:

> "You!" She looked incredulously at the dapper young gentleman who spoke. "You--why, it's a workman's job."
> "All right, I am a workman--though that is not the only sort of work I do. Let me explain. I am an Australian, and, as we have to move about fast, we are all trained to farriery and such mechanics as come into travel--and I am quite at your service." (30)

Like Lord Athlyne who is able to repair his own motorcar and Rupert Sent Leger who flies his own airplane, Adam Salton has allied himself with the most advanced technological thinkers.

Certainly, *The Lair of the White Worm* continues to present the triumph of civilization: white men over black men, dynamite over dinosaurs, men's women over women alone. Oolanga, who dies relatively early in the novel, is presented as an example of the human being at its most primitive:

The diversion was welcome to all; the two Saltons and Sir Nathaniel were shocked at Caswall's face--so hard, so ruthless, so selfish, so dominant. . . . But presently his African servant approached him, and at once their thoughts changed to a larger toleration. For by comparison with this man his face seemed to have a certain nobility hitherto lacking. Caswall looked indeed a savage--but a cultured savage. In him were traces of the softening civilization of ages--of some of the higher instincts and education of man, no matter how rudimentary these might be. But the face of Oolanga, as his master at once called him, was pure pristine, unreformed, unsoftened savage, with inherent in it all the hideous possibilities of a lost-devil-ridden child of the forest and the swamp--the lowest and most loathsome of all created things which were in some form ostensibly human. (34-35)

Given this attitude to people of color, it is not surprising that no one--Adam Salton, Lady Arabella, Edgar Caswall, Sir Nathaniel, or even Stoker himself--is overly concerned by the horrifying death of Oolanga. What is somewhat surprising is the fact that Mimi Watford Salton is also presented as a woman of color. Unlike Oolanga, however, Mimi has totally accepted the tenets of Western Civilization.

The novel also examines gender. As they prepare to destroy the White Worm, Sir Nathaniel and Adam consistently describe it in terms that combine femininity and primitiveness:

I never thought this fighting an antediluvian monster was such a complicated job. This one is a woman, with all a woman's wisdom and wit, combined with the heartlessness of a *cocotte* and the want of principles of a suffragette. She has the reserved strength and impregnability of a diplodocus. We may be sure that in the fight that is before us there will be no semblance of fair-play. . . . Now, Adam, it strikes me that, as we have to protect ourselves and others against feminine nature, our strong game will be to play our masculine against her feminine. (206)

In the end, the only woman to survive is Mimi, who has linked her fortune to Adam Salton by marrying him. Both her cousin Lilla, who had chosen to battle wills with Edgar, and Lady Arabella, who had attempted to control her own destiny and those of the world around her, are dead. In fact, the success of the dark-skinned Mimi (her mother had been Burmese though her father was English) suggests that skin color is less important than accepting the dictates of Western European civilization; and Mimi is in every way a man's woman--a woman who has accepted the conventional wisdom of patriarchal civilization including its embrace of law and technology. Early in the novel, the wise old Sir Nathaniel warns Adam against falling in love with Lady Arabella and tells him that Mimi would be an acceptable wife:

She is indeed a very charming lady. I do not think I ever saw a girl who united in such perfection the qualities of strength of character and sweetness of disposition. (189)

In fact, the novel suggests that the monstrous female must be destroyed before the world is safe for Mimi. Once the primeval monster (and the aggressive independent woman) is destroyed, the novel concludes with a return to domesticity:

But all's well that ends well. We had better hurry home. Your wife may be waking by now, and is sure to be frightened at first. Come home as soon as you can. I shall see that breakfast is ready. I think we all want it. (324)

Thus the novel concludes with breakfast and the expectations that Adam will use his already substantial fortune to produce a profit from the white clay he had discovered on Lady Arabella's property.

Stoker's contemporaries seemed not to know what to do with this strange novel; and twentieth-century responses to Stoker's last novel reveal that they also find it difficult and baffling. Ludlam observes that it seems to reveal "some deep mystery between the lines--the mystery of the mind of the man who wrote it" (165). Leonard Wolf, who also notices "the signs of confusion and loneliness the narrative obtrudes," [40] points out the sexual message in *Lair*; and both he and Daniel Farson comment on the creepy sexuality of Stoker's last novel. Finally, Rosemary Jackson in *Fantasy: The Literature of Subversion* and Gregory Waller in *The Living and the Undead* examine the novel's political ideology.

DRACULA'S GUEST--AND OTHER WEIRD STORIES   (1914)

Stoker was sifting through his earlier short fiction to prepare several anthologies when he died, and Stoker's widow saw this one to press. As Florence Stoker's brief preface observes, Stoker was working on several projects when he died: He had "planned three series of short stories for publication, and the present volume is one of them."[41] The widow notes that she added an episode from *Dracula* which was originally excised owing to the length of the book" and explains that it "may prove of interest to the many readers of what is considered my husband's most remarkable work." [42] She concludes her preface by indicating that she had made no other changes to his plans:

Had my husband lived longer, he might have seen fit to revise this work, which is mainly from the earlier years of his strenuous life. But, as fate has entrusted to me the issuing of it, I consider it fitting and proper to let it go forth practically as it was left by him.

The collection includes the following short stories--"Dracula's Guest," "The Judge's House," "The Squaw," "The Secret of the Growing Gold," "A Gypsy Prophecy," "The Coming of Abel Behenna," "The Burial of the Rats," "A Dream of Red Hands," and "Crooken Sands." As Florence Stoker observes, these

stories were "mainly from the earlier years of his strenuous life." Thus, they do not represent the culmination of his development as a writer. Moreover, "Dracula's Guest" was a chapter that he deliberately chose *not* to include, for it was discovered only after his death.

Although the stories in the collection do not all deal with the supernatural, most of them reveal Stoker's interest in the weird and macabre. In fact, the title of the first edition was *Dracula's Guest and Other Weird Stories* though subsequent editions have dropped the phrase "and other weird stories." "The Judge's House" (first published in the December 5, 1891 issue of the *Illustrated Sporting and Dramatic News*) includes a haunted house, a haunted portrait of the cruel judge who had once owned the house, and rats, one of whom seems to have taken on the character of the judge. This chilling story ends with the death of the young student who had chosen to live in the judge's house. A Jonathan Harker-like figure, he had chosen to ignore the warnings of other residents of the community. When they finally break into the house, they find him hanging at the end of the same rope the hangman had used for the judge's victims.

Reminiscent of Poe, "The Secret of the Growing Gold" includes a love triangle and a murdered wife, whose blond hair continues to grow after her husband had attempted to conceal her body under the floor. Although the first wife had sought vengeance on her unfaithful husband, she is able to extract vengeance on him and his second wife only after her death.

"The Squaw," the most anthologized of Stoker's stories, was originally published in the December 2, 1893 issue of the *Illustrated Sporting and Dramatic News*. Another tale of vengeance, it focuses on a mother cat, who achieves vengeance against a man, Elias P. Hutcheson, who accidentally killed her kitten. (Hutcheson, a jovial traveler from Nebraska, bears some resemblance to some of Stoker's American adventurers, for he is brash and unpolished; and Arata would probably read his horrible death as a punishment on a colonial.) The conclusion, which is narrated by another tourist who witnesses Hutcheson's death in the Nurnberg Virgin, is grisly in the extreme:

As the door closed I caught a glimpse of our poor companion's face. He seemed frozen with terror. His eyes stared with a horrible anguish as if dazed, and no sound came from his lips.
And then the spikes did their work. Happily the end was quick, for when I wrenched open the door they had pierced so deep that they had locked in the bones of the skull through which they had crushed, and actually tore him--it--out of his iron prison till, bound as he was, he fell at full length with a sickly thud upon the floor, the face turning upward as he fell. (65)

The story reinforces the conflict of cultures, for the title refers both to the vengeful mother cat and to an Apache squaw who Hutcheson watched torture the man who had killed her baby. Thus the story looks at animal response, primitive behavior, the behavior of the frontiersman, and the response of the civilized European couple.

"The Gipsy Prophecy" and "The Coming of Abel Behenna" combine love stories with weird events. In the first of these, a young husband visits a Gipsy fortuneteller who reads the following fortune in his hand:

'I see here the flowing of blood; it will flow before long; it is running in my sight. It flows through the broken circle of a severed ring. . . . This is the hand of a murderer-- the murderer of his wife." (88)

When he tells his wife of the prophecy, she too goes to the Gipsy camp only to hear a similar prophecy--that she will lie at her husband's feet and that his hands will be red with blood.

To avert the prophecy, the young wife dulls all the knives in the house. Although Stoker prepares the reader for a grisly conclusion, the story ends happily when she falls on her husband's Ghourka knife, a fall that severs her wedding ring and cuts her hand. Thus the Gipsy's prophecy ironically comes true.

"The Coming of Abel Behenna" does not end as happily. Here two young men agree to a contest for the hand of a fickle young woman (an echo of *Dracula's* Lucy Westenra). However, one of the young men dies, and the other goes mad when he sees the drowned body of his rival.

"The Burial of the Rats," a story of purely human evil, tells of a young man's experience when he is trapped by a group of desperate people who wish to rob and murder him. One of Stoker's courageous young men, he manages to elude his predators and even to wreak some vengeance against them. Moreover, because the predators are associated with the violence of the French Revolution, this story--like *Dracula*--suggests a conflict between past and present. "A Dream of Red Hands" (originally published in July 11, 1894 in the *Sketch*, Vol. 6) and "Crooken Sands" (published in the December 1, 1894 issue of the *Illustrated Sporting and Dramatic News*) are moral tales. In the first, a man is beset by bad dreams for a crime he had accidentally committed in his youth. However, he manages to expiate his crime by courageously saving the life of another man. "Crooken Sands" includes a double image and a man who is able to conquer his own pride.

Of the stories in this collection, "Dracula's Guest" has received the most attention from recent critics, many of whom note Stoker's debt to fellow-Irishman Joseph Sheridan Le Fanu's *Carmilla*.[43] Obviously Florence Stoker 's awareness that people would continue to regard *Dracula* as her husband's best work motivated her decision to include it in this collection.

Although scholarly interest in these stories has been modest at best, other people have managed to capitalize on the continued popular interest in *Dracula*. For example, the collection was reprinted in 1927 in a special souvenir edition that was presented to "the audience at the Prince of Wales Theatre for the 250th London performance of the play *Dracula*." When members of the audience opened their packet, they found a copy of *Dracula's Guest* and "inside the book's cover, a black bat, powered by elastic, which flew out as the book was opened" (Publishers' Note to the 1966 edition).

THE CRITICAL RECEPTION TO STOKER'S WORKS

Examining the critical response to Stoker's works reveals that attitudes toward his fiction have changed over the past century. Stoker's contemporaries were much more tolerant of his frequent sentimentality, less tolerant of the sexuality that so often appears in his works and less intrigued by the way that Stoker combines Gothic elements with an interest in science and technology. More recent critics are likely to explore that very sexuality through they may well find his attitudes perplexing; and recent critics are certainly both aware of and interested in Stoker's concern with topical issues: gender, ethnicity, imperialism, and scientific and technological development.

Since *Dracula* has become so thoroughly a part of Anglo-American consciousness, it is likely that Stoker himself will never be completely forgotten. That so many of the other works he wrote remain either out of print or available only in truncated paperback editions probably means that he will remain in the ranks of the second-rate writers. Having spent so much time with Stoker's work, I believe such a fate is undeserved. Although some of what he wrote is dated and often hurriedly prepared, other works continue to speak on issues that continue to perplex readers poised on the verge of the twenty-first century. Bram Stoker deserves better, and so do contemporary readers.

NOTES

[1] Carol A. Senf, The Vampire in Nineteenth-Century Fiction. (Bowling Green, Ohio: Popular Predss, 1987).

[2] Margaret Drabble, ed., *The Oxford Companion to English Literature*. 5th Ed. (New York: Oxford University Press, 1985).

[3] Joseph S. Bierman, "The Genesis and Dating of *Dracula* from Bram Stoker's Working Notes," *Notes and Queries* 24 (1977): 39.

[4] Daniel Farson, *The Man Who Wrote Dracula: A Biography of Bram Stoker* (New York: St. Martin's Press, 1975): 234.

[5] Kenneth W. Fair, "About Bram," *The Romantist*, IV-V (1980-1981): 39.

[6] Phyllis A. Roth, *Bram Stoker* (Boston: Twayne, 1982): 38.

[7] For a good bibliography of films, see Raymond T. McNally, *Dracula was a Woman* (New York: McGraw-Hill, 1983): 234-44.

[8] *Dracula: The Vampire and the Critics* (Ann Arbor: UMI Research Press, 1988).

[9] Clive Leatherdale, *Dracula: The Novel and the Legend* (Wellingborough: Aquarian Press, 1985).

[10] There are two biographies of Stoker: The first is Harry Ludlam, *A Biography of Dracula: The Life Story of Bram Stoker* (London: W. Foulsham, 1962). The second was prepared by Daniel Farson, Stoker's grand-nephew.

[11] Richard Dalby, *Bram Stoker: A Bibliography of First Editions* (London: Dracula Press, 1983).

[12] Bram Stoker, *Under the Sunset.* 1882. rpt. North Hollywood, CA: Newcastle Publishing Co., 1978, 71. All references will be to this edition and will be included in the text.

[13] "Review of *Under the Sunset,*" *Punch* (December 3, 1881): 261.

[14] Joseph S. Bierman, "*Dracula*: Prolonged Childhood Illness and the Oral Triad," *American Imago* 29 (1972): 186-98.

[15] Bram Stoker. *The Snake's Pass.* 1889. rpt. Brandon Ireland, County Kerry, Ireland: Brandon, 1990, 26. Future excerpts to this novel will be from this edition and will be included in the text.

[16] "Review of *The Snake's Pass,*" *Punch* 99 (December 6, 1890): 269.

[17] "Review of *The Snake's Pass,*" *Atheneum* 96 (December 20, 1890): 85.

[18] Bram Stoker, *The Watter's Mou'.* 1895; rpt. *The Bram Stoker Bedside Companion,* ed. Charles Osborne. New York: Taplinger, 1973. p. 167. Future quotations will be to this edition and will be included in the text.

[19] Bram Stoker. *The Shoulder of Shasta.* London: Macmillan's Colonial Library, 1895, 4. Future quotations will be included in the text.

[20] Bram Stoker, *The Annotated Dracula,* ed. Leonard Wolf. New York: Clarkson N. Potter, 1975. 39-41. Future references will be to this edition and will be included in the text.

[21] "Review of *Dracula,*" *Spectator* 79 (July 31, 1897): 151.

[22] Stoker's relationship to these so-called "New Women" novelists is addressed in the following essay: Carol A. Senf, "*Dracula*: Stoker's Response to the New Woman." *Victorian Studies* 26 (19982), No. 1, 33-49.

[23] Bram Stoker. *Miss Betty.* 1898. rpt. London: New English Library, 1974, 130. Future quotations will be to this edition and will be included in the text.

[24] "Review of *Miss Betty,*" *Punch* 114 (March 5, 1898): 105.

[25] Bram Stoker, *Snowbound: The Record of a Theatrical Touring Party.* 1899 and 1908; rpt. Ann Arbor, Michigan: University Microfilms International, 1977. (This edition is an authorized facsimile of the original book). All quotations will be from this edition and will be included in the text.

[26] Charles Osborne, ed., *The Bram Stoker Bedside Companion.* (London: Quartet, 1972): 13.

[27] Bram Stoker. *The Mystery of the Sea.* 1902. London: Rider & Co., no date (though Dalby notes that it was printed in October 1929 and also observes that this inexpensive edition was somewhat abridged from the first edition), 209. Future quotations will be taken from this edition and will be included in the text.

[28] "Review of *The Mystery of the Sea,*" *Bookman* 23 (October 1902): 32.

[29] Bram Stoker. *The Jewel of Seven Stars.* London: William Heinemann, 1903. 172. All quotations will be taken from this edition and will be included in the text.

30 Bram Stoker. *The Man*. London: William Heinemann, 1905. 435-36. All quotations will be to this edition and will be included in the text.

31 "Review of *The Gates of Life*," *Nation* 87 (August 20, 1908): 163.

32 "Review of *The Man*," *Bookman* 29 (October 1905): 39.

33 Bram Stoker. *Personal Reminiscences of Henry Irving*. 1906 (rpt. Westport, Ct: Greenwood Press, 1970). I:61-62. All quotations will be to this edition and will be included in the text.

34 Bram Stoker. *Lady Athlyne*. New York: Paul R. Reynolds, 1908, p. 124. (Dalby does not mention this edition though it seems to have the same number of pages as the first edition.) All quotations will be to this edition and will be included in the text.

35 Bram Stoker. *The Lady of the Shroud*. London: Heinemann, 1909, p. 269. All future quotations will be taken from this edition and will be included in the text.

36 W.F. Purvis, "Bram Stoker's Latest Novel." *Bookman* 37 (January 1910): 194.

37 Bram Stoker. *Famous Impostors*. New York: Sturgis and Walton, 1910, p. 227. All future references will be to this edition and will be included in the text.

38 Dalby: 63-65.

39 Bram Stoker. *The Lair of the White Worm*. London: Rider and Son, 1911, pp. 31-32. All future quotations will be to this edition and will be included in the text.

40 Leonard Wolf, *A Dream of Dracula* (Boston: Little, Brown, 1972): 256.

41 Bram Stoker. *Dracula's Guest*. 1914; rpt. London: Jarrolds Publishers, 1966, preface. Future quotations will be taken from this edition and will be included in the text.

42 According to Ludlam, Stoker's literary executor discovered the manuscript of the story that has become known as "Dracula's Guest" while he was going through Stoker's papers (169). There are also obvious differences, including the fact that the young male character in the story is *not* named Jonathan Harker and the fact that his adventure takes place in a totally different country. These differences merely suggest that Stoker worked on *Dracula* over a period of years and obviously changed his mind about the novel more than once.

43 In fact, Ludlam notes that "Dracula's Guest" is too derivative of the earlier work:

Sheridan Le Fanu's female vampire 'Carmilla' was a Countess. She also pursued her macabre errands in Styria. And she was a suicide, laid in such a tomb. . . . It was the only piece in the story that was not wholly the product of his own vivid imagination and imaginative research. (128)

Under the Sunset

"REVIEW OF *UNDER THE SUNSET*," *SPECTATOR* 54 (NOVEMBER 12, 1881), 1440-41.

How much do children understand of the fanciful and often beautiful books that are written for their delectation at the present time? To what extent do they appreciate them? These are questions which our own experience cannot help us to answer, for, besides that the remembrance of one's childhood is rarely vivid in these respects, there were no such books in those far past days. After *Robinson Crusoe*, and the few immortal stories, such as *Jack the Giant Killer*, *Red Riding Hood*, *Puss in Boots*, and some others which we can all remember, literature for children was poor stuff, mostly consisting of dreadful little moral tales of the Tommy-and-Harry order, relieved only by the ever-glorious exception of *Peter Parley's Annual*. *That* was a book to make one rebel against the ordinance of Nature which decreed that Christmas should come only once a year. What a treat it was, and how we loved it! But even Peter Parley did not appeal to and cultivate the imagination of children as the writers of the present day do. Peter Parley gave only stories of sea and land, of sharks and whales, of deserts and their denizens, of fights and victories, of pleasant school-days, and the peaceful pursuits of home. "P.P." was great in puzzles, and the farther one was from guessing them the nicer they were; but in the purely imaginative, he did not deal. Then there was *Gammer Grethel*, a book for which the world can never be too grateful; but though it was fanciful, inasmuch as it dealt with dwarfs and sprites, wood-goblins, kings, queens, and princesses, it was realistic, too, in the matter-of-fact German way, and put upon the minds of its young readers none of the strain of high, sentiment and ingenious allegory.

What a gulf divides the days of *Grammer Grethel*, and even those of *The Story Without an End* (always, we fancy, over the heads of children, unless they were the spectacled sages of German nurseries), and those of *Lilliput Levee*, *Alice in Wonderland*, and the beautiful book which lies before us, *Under the Sunset*, by Mr. Bram Stoker, in whom the children of this year of grace have a new and generous friend. As, however, in that gulf lie buried our own childhood and youth, we ask,--Do the children of this generation appreciate the books that are written for them? If they do, what a long way ahead of us they must be, at their very first start in reading and thinking life. There is an educational process for the eye, a refining influence over the taste, in a book like this one, which are not to be lightly estimated, if we are inclined to take anything into consideration with regard to a book for children except whether it will please and amuse them. There is, we think a test which may be depended upon by which to try the value of a volume of this kind of the little ones. Try it with the big. There are more ardent lovers or frequent quoters of *Alice in Wonderland* among grown men and women, than among the children to whom the Rabbit and the Jabberwock are quite real and possible; and, indeed, we do not think the humour of the Mock-turtle, or the Walrus and the Carpenter, is to be apprehended of the little people.

Under the Sunset may be tried with the grown-up world with perfect success. To its intellectual and critical perception, the literary charm of the stories--all strung upon a slender, gathering thread, like a pearl necklace or a daisy chain--will commend themselves highly; while the hearts of the small readers of the chronicles of that beautiful, angel-guarded "Country under the Sunset" will surely respond to the touch of Prince Zaphir and Princess Bluebell.

Here is the introduction to the scene of the poetical and attractive stories which Mr. Bram Stoker tells, with such delightful skill that all children will accept them with entire good-faith, while if we, the wiser and the sadder ones, hear the minor music of them, it will be with no pain :

"Far, far away there is a beautiful country try which no human eye has ever seen in waking hours. Under the sunset it lies, where the distant horizon bounds the day, and where the clouds, splendid with light and colour, give a promise of the glory and beauty which encompass it. Sometimes it is given us to see it in dreams. . . . No one can leave the country Under the Sunset except in one direction. Those who go there in dreams, or who come in dreams to our world, come and go they know not how; but if an inhabitant tries to leave it, he cannot, except by one way. . . . This place is called the Portal, and there the angels keep guard.

Pure and beautiful are the beings with whom the Country under the Sunset is peopled, odd and humorous, too; and the tale of their loves and their deeds is in the best style of imaginative narrative, with charming little touches of nature and reference to every-day things, so that the loftiness of its meaning (which is also quite simple) shall not be too sustained a strain upon the small reader, nor his attention be fatigued or puzzled. For instance, there is a delightful passage in the description of the little, motherless prince, Zaphir, about his faithful dog "Gomus," and about the talk of the angels on guard at the portal. "If we knew the no-language that the Angels were not-speaking, we should have heard thus," says the author, and could anything be more happily said in a story of the kind? The angels, too, are such beautiful creatures in the illustrations to the book, so grand, calm, and powerful, their majestic might reducing the city, with its towers and battlements, its stately castle, and the grand dark portal, to insignificance. Then the giant whom Prince Zaphir slays is such a terrible creature in the story, and in the picture in the latter he resembles the powerful drawing of the monster in *La Maison Forestiere*, the grimmest conceit of the Erckmann-Chatrian *Romans Populaires*. And the old King is so noble and fatherly, the romance of love and war has rarely been so happily blended. In the story of the Prince and the Giant the author uses simple though poetical language; but one word occurs which we had never previously met with. "As the Giant fell, he gave a single cry, but a cry so loud that it rolled away over the hills and valleys like a peal of thunder. At the sound, the living things cowered again, and sagged with fear." What is "to sag"?

Nothing in this charming book is better than the "knowledgeable" and sympathetic treatment of the "living things." Animals are the friends and companions of the people in the stories; the small traits of their characters are dexterously indicated, and the sympathy between them and man is brought out with great skill. Mr. Bram Stoker has dedicated his book to his little son. It is well done to set such lessons, such illustrations of the precept,

> "He prayeth best who loveth best
> All things, both great and small,"

before the baby mind, that they may sink into the child's heart, and bear their fruit in the man's practice. There is strife in these stories, fight for a good cause, sacrifice, bravery, and glory; but there is not a line to inculcate the love of killing anything made to live by the Creator, or an opportunity lost of drawing out the sympathy of children with the beauty, the intelligence, and the purposes of the animal world. The dogs are very amusing, and admirably differentiated. There is 'Gomus,' quite a boy's dog, who knows when his master is rather solitary in his thoughts, at the hour which is rest-time in the Country under the Sunset, and accordingly wags his tail to say:--"Here I am, prince; I am not asleep either;" and there is 'Sumog,' quite a girl's dog, and 'Bluebell's' property. "This dog," the author tells us gravely, "was at first called 'Sumog,' because Zaphir's dog was 'Gomus,' and this was the name spelled backwards. But then it was called 'Smg,' because this was a name that could not be shouted out, but could only be spoken in a whisper. "Bluebell" had no need for more than this, for 'Smg' was never far away, but always stayed close to his mistress, and watched her."

The illustrations are all real works of art, and one, "The Castle of the King," in the midst of a great waste, is of very rare beauty, as poetical and as solemn as the story of the poet, and his lost-love which it illustrates, and which is not, we should think, at all within the reach of childish readers. "The Shadow Builder" is another delicate, refined, and pathetic conceit, touched with a tenderness that never strays into affectation; but happily, the little ones lack the knowledge that will enable its readers of a larger growth to feel its solemn beauty and irresistible truth.

The element of fun, and the pure whimsicality in which Hans Christian Anderson's stories abound, are abundantly present in Mr. Bram Stoker's. "How 7 went Mad" might be ranked with the famous "Tin Soldier," in pleasant unreason; and there is a raven in it--his name is "Mr. Daw"--the honour of whose acquaintance we should greatly like to have. "The Wondrous Child" is what may be called the youngest story in the volume. In its keen sympathy with the fancies, and perception of the absence of proportion in a child's mind, it is also the cleverest. The volume is beautifully printed, and tastefully bound in white vellum, with red-and-gold lettering and edges; it is, as compared to the children's books of our time, what the dolls of the period are to the Dutch darlings of the past.

"REVIEW OF *UNDER THE SUNSET*," *PUNCH* 81 (DECEMBER 3, 1881), 261.

Get *Under the Sunset* . . . by Mr. BRAM STOKER, M.A. It's very pretty to look at, as to binding, pictures, and general get-up. Our Special Child-Critic says, "Oh yes, I like it, but it's rather too goody-goody. One of the stories reminds me of David and Goliath,"--("Tell it not in Gath," Mr. STOKER)--"and there's not very much to laugh at." A charming book for all that, though, perhaps, somewhat above the heads of those who are only three feet and a half high.

JOSEPH S. BIERMAN, "*DRACULA*: PROLONGED CHILDHOOD ILLNESS AND THE ORAL TRIAD," *AMERICAN IMAGO* 29 (1972), 186-98.

In the early summer of 1895, Bram Stoker, the author of *Dracula* had a nightmare which he attributed to eating too much dressed crab at supper one night. He dreamed about a vampire king rising from the tomb to go about his ghastly business (Ludlam, 1962). Inspired by this dream, he set to work writing the novel, *Dracula*. By the fall of 1895, he was writing his first draft. Since it first appeared in London in 1897, *Dracula* has not been out of print. I would like to present one key answer, summarized from a wider study, to the question of what enabled and forced Stoker to write *Dracula*. The answer is based on an analysis of two autobiographical stories from an earlier book for children that can be considered as associations to his dream novel. The material of *Dracula*, and these stories, lend themselves to the application of Lewin's concept of the oral triad--i.e., the wish to eat, be eaten and sleep.

Stoker's distinctive early childhood is mirrored in both *Dracula* and one of these short stories. The distinction is that Stoker was expected to die from the moment of birth on. He himself says: "In my babyhood I used, I understand, to be often at the point of death. Certainly, until I was about seven years old, I never knew what it was to stand upright (Stoker, 1906)." By the time young Stoker was able to walk at age seven, the Stokers had had four additional children. The nature of this very long illness is unknown, and is made all the more puzzling by the fact that recovery was so complete that Stoker was to become the Athletic Champion of Dublin University. . . .

After Stoker recovered from his long illness, he went to a private religious school in Dublin and then went on to Trinity College of the University of Dublin. There, he took honors in writing, science and mathematics. After graduation, he joined his father as a Civil Servant in Dublin Castle. In the next few years, he earned a Master of Arts degree, worked as an editor of the newspaper, wrote some "cliff hangers" for a newspaper, and also became the drama critic for one of the dailies in Dublin. In December 1878, he joined Henry Irving, who was then the foremost Shakespearean of his time, as the acting manager of the Lyceum Theatre in London. He was to be Irving's factotum and *alter ego* for the next 27 years. His duties included reading and editing plays, accounting, being in charge of arrangements for tours, and greeting guests. Among the celebrities he was to meet in these 27 years was Sir Richard Burton, the famed orientalist, translator of the Arabian Nights and also translator of a book of Indian vampire stories. Stoker was to write later how impressed he was by Burton's canine teeth (Stoker, 1906). Right before joining Irving in London in 1878, Stoker married a girl from Clontarf, and a year later, the couple had their only child, a son named Noel. It was to this son that Stoker dedicated his first book of fiction--in 1881--a collection of short stories for children entitled, *Under the Sunset* (Stoker, 1882).

Under the Sunset is the land that people visit in their dreams. "A beautiful country which no human eye has ever seen in waking hours." All of the stories take place in this land in which live both a good king with his palace and people and the King of Death with his castle. One of the stories, *The Castle of the King*, is about the King of Death and has some phraseology that is repeated almost verbatim in the description of Dracula's castle. In this story, a poet dies when he sees the face of the King of Death. The dedication of the book to Stoker's son would seem to refer to this story--TO MY SON WHOSE ANGEL DOTH BEHOLD THE FACE OF THE KING--and reveals some death wishes toward his son. Themes from *Under the Sunset* are recognizable in almost all of Stoker's 14 books. It is as if he had to tell these stories again and again. . . .

I shall relate two stories from *Under the Sunset* that help explain the blood sucking, madness, the psychiatrist and the insane asylum, the sleep disturbances, and the constant feeling of approaching horror in Dracula.

The first story is *How 7 Went Mad*. It contains blood letting, madness and sleep disturbances and, at the same time, manages to be quite humorous. It is about a school boy named Tineboy and his lame pet raven, Mr. Daw. One day, Tineboy was at his sums in school, and instead of tending to what he was doing, he was trying to make his pet raven come in through the window. His problem was to multiply 117,649 by seven. After struggling unsuccessfully, he then said, "Oh, I don't know--I wish number seven had never been invented." "Croak," said Mr. Daw. Tineboy suddenly became very sleepy and had a dream in which his teacher was about to tell the story about how 7 went mad. The raven kept his head on one side, "closed one eye--the eye nearest the school room so that they might think him asleep--and listened harder than any of them. The pupils were all happy--all except three--one because his leg went to sleep; another because she had her pocket full of curds and wanted to eat them and couldn't without being found out, and the curds were melting away; and the third, who was awfully sleepy, and awfully anxious to hear the story, and couldn't do either because of the other." The teacher's story starts out with the alphabet doctor being called in to see a patient at night, poor number seven. The alphabet doctor attended to "the sicknesses and diseases of the letters of the alphabet"--like a capital A with a lame leg. No. 7 "is mortal bad. We don't think he'll ever live through it. He was foaming at the mouth and apparently quite mad. The nurse from the grammar village was holding him by the hand, trying to bleed him. The footsmith, the man who puts the feet on the letters and numbers to make them able to stand upright without wearing out, was holding down the poor demented number."

The doctor then examined 7. He used the stethoscope, telescope, microscope and horoscope "to find the scope of the disease." Tineboy asked what "the horror scope" is, and was corrected and told to look it up in the dictionary. In this prophetic pun, horror is attached to the activities of the doctor and to the horoscope. This exchange is italicized in the book.

After this examination, the doctor interrogated No. 7 and found out what makes him mad. No. 7 said the treatment he got made him mad. He was: "wrong added, wrong divided, wrong subtracted, and wrong multiplied. Other numbers are not treated as I am and besides they are not orphans like me." No. 7 said he was a number without kith or kin. Tineboy asked," How can he have no skin?" "Kin, my child, kin, not skin," said the teacher. "What is the difference between kin and skin?" asked Tineboy. "There will be but a small difference," said the teacher, "between this cane and your skin if you interrupt."

At that time, Tineboy had a change of heart. "I want poor old 7 to be happy. I will give him some of my lunch and share my bed." (This interchange is also italicized.) By the end of the teacher's story, No. 7 had promised not to be mad, and he got better. Ruffin, the bully boy, then told the teacher that he didn't believe the story and, "if it is true, I wish he had died. We would be better without him." Mr. Daw, the raven, who did not like Ruffin, then stayed in school that night stealing all the number sevens with his beak and swelling to seven times his natural size. Because the raven had stolen all the number sevens, seven o'clock was missing the next morning, and neither the teacher nor the pupils could even remember that there was a number seven. The teacher accused Ruffin of causing this state of affairs by wishing No. 7 had died in a madhouse. After Mr. Daw started to drop the sevens from his beak, the students were then able to use them for multiplication. After the third seven was dropped, the raven began to swell. At this point, very close to the end of the story, Stoker makes a slip. When the raven dropped the fourth seven, which will give seven to the fourth power, the spelled out answer given is wrong. Stoker has done what number seven complained of--wrong multiplied. The mistake is substituting a three for a four.

The parallels and similarities of this story to parts of *Dracula* are very apparent. In *Dracula*, there is the mad man who is in an insane asylum and who actually dies in an insane asylum of broken bones; there is the doctor who treats the mad man. . . . *How 7 Went Mad* is, of course, another tale of medical detection. Number seven represents Stoker as a child with his near mortal illness, his inability to stand on his two feet, and the feeling of being different from his siblings. The story, then, if one assumes this parallel between No. 7 and Stoker, gives a hint as to the kind of medical treatment which might have been instrumental in laying the groundwork for Stoker's dreaming about a vampire. That is, Stoker might have bled just as No. 7 was bled. This was a practice that was extremely common in Ireland in the 1840's. The association in the story between madness and bleeding would then suggest that Stoker became "mad" when he was bled. Certainly in *Dracula* the "zoophagous mania" combines madness and blood.

There is another theme in addition to the one of Stoker as the sick, different child that is furnished by an analysis of the slip in the multiplication of seven to the fourth power in which a three is substituted for a four. The swelling and shrinking in size of the raven, the stress on kith and kin, and on the horoscope suggest very strongly that the powers of seven represent the birth order of the seven Stoker children. After the third power the raven swells, and then starts to shrink to his natural size after the fourth seven is dropped. In oral terms this sequence suggests his mother's pregnancy with the fourth born Tommy who was delivered when Stoker, the third born, was twenty-one months old. This mathematical error by a man who had received honors in mathematics at Trinity College implies not only that he felt Tommy was a mistake, who should have been "wrong multiplied" as No. 7 was, but also that Tommy, number four, should not have been the product of the multiplying, i.e., should not have been born, but that he number three, should have taken his place. In fact, when we look at the original sum that causes Tineboy to wish that number seven had never been invented, we find that it is seven to the seventh power which would represent George, the youngest brother, who was born when Stoker was seven. Stoker must have wished, as Mr. Daw did, that George would croak, a word which in Victorian England, also, meant 'die.' This wish is carried out by eating and swallowing and is undone by regurgitation. The death wishes toward his baby brothers, Tom and George, may be found in *Dracula* in the form of three instances of infanticide by eating and sucking and the frequent usage of the names Tom and George for different minor characters and events. For example, Harker arrives at Dracula's castle on St. George's Eve. Even the novel itself is dedicated to a Tommy--to Thomas Hall Caine, a novelist friend of Stoker's.

After Tineboy wishes that number seven had never been invented--that is, after he wishes George were dead--he uncontrollably falls asleep, and even in his dream, the students have some sleep disturbances, including a girl who wants to eat her milk curds. This combination of killing, which is equated with eating in the dream, milk and sleep brings to mind Lewin's oral triad of the wish to eat, be eaten and sleep. There is a very striking passage in *Dracula* that demonstrates the concept of the oral triad at work and that refers back to another story in *Under the Sunset* called *The Wondrous Child*. . . . .

This story concerns a brother, Sibold, and a sister, May, who want to have a baby of their own on the day that a baby brother arrives in their home.

The older brother has a theory that babies are to be found on a bed of parsley after they have come from over the sea. After having a picnic lunch of the new baby who is called the King of the Feast, they fall asleep amidst scarlet poppies and dream that they find a baby brother on an island and placed on a bed of parsley. They become angry with each other over whose baby he is. These angry thoughts cause the baby to die. Only when they repent does the baby come alive again. Wondrously, the baby begins to talk to his brother and requests that May sing to him. When a cow suddenly appears, May thinks that the baby wants to be fed. But both she and her brother have forgotten how to milk a cow. Then follows the part that would seem to be referred to in *Dracula*. "All at once, without knowing how it came to pass, she felt herself pouring milk out of a watering pot all over the baby, who lay on the ground, with Sibold holding down its head." The baby then proves to be additionally wondrous in his ability to tame wild beasts, such as a dragon and snake. This story contains themes similar to those in *How 7 Went Mad*. There is the death of the baby brother and his revival, an oral theory of birth, the sleeping and dreaming after eating, even the falling asleep associated with scarlet--the color of blood.

There are, of course, other references to *The Wondrous Child* in *Dracula*, such as Dracula himself being called a child and wondrous.

Parts of the novel and the two stories that are associations to it suggest that *Dracula* concerns itself with death wishes toward younger brothers, nursing at the breast, and primal scenes expressed in nursing terms. All are associated with sleep disturbances. Lewin's concept of the oral triad--the wish to eat, be eaten and sleep--and the manic defense against sleep because of the fear of dying and being eaten suggest the way to synthesize these themes. Lewin (1950) feels that the genetic linkage of the three wishes of the oral triad causes them to be reactivated together, i.e., "the reactivation of one would be the reactivation of all three." Sleep, as expressed in Harker's stupor, would be a first line of defense against being awakened by the primal sounds, but the wishes to eat and be eaten would also arise; and thus the stage would be set for intercourse being seen in terms of sucking and being sucked. Stoker, like Harker, or Dracula might have been in the parental bedroom and would have wanted to get rid of the baby-making sounds in order to stay asleep. At age twenty-one months, Tommy was born and Stoker would have seen him nursing at the breast. This would have aroused great feelings of rivalry and the wish to get rid of Tommy, the wish that he would die. Because of being bedridden, Stoker would not have had the usual outlet of motility for his aggression but would have had to express it orally. Killing would have been seen as eating up, as was the case in *How 7 Went Mad*. The eating up wishes would also have activated the other two parts of the triad--the wish to be eaten and to sleep. Because of their unacceptability to young Stoker, these passive wishes would in turn have generated anxiety and fear of sleep and death, i.e., a feeling of approaching horror. Perhaps this was another part of his and No. 7's night madness. . . .

Stoker was to experience the birth of four children before he himself was able to get out of bed. The last birth, the birth of George, coincided with his leaving his bed. This may account for Tineboy's remark about sharing his lunch and bed with Number Seven. The reluctance to give up the baby position to

George when he was finally able to walk must have accentuated his hostile rivalrous feelings toward this younger brother.

We are now in a position to analyze the association to the vampire dream--that it was caused by eating too much dressed crab. The two stories, *The Wondrous Child* and *How 7 Went Mad* furnish us with a basis for this analysis, by combining the fantasy of the baby coming from over the sea and being found on a bed of parsley with the stress on the horoscope. Dressed crab was classically served in England at that time on a bed of parsley. Crab, when viewed horoscopically for this horror tale, is that sign of the Zodiac that covers the period between June 23 and July 23. George, Stoker's youngest brother, was born under the sign of the crab on July 20th. Eating the dressed crab meant, unconsciously eating up and killing baby George.

Something then, in the spring of 1895, must have happened that generated some rivalrous feelings in Stoker and brought into play earlier rivalries toward his son and brothers. I would propose that the 'something' was the act of Queen Victorian bestowing knighthood in that spring on both Henry Irving for his acting, and on Dr. William Stoker, Bram's older brother, for his accomplishments as a physician. . . .

In summary: When Queen Victoria knighted both Stoker's actor-employer and physician-brother, she revived memories of earlier times when he felt the threat that he would lose the favors of his family Queen to his younger brothers. These memories had been put in story form when they had been revived by the birth of his son, his new rival; and, in this form, they were available for his dream and novel. In his dream, he could be the King who would be entitled to have a Queen of his own; and in his novel, he could appropriate for his sucking pleasure the women of other men, and have them feel threatened with the loss instead of himself. But Stoker was too threatened by his own wishes--and thus the nightmare quality of the dream. To find relief, Stoker had to write his novel in which the vampire's victim could rise, disgorged from the tomb, while the Dracula is Stoker could be laid to eternal rest, unable to rise again to go about his ghastly business.

The Snake's Pass

"REVIEW OF *THE SNAKE'S PASS*," *PUNCH* 99 (DECEMBER 6, 1890), 269.

The Snake's Pass, by BRAM STOKER, M.A. (SAMPSON LOW), is a simple love-story, a pure idyl of Ireland, which does not seem, after all, to be so distressful a country to live in. Whiskey punch flows like milk through the land; the loveliest girls abound, and seem instinctively to be drawn towards the right man. Also there are jooled crowns to be found by earnest seekers, with at least one large packing-case crammed with rare coins. The love-scenes are frequent and tempting. BRAM has an eye to scenery, and can describe it. He knows the Irish peasant, and reproduces his talk with a fidelity which almost suggests that he, too, is descended from one of the early kings, whereas, as everyone knows, he lives in London and adds grace and dignity to "the front" of the Lyceum on First Nights and others. He is perfectly overwhelming in his erudition in respect of the science of drainage, which, if all stories be true, he might find opportunity of turning to account in the every-day (or, rather, every-night) world of the theatre. In his novel he utilises it in the preliminaries of shifting a mighty bog, the last stages whereof are described in a chapter that, for sustained interest, recalls CHARLES READE'S account of the breaking of the Sheffield Reservoir. The novel reader will do well not to pass by *The Snake's Pass*.

"REVIEW OF *THE SNAKE'S PASS*," *ATHENAEUM* 96 (DECEMBER 20, 1890), 85.

The reader of 'The Snake's Pass' is tempted to exclaim with Madame de Longueville, after a literary performance at the Hotel Rambouillet, "Que cela est beau! et, mon Dieu, que cela est ennuyeux!" so long, so good, and so dull is Mr. Bram Stoker's new novel. The scene of action is laid in the west of Ireland, whose beautiful coast is as well described as the strange phenomenon of the shifting boy which plays so large a part in the story. The two heroes are almost equally high-minded, scrupulous, and self-sacrificing; in fact, they carry these virtues to a pitch which amounts to absurdity in their dealings with the villainous Murtagh Murdock. Andy, the car-driver, is quite the most amusing character in the book, and very good company as a rule. His dialect is occasionally oppressive, but possibly accurate. The writer shows himself so thoroughly capable of entering into the delightful humour and light-heartedness which constitute the charm of the Irish character to the benighted Saxon, that it is an additional pity he should have altogether denied Norah Joyce her birthright in this respect. The two young men also are quite overweighted by the burden of their solid virtues, without one redeeming weakness or the smallest sense of humour.

The Watter's Mou'

"REVIEW OF *THE WATTER'S MOU'*," *PUNCH* 108 (JANUARY 19, 1895), 29.

Says the Baron, "What I who have read Mr. BRAM STOKER'S latest romance could tell you about *The Watter's Mou'* would make your mou' watter with longing desire to devour it. It is excellent: first because it is short; secondly, because the excitement is kept up from first page to last; and thirdly, because it is admirably written throughout; the scenic descriptive portion being as entrancing as the dramatic. It is brought out in the Acme Series in charge of A. CONSTABLE, and its full price is only one shilling.

"REVIEW OF *THE WATTER'S MOU'*," *ATHENAEUM* 105 (FEBRUARY 23, 1895), 246.

There is some good descriptive writing in this little tale about smuggling and love and duty nobly done. The storm and Maggie's wild sail to save her father's honour are told with much power and excitement, and the coastguardsman's victory over temptation is finely conceived. The chief defect of the book, inevitable perhaps from the author's associations, is a tendency to melodramatic and stagey writing is some of the speeches and situations. A phrase like the following, for example, which is rather typical of the scene between Maggie and her lover, seems more adapted for the Adelphi stage than for a discussion between two Scotch lovers: "What is it that you would make of me? Not only a smuggler, but a perjurer and a traitor too. God! am I mistaken?" But in spite of a certain air of unreality about the whole tale, it has interest and movement enough to arouse and sustain the attention.

"REVIEW OF *THE WATTER'S MOU'*," *NATION* 62 (FEBRUARY 27, 1896), 183.

There is only one rational excuse for the use of dialect in stories, and that is when the dialect helps out the story--when, in fact, you couldn't have the story without it. No such limitation has embarrassed the mind of the author of 'The Watter's Mou'. The smuggler's daughter, her father and brothers and friends, would be just as theatrical and conventional in English as they are in intermittent Aberdeenshire Scotch. The central incident has a thrill in its heart which loses force by the author's artificial treatment, and never have sky, sea, and wind lowered, raged, and roared with more amazing spectacular effect, not only o'erstepping, but quite putting to shame, the modesty of nature.

The Shoulder of Shasta

**"REVIEW OF *THE SHOULDER OF SHASTA*," *ATHENAEUM*
106 (NOVEMBER 16, 1895), 677.**

MR. BRAM STOKER'S story, 'The Shoulder of Shasta,' will not, it is to be
feared, increase his literary reputation, nor appeal to many readers. The
"Shoulder" must be a particularly beautiful spot, amid admirable natural
surroundings, but the people placed there are, in spite of the author's genial and
kindly manner, scarcely worthy those surroundings. Not a little crudity in them
and in the treatment of what does duty for a story is unfortunately but too
visible. This want of maturity and sense of humour may be due to haste, for the
book bears the stamp of being roughly and carelessly put together. Mr. Stoker
can probably do much better work than this; so perhaps the less said about 'The
Shoulder of Shasta' the better for every one concerned.

**"REVIEW OF *THE SHOULDER OF SHASTA*," *SPECTATOR*
76 (FEBRUARY 22, 1896), 273.**

The scene of Mr. Bram Stoker's vigorous, clever, pleasant, and distinctly out-of-
the common new work, *The Shoulder of Shasta*, is laid chiefly at a remote part
of a Californian mountain, where a San Franciscan lady goes to spend the
summer for the health of her anaemic, romantically inclined daughter, Esse,
whose unsatisfied young life had hitherto "watched and waited at the shrine of
nature, not knowing what she sought or hoped for, whilst all the time the deep,
underlying, unconscious forces of her being were making for some tangible
result which would complete her life." On their arrival the immediate effect

produced on the impressionable young lady by the glorious scenery of her wild surroundings is a determination "to let her feet lead her where instinct took them;" and as fate just then throws her into almost daily contact with Dick, "a picturesque hunter, massive of limb and quaint of speech," there is for some time a considerable likelihood that the above-mentioned tangible result to complete her life will be found in her very excusable infatuation for him, whose rise, progress, and fall are depicted with a skill making one fancy that Mr. Stoker must have bestowed especial study on girls of Esse's hysterical, emotional temperament. As Dick, though a splendid specimen, both in body and mind, of unsophisticated humanity, chivalrous, brave, large-hearted, and true to himself in all cases (alike when exposed to deadly peril from grizzly-bears, or to the gibes of a roomful of smart people), is nevertheless, a rough trapper, with a weakness for "painting red spots" over any town he happens to visit, and no more elevated idea of amusement than a music-hall, he is clearly hardly adapted to mate with the refined, fastidious, and highly cultured Esse. But even if he be a trifle uncivilised, he is far and away too good to be sacrificed to a delicate girl's sickly fancy, and conquers our esteem and liking so thoroughly that we rather grudge his being involved in any discomfort at all through her, even though it be nothing more serious than finding himself for a few minutes in a false position. However, it is very soon over, and as he fortunately remains heart-whole, and is never once touched by any tenderer feeling for her than unbounded loyalty and kindly devotion, everything ends happily. His racy, quaintly expressive mountain way of talking adds zest to the book; and there is much humour and freshness in the episode of Miss Gimp and the Indians, whose profound respect for her she attributes entirely to her own personal merits, whereas it is due really to their conviction that her talking parrot is a god, and their belief (as Dick explains to Esse) that Miss Gimp is "the sachem, the medicine-man, the witch, and they want to make themselves solid with her, because they think she can square him."

Dracula

"REVIEW OF *DRACULA*," *ATHENAEUM* 109 (JUNE 26, 1897), 835.

Stories and novels appear just now in plenty stamped with a more or less genuine air of belief in the visibility of supernatural agency. The strengthening of a bygone faith in the fantastic and magical view of things in lieu of the purely material is a feature of the hour, a reaction--artificial, perhaps, rather than natural--against late tendencies in thought. Mr. Stoker is the purveyor of so many strange wares that 'Dracula' reads like a determined effort to go, as it were, "one better" than others in the same field. How far the author is himself a believer in the phenomena described is not for the reviewer to say. He can but attempt to gauge how far the general faith in witches, warlocks, and vampires-- supposing it to exist in any general and appreciable measure--is likely to be stimulated by this story. The vampire idea is very ancient indeed, and there are in nature, no doubt, mysterious powers to account for the vague belief in such beings. Mr. Stoker's way of presenting his matter, and still more the matter itself, are of too direct and uncompromising a kind. They lack the essential note of awful remoteness and at the same time subtle affinity that separates while it links our humanity with unknown beings and possibilities hovering on the confines of the known world. 'Dracula' is highly sensational, but it is wanting in the constructive art as well as in the higher literary sense. It reads at times like a mere series of grotesquely incredible events; but there are better moments that show more power, though even these are never productive of the tremor such subjects evoke under the hand of a master. An immense amount of energy, a certain degree of imaginative faculty, and many ingenious and gruesome details are there. At times Mr. Stoker almost succeeds in creating the sense of possibility in impossibility; at others he merely commands an array of crude statements of incredible actions. The early part goes best, for it promises to unfold the roots of mystery and fear lying deep in human nature; but the want of skill and fancy grows more and more conspicuous. The people who band themselves together to run the vampire to earth have no real individuality or being. The German man of science is particularly poor, and indulges, like a German, in much weak sentiment. Still Mr. Stoker has got together a number of "horrid details," and his object, assuming it to be ghastliness, is fairly well fulfilled. Isolated scenes and touches are probably quite uncanny enough to please those for whom they are designed.

"REVIEW OF *DRACULA*," *SPECTATOR* 79 (JULY 31, 1897), 150-51.

Mr. Bram Stoker gives us the impression--we may be doing him an injustice--of having deliberately laid himself out in *Dracula* to eclipse all previous efforts in the domain of the horrible,--to "go one better" than Wilkie Collins (whose method of narration he has closely followed), Sheridan Le Fanu, and all the other professors of the flesh-creeping school. Count Dracula, who gives his name to the book, is a Transylvanian noble who purchases an estate in England, and in connection with the transfer of the property Jonathan Harker, a young solicitor, visits him in his ancestral castle. Jonathan Harker has a terrible time of it, for the Count--who is a vampire of immense age, cunning, and experience--keeps him as a prisoner for several weeks, and when the poor young man escapes from the gruesome charnel-house of his host, he nearly dies of brain-fever in a hospital at Buda-Pesth. The scene then shifts to England, where the Count arrives by sea in the shape of a dog-fiend, after destroying the entire crew, and resumes operations in various uncanny manifestations, selecting as his chief victim Miss Lucy Westenra, the fiancee of the Honourable Arthur Holmwood, heir-presumptive to Lord Godalming. The story then resolves itself into the history of the battle between Lucy's protectors, including two rejected suitors--an American and a "mad" doctor--and a wonderfully clever specialist from Amsterdam, against her unearthly persecutor. The clue is furnished by Jonathan Harker, whose betrothed, Mina Murray, is a bosom friend of Lucy's, and the fight is long and protracted. Lucy succumbs, and, worse still, is temporarily converted into a vampire. How she is released from this unpleasant position and restored to a peaceful post-mortem existence, how Mina is next assailed by the Count, how he is driven from England, and finally exterminated by the efforts of the league--for all these, and a great many more thrilling details, we must refer our readers to the pages of Mr. Stoker's clever but cadaverous romance. Its strength lies in the invention of incident, for the sentimental element is decidedly mawkish. Mr. Stoker has shown considerable ability in the use that he has made of all the available traditions of vampirology, but we think his story would have been all the more effective if he had chosen an earlier period. The up-to-dateness of the book--the phonograph diaries, typewriters, and so on--hardly fits in with the mediaeval methods which ultimately secure the victory for Count Dracula's foes.

"REVIEW OF *DRACULA*," *BOOKMAN* 12 (AUGUST 1897), 129.

Since Wilkie Collins left us we have had no tale of mystery so liberal in matter and so closely woven. But with the intricate plot, and the methods of the narrative, the resemblance to stories of the author of "The Woman in White" ceases; for the audacity and the horror of "Dracula" are Mr. Stoker's own. A summary of the book would shock and disgust; but we must own that, though here and there in the course of the tale we hurried over things with repulsion, we read nearly the whole with rapt attention. It is something of a triumph for the writer that neither the improbability, nor the unnecessary number of hideous incidents recounted of the man-vampire, are long foremost in the reader's mind, but that the interest of the danger, of the complications, of the pursuit of the villain, of human skill and courage pitted against inhuman wrong and superhuman strength, rises always to the top. Keep "Dracula" out of the way of nervous children, certainly; but a grown reader, unless he be of unserviceably delicate stuff, will both shudder and enjoy from p. 35, when Harker sees the Count "emerge from the window and begin to crawl down the castle wall over that dreadful abyss, *face down*, with his cloak spreading out around him like great wings."

ROYCE MACGILLIVRAY, "BRAM STOKER'S SPOILED MASTERPIECE," *QUEEN'S QUARTERLY* 79 (1972), 519-527.

Bram Stoker's *Dracula* has never been much praised for its literary merits. Yet this horror novel, first published in May 1897, survives today, after more than seventy years of popularity, as one of the little group of English language books from the nineties still read by more than scholars. Because of the succession of horror films based on it, whether *Dracula* would have achieved this success solely through its intrinsic merits is uncertain. Certainly without the films it is hard to believe that Dracula would be one of the few proper names from novels to have become a household word, known even to people who have never heard of the novel. Stoker created a myth comparable in vitality to that of the Wandering Jew, Faust, or Don Juan. This myth has not, so far, been crowned with respectability by its use in great literature, yet is it too much to suggest that in time even that may be achieved? Such a myth lives not merely because it has been skillfully marketed by entrepreneurs but because it expresses something that large numbers of people feel to be true about their own lives.

In the following pages I want to examine *Dracula* with more attention than is usually given to it. Since the novel will probably have readers for many years to come, it is best that it be read with understanding. This understanding can be best achieved by scholarly debate, to which the following is a contribution. [1] While the idea of scholarly study of a horror novel may initially seem ridiculous, I think I can show that *Dracula* is substantial enough to deserve the attention of scholars. Even if the novel should seem to most others less impressive than it has seemed to me after a number of readings, I suggest that the historian and sociologist will find it worthwhile to pay attention to the contents of a novel that has been so influential in our century. . . .

Stoker, who sets his narrative uncompromisingly in the framework of the technologically advanced and modern-minded Victorian civilization, weaves into it the commonplace details of everyday life precisely where we expect them least. It is absurd, and yet convincing, to find that Dracula has a sizeable library in his vampire castle, from which he has been quarrying information about the customs, laws, and so forth of England. Coming into the room one evening, Harker finds him lying on a sofa reading Bradshaw's railway guide. In the castle, where no servants are ever seen, Harker glimpses Dracula making Harker's bed and setting his table. As we read of the meals which Harker was served ("an excellent roast chicken," "an excellent supper") we wonder, as Stoker probably intends we should, whether Dracula also did the cooking. It is touching that when the pursuers break into the house Dracula has bought in Piccadilly they find his clothes brush and brush and comb there--necessary implements, it seems, even for someone who lives in a coffin. While they wait at his house, Mrs. Harker, with pleasing impudence, sends them a telegram there to warn them that Dracula may be approaching. When Dracula, intent upon fleeing from England, meets a sea captain to commission him to ship his one remaining box of earth out of the country--the captain of course does not know that the stranger who is addressing him is a vampire and will be hiding in the box--Dracula is seen to be wearing a straw hat, which, as Van Helsing remarks in his imperfect English, "suit not him or the time." Perhaps this element of the incongruous in the novel is intended only as a gentle form of self-parody, or of mockery at tales of the supernatural. I think, however, that it plays a rather more important role than this. We live daily, Stoker seems to say, with the incongruous, with the ironies, contradictions, and wild absurdities of life. We have no reason then to be surprised if the most preposterous events should come upon us at the very moment when life seems most sober, rational, and humdrum.

Stoker created in Dracula a towering figure who dominates the novel and appears utterly convincing. It was unfortunate for Stoker that he did not live early enough to write his novel at the beginning rather than the end of the nineteenth century. Had Dracula come to literary life in the age of Romanticism and the Gothic novel, one imagines that he would have been received rapturously into the literary tradition of western Europe instead of being sternly restricted, as he has been, to the popular imagination.[2] In view of the extraordinary pains Stoker took to make the geographical and social background of the novel as accurate as possible--his description of Whitby, where Dracula landed in England in the midst of an immense storm, is a reliable guide for tourists today--it is not surprising to find that he selected for his vampire a real historical figure, Vlad the Impaler, also known as Dracula, who was voivode or prince of Wallachia from 1456 to 1462, and again in 1476. In real life Dracula was known for his horrifying cruelty, but Stoker, who wanted a monster that his readers could both shudder at and identify with, omits all mention of the dark side of his reputation and emphasizes his greatness as a warrior chieftain. As Dracula entertains young Harker in his castle, he cannot refrain from reminiscing about the campaigns in which he took part. Though he pretends to be merely talking about the history of his part of Europe and conceals all personal involvement, a telltale sign appears: "In his speaking of things and people, and especially of battles," Harker notes, "he spoke as if he had been present at them all."[3] When Van Helsing has had a Budapest correspondent make enquiries into the identity of the historical figure whose living corpse they are pursuing, he is able to report:

He must, indeed, have been that Voivode Dracula who won his name against the Turk, over the great river on the very frontier of Turkey-land. If it be so, then was he no common man; for in that time, and for centuries after, he was spoken of as the cleverest and the most cunning, as well as the bravest of the sons of the "land beyond the forest." That mighty brain and that iron resolution went with him to his grave, and are even now arrayed against us. The Draculas were . . . a great and noble race, though now and again [there] were scions who were held by their coevals to have had dealings with the Evil One. They learned his secrets in the Scholomance, amongst the mountains over Lake Hermanstadt, where the devil claims the tenth scholar as his due. In the records are such words as "stregoica"--witch, "ordog," and "pokol"--Satan and hell; and in one manuscript this very Dracula is spoken of as "wampyr," which we all understand all too well. There have been from the loins of this very one great men and good women, and their graves make sacred the earth where alone this foulness can dwell. For it is not the least of its terrors that this evil thing is rooted deep in all good; in soil barren of holy memories it cannot rest.

Fixing himself on this biographical basis, Stoker gives his vampire story an unexpected and, in view of later exploitations of the Dracula theme in films, a remarkably sophisticated psychological interest, and even a degree of pathos. Anyone who compares Stoker's portrait of Dracula with the lore that Montague Summers has collected in his two volumes on vampires will find that Dracula, a polished and eloquent gentleman as well as a wily antagonist, is untypical.[4] In their non-fictional existence, as described by tradition, vampires tend, it seems, to be squalid and animal-like. But for the superiority of Dracula there is a reason beyond that of his superiority in life. Dracula, we are led to believe, has been slowly recovering his faculties since the time of his death, when they were partly destroyed. While the execution of his elaborate project for transferring himself to England, where multitudes exist to be his prey, is the highest achievement that his process of self-development has yet yielded, there are possibilities that if he survives he will become more dangerous still. "What more may he not do," Van Helsing asks, "when the greater world of thought is open to him?" Dracula's power to grow intellectually is, however, barren. No matter what he grows into, he must remain painfully and utterly separated from the surrounding world of men and its values.

Dracula though at a lower level of literary achievement, is--like *Steppenwolf, L'Etranger,* and *La Chute* a novel of alienation. The depiction of Dracula as an alienated figure derives from the traditional vampire legends, the Gothic novels, and the idea of the romantic hero, as well as from Stoker's psychological acumen. When we have seen Dracula in this light, we can grasp the double irony of his statement to Harker in the castle that "I long to go through the crowded streets of your mighty London, to be in the midst of the whirl and rush of humanity, to share its life, its change, its death, and all that makes it what it is." This touching sentimentality, which masks the fact that he wants to be among these people to prey on them, also masks his defeat. Though he has retained and recovered some human characteristics, he can no more share the people's "whirl and rush" and life and change than he can ever see again the armies he commanded so long ago. Dracula's disastrous expedition to England can even be seen as unconsciously suicidal, as his attempt to extinguish his anguish in a lasting death.

Besides being an alienated figure, Dracula is, as Maurice Richardson has said in his remarks on the novel, "a father-figure."[5] The theme of Dracula as a father figure is less overt than the theme of alienation, and one feels that in inserting it in the novel Stoker was not fully conscious of his own feelings. Dracula is the patriarch of his castle, for as a little sifting of the evidence will show, the three female vampires who share it with him are his wife and two daughters, perhaps by another marriage, or his wife and two sisters. Rather more importantly for the emotional undercurrents of the novel, Dracula even aspires to be, in a sense, the father of the band that is pursuing him. Because he intends, as he tells them, to turn them all into vampires, he will be their creator and therefore "father."

This only means that they will become a different kind of "family": as a little examination will show, they are already a "family." They even participate in a kind of group marriage--one is tempted to say a kind of group sex--when four of them give blood by transfusion from their own veins to Dracula's victim Lucy Westenra. The significance of the blood transfusion is pointed out for any reader who might have missed it when Arthur, who mistakenly supposes that he alone has given blood to Lucy, speculates that the blood transfusion has made Lucy his wife in the sight of God. Somewhat ludicrously, no fewer than three of them had previously proposed to Lucy all in one day. At the end of the novel this closely knit band of pursuers even manages to produce a baby in the form of the Harkers' child Quincy, whose "bundles of names," we are told, "links all our little band of men together." Van Helsing, the guide of this family, is, as Richardson says, a good father figure.[6] While Van Helsing actually seems more a kindly elder brother than a father, his nearness to the father role is one of the things that make him faintly resemble Dracula and thus tinge him slightly with moral ambiguity. (Perhaps the reason why he is so thin as a character is that too much of him consists of materials left over from creating the vast figure of Dracula.)

The theme of Dracula as father figure gains psychological interest from the framework of references to the death or murder of parents in which it is inserted. One of Dracula's earliest victims in the novel is a mother who comes to the castle to demand the return of her abducted child. In a horrifying scene which Harker watches from a castle window she is torn to pieces by the wolves who are at Dracula's call. An old man, another father figure, is found dead with a broken neck in the churchyard at Whitby shortly after Dracula's landing at that port. Then there are the deaths from natural causes of Arthur Holmwood's father; of Harker's employer and patron, who had been a father to him and to Mrs. Harker; and of the mother of Lucy Westenra. It is suggestive of the emotional significance the parricide theme seems to have had for Stoker that the last three of these deaths are incidental to his narrative, which would be improved by their omission. Even Quincey Morris, who is killed at the end of the novel in the final struggle against the vampire, becomes a retrospective father when the Harkers' baby Quincey, is born on the anniversary of his death and perpetuates his name.

The counterpart to this theme of parricide is the theme of the murder of children by their parents. Stoker introduces anecdotally the story of a hunchbacked son who committed suicide in revenge for his mother's hatred. We are led to believe that the mother of Lucy Westenra was partly responsible for her daughter's death by failing to follow the instructions laid down by Van Helsing for Lucy's protection from the vampire. Dracula himself appears in the role of murderous parent: to turn people into vampires, in effect to make them his children, he must first kill them. In a dialogue with overtones of incest, it is hinted that Dracula, in accordance with the rule that vampires begin their careers by preying first on their nearest kin, has made his daughters or sisters into vampires. The sequence of birth and infanticide is represented by the scene in the castle in which Dracula, who has been out hunting, produces a child from a sack and hands it over to the female vampires to be their victim.

The theme of parent-child conflict reaches its culmination at the end of the novel with the destruction of Dracula himself at the hands of his intended children, his pursuers. As Richardson reminds us, what Stoker has described is similar to the destruction of the father of the primal horde by his offspring as imagined by Freud in *Totem and Taboo*.[7]

The popularity of the Dracula myth in this century suggests that many persons find a resemblance between themselves and Dracula and between themselves and vampires in general. It is hard not to suggest that vampire stories, including *Dracula*, reflect, in a sensationalized but recognizable form, the truth that the close association of any two persons is almost certain to involve, however faintly, some "vampirish" exploitation, be it economic, intellectual, or emotional, of one of them by the other.

Who was Bram Stoker? He was born in Ireland in 1847, and began his career by following his father into the Irish civil service. Some years later he gave up his civil service employment to migrate to England as the acting-manager of the great actor, Henry (later Sir Henry) Irving. Meanwhile, he had dabbled in journalism and unpaid dramatic criticism and laboured on his first book, a legal manual on the duties of clerks of petty sessions in Ireland. For well over a quarter of a century he served Irving diligently. . . . Stoker seems to have been the very reverse of sinister or exotic. . . . One can see, however, certain parallels between Stoker's life and the fictional Dracula's which must have assisted him in creating his hero-villain. After a sickly childhood in which he was unable to leave his bed and stand on his own feet until he was in his eighth year, Stoker became a champion athlete at Trinity College, Dublin. . . . In his own development Stoker must have found clues for his depiction of Dracula as someone who developed in the tomb, slowly groping his way toward the full mastery of the possibilities open to him. Similarly, Stoker's migration from Dublin, where he must have felt isolated with his youthful literary ambitions, to London, the intellectual capital of the British Isles and the hub of a vast empire, parallels Dracula's migration from his thinly populated Transylvanian feeding-grounds to the same city and its teeming human life. In his isolation in Dublin and in his later role as an Irishman in England, Stoker must have picked up clues for his depiction of Dracula as an alienated figure. Even the cumbersome train of baggage that Irving and his acting company carried with them as they toured the provinces and America may have been in his mind when he described Dracula's movements with his boxes of earth.

One of the defects of the novel is the Victorian emotionalism which occasionally makes the modern reader wince. A far graver defect, however, is its weakness of characterization, a rule whose only exception is the magnificent and convincing figure of Dracula. This weakness is especially evident in all six of the little band of heroes pursuing Dracula. Harker is the most convincing, principally because Stoker has not tried to give him a distinct character but has been content to let him be a transparent object through which events are viewed. Part of the reason why the first fifty or sixty pages of the novel, which deal with Harker's experiences in Transylvania, are so much better than the remainder of the work is that no characters but the superior Dracula and Harker appear in them, except briefly. After these first pages, in which he is introduced in great detail, Dracula is removed almost completely from the direct view of the reader. In this way Stoker maintains in the reader a sense of the ominous--not, be it noted, a sense of the mysterious, which is little awakened because the approach which the heroes of the novel take to the reemergence of vampires in modern society is severely practical and rationalistic--but he deprives himself of the full use of his strongest creation.

The only character in the novel who comes close to being boring is, oddly enough, slightly better developed than most of Stoker's characters. This is Renfield, the zoophagous patient in Dr. Seward's lunatic asylum. Renfield's repulsive desire to eat flies, birds, and other small living creatures, and all the other details of his malady and daily life are described with surprising relentlessness. Eventually he is allowed to play a feeble part in the action by admitting Dracula into the asylum when his prospective victim, Mrs. Harker, is visiting there; according to the rules which tradition tells us govern a vampire's actions, he cannot enter a house until one of its occupants has admitted him, but thereafter he can come and go as he pleases. As Stoker is a story teller par excellence, it is strange that he does not enliven the sections which deal with Renfield by including more action, perhaps in the form of a subplot based on

Renfield's past life. But if the treatment of Renfield is unsuccessful, that is not because he is irrelevant to the novel. I suggest we should regard him as a good idea which does not quite succeed. His simplest function is to tie together disparate parts of the narrative through his presence. Stoker may also have felt the need of a sluggishly unfolding account of Renfield to contrast with the usual swift pace of his narrative. But most importantly, Renfield joins Dracula and his pursuers in a triangular relationship in which he heightens our awareness of their character and position.

As we seek to define the most important role he plays in this relationship, it becomes evident that he is the sad anti-Dracula of the novel. Along with his desire to feed on living things, he has dim hopes of becoming a vampire. Meanwhile his madness and his prison walls confine him as much as Dracula is confined by his alienation and the rules that restrict the actions of a vampire. We are constantly aware of Renfield's exclusion from the band of pursuers and thus see in him an echo of Dracula's alienation. In the same way, it may be mentioned in passing, Dracula's alienation is mocked by the clubbiness and family feeling of the pursuers. The anti-Dracula may at the same time be seen as a participant in a parent-son conflict of unusual sterility. He plays the role of son and Dr. Seward of father, but the age relationship of father and son is reversed, with the doctor being younger than his "son." In this way, just as Dracula is a kind of super-father, Renfield is a father broken and made harmless-- so much reduced from his rightful fatherhood that when he is murdered by Dracula it is hard to be sure whether we are even entitled to count him as another of Stoker's murdered parents. Since the quest of the vampires for blood seems often to be in some undefined way a sexual quest, it is tempting to see Renfield, the would-be vampire, as suffering from sexual frustration, and it is not only tempting but plausible to suggest that sexual frustration was one of the elements that Stoker drew on in creating him.

Dracula is a thoroughly unpolitical novel.[8] This statement is true both in the sense that Dracula ignores the party issues of the day and in the more general sense that it ignores the strains of the class society of late Victorian England. To the historically minded, however, it is interesting for its expression of certain attitudes belonging to Stoker's part of the Victorian period, and for its anticipations of the intellectual climate of our century. The alienation theme in the novel is especially relevant to the twentieth century--indeed, is brought out in the novel with a sharpness which seems almost anachronistic and which deserves close examination by the historians of the development of the English novel--but the novel expresses also the disquiet of many Victorian intellectuals about the atomizing and dehumanizing effects of their own time. While the novel's parent-child conflicts are presumably rooted in Stoker's private feelings, one can see interesting parallels with the twentieth-century revolt against the Victorian father and the whole Victorian heritage as expressed, for instance, in Butler's *The Way of All Flesh* and Gosse's *Father and Son*. The novel also reflects the foreboding with which some Victorians faced the new century. Surely some ill-fortune would take away the good things which had been so unstintingly poured upon Victorian England? Dracula may have partially symbolized for contemporaries this nameless threat. The vampire theme has special relevance, too, to the Victorian problem of loss of faith. The abandonment of traditional Christianity reopened the whole question of what becomes of a person after death. In our time *Dracula* probably gains part of its impact from the intense fears which have clustered, more in this century than in any other, about the problem of growing old, a problem which vampires, who are capable of living forever, have solved.

But of all that is historically interesting in *Dracula*, nothing is more curious than its combination of the Victorian preoccupation with death and an almost twentieth-century preoccupation with sex. This combination is found, for example, in the hunting activities of the vampires, who belong to the dead but pursue the living in what often seems to be a spirit of blatant sexuality, and in the destruction of beautiful female vampires by driving stakes through their hearts as they sleep in their tombs.

I must not allow my remarks on the faults of this novel to conceal the remarkable skill with which it is written. It is hard to believe that anyone who has observed the power Stoker shows in *Dracula* of setting a scene and developing its action with a maximum of conciseness and vividness could dismiss him as a mere writer of thrillers. It is even harder to believe that anyone who has examined this novel's extraordinary richness of detail and Stoker's ability to subordinate this richness to a severely disciplined plot could regard him as deficient in inventiveness, intellectual power, or a sense of literary design. The long passage I quoted earlier shows that his language rises at times to a kind of poetry. Had Stoker been able to overcome the single problem of his weakness in characterization, there is no reason why *Dracula* should not have been one of the minor masterpieces of English fiction. Even in its imperfect form it deserves to be known to scholars as more than a source of sensational films.

WILLIAM PATRICK DAY, *IN THE CIRCLES OF FEAR AND DESIRE: A STUDY OF GOTHIC FANTASY.* CHICAGO: UNIVERSITY OF CHICAGO PRESS, 1985, 143-49.

The tradition reaches its logical fulfillment at the end of the nineteenth century in *Dracula*. Bram Stoker attempts to resolve the central anxieties expressed in the genre, the twin fears of pleasure and androgyny. In *Dracula*, Stoker creates a pair of androgynes, Count Dracula and Mina Harker, and in doing so, seeks to liberate the desire for androgyny from the fear of sensual pleasure. In this strategy, Stoker fails; in fact, he renews the dynamics of the Gothic fantasy in such a way as to transform its parodic impulse into a mythologizing one. Dracula becomes the archetypal representative of the Gothic world, the primal creature of the Gothic abyss, and he is in himself complete and whole, a true alternative to human identity. Though that alternative may be horrific, it is nonetheless powerful, for Dracula escapes the fragmentation that the doubled human identity faces, even if he does so by embracing terror as a way of existence. In him, death becomes, not the end of the crisis of identity through the destruction of the self, but rather the monstrous gateway into a completely new kind of identity. Dracula's difference in kind, rather than simply in degree, from the humans in the story makes him a truly mythological figure.

Stoker's novel dramatizes the conflict between two communities. . . . The community of the vampires stands as the single example in the tradition of beings who have settled fully and completely into the Gothic world. Dracula himself, as we have seen, has fully internalized the sadomasochistic aspects of masculine identity, as has his harem of female vampires. They live in an underworld in which the masculine and feminine have come together on terms dictated by the former, and the resolution of the dichotomies between the two patterns of identity is the creation of a whole world of monstrous androgynes. Because Dracula has recreated his three human lovers as vampires, he is not only their lover but their parent. Thus the motif of incest continues in the vampire world. In his obsession with blood and his horrific immortality, in Renfield's references to him as "the Master," Dracula shows that he is a parody of Christ. He has gone beyond seeking to hear God's voice or to become God, he now is God, the Savior, at least in his own realm. At the heart of that realm is the perversion of love, the transformation of the affective impulse into an act of destruction that is also a perversion of sexuality. Neither Dracula nor the female vampires have any particular sexual orientation: they will suck the blood from anyone, man, woman, or child. Their magnetic sexual attractiveness does not work on each other, only on humans, because the humans find in them, not only the call to death that lurks in the patterns of identity we have been exploring, but a resolution of the conflict between self and Other.

The vampire's transformation of love into sadism can best be seen early in the novel, in the scene in which female vampires lust after the blood of Jonathan Harker. Dracula forbids them their victim, and they reply, "You never love, no, you never love." He replies, "You know well I loved once." At first this appears to be a grotesquely pathetic moment, in which the vampires yearn for love as pale echoes of their lost human identities. In fact, though, the exchange is sinister and obscene when we realize that what the vampire means by "love" is literally the sucking of the victim's blood. Sexuality and love have become the act of feeding. Dracula has made literal the romantic trope that for the lover, love is food and drink. The vampires are androgynes, but their androgyny is an expression, not of increased sympathy and widened identity, but of an indifference to everyone but themselves. The androgyne grows out of the conceptions of masculine and feminine that dominate the real world and have their negative image in the Gothic fantasy. The Gothic gives back, not only the terrifying parody of male and female, but a monstrous vision of the androgyne that is their unacknowledged offspring. When Dracula stands over Mina, having forced her to drink his blood in a blasphemous sacrament, he calls her "my wine press," and the female vampires greedily suck the blood from a child that Dracula has brought them as a substitute for Harker. Conventional ideas of masculine and feminine identity can only form a parody of the androgyne.

In contrast, the humans who oppose Dracula are bound together by ties of love and friendship; their relationships are so spiritually uplifted in standard Victorian fashion that the modern reader may find them somewhat hard to take.

This human group, a voluntary family opposed to Dracula's conscripted one, has no true patriarch; its roots are in the feminine ideal. Van Helsing does take some of the functions of the patriarch, for he knows more about vampires than do the rest, but his leadership rests on his particular knowledge and wisdom, not on his status as eldest male. All of the men who were Lucy's lovers, Seward, Holmwood, and Morris, are apparently adventurers, but they, too, subordinate themselves to the feminine ideal of the family. They do this in part because they worshipped Lucy and hold their own sacrifices of blood to her, through transfusions, sacred. In this attitude there is a genteel and benign paternalism, perceiving women as passive victims to be protected. The men attempt to place Mina Harker in this category, and had they succeeded, their community would have been a glossed-over version of traditional male hegemony over the feminine. But in fact, Mina becomes the most powerful figure in the group; if anyone dominates, it is she. By initially excluding her from the witch hunt for Dracula, the men in fact make her more vulnerable to his attacks. When they recognize this, they must take her into the circle as an equal, and Mina, with what Van Helsing calls her "man's brain and woman's heart," really plans the pursuit of Dracula; her courage far outstrips that of her male comrades', for she is in danger of losing her soul as well as her life. Mina is a far more attractive androgyne than Dracula, combining intelligence, decisiveness, and efficiency with tenderness. She can succeed in making her place in the band of male questers exactly because her presence converts them from would-be quest heroes to members of a true family. She serves as sister-mother-confessor to all, though wife to only Harker. As in *Uncle Silas*, the affectional "family" can absorb masculine power if the bonds of the real family don't interfere. Parents and parent figures, die with remarkable frequency; the old solicitor who is like Harker's father, Lucy's mother, and Holmwood's father all die in the course of the novel. The voluntary family takes the place of the biological family.

Emancipation from the biological family relieves the characters of anxiety about the sexuality it embodies: the relationships of the vampires are coldly androgynous, and those of human family are purely spiritual. However, we must also note that Mina is the only female Gothic character who is not a virgin. The fact that she is a sexual being as well as a friend to the men suggests that some of her power stems from her ability to act on her own sexual desires. Lucy, who is a virgin when Dracula makes her his victim, is a target because of her repressed, though extremely sensual, nature. Her fantasies about marrying all three of her suitors and her sleepwalking betray an erotic restlessness on which Dracula seizes. Sensual but chaste, Lucy's sexuality has no outlet, no mode of expression. In Mina, the Gothic heroine has truly made the transition from girl to woman. She comes closest to a fully integrated and stable identity as any character in the genre, with the exception of Dracula himself, her monstrous, masculine enemy.

In the end, Mina and her companions succeed: Dracula is destroyed and the curse is lifted, not only from the humans, but as Mina asserts at the last moment when Dracula smiles, from the vampire himself. The novel has dramatized the conflict between two versions of identity, two versions of the family, and crystalized the themes of the Gothic fantasy in their most direct and powerful form. In Dracula, Stoker created a character who has become one of the dominate icons of the twentieth-century imagination. The count refuses to stay dead; he returns over and over in films, novels, and television, in literally hundreds of incarnations and revisions. We have taken the villain of *Dracula* and made him our own, made him, I would argue, one of our images of what we are. If *Dracula* is an an attempt to solve the central issues of the Gothic on their own terms, it has the strange effect of transforming the genre from a parody to a myth. We accept Dracula as he seems himself, as a whole and powerful identity, not an aspect of our old and worn-out images, but a clear reflection of our true selves. Awful as he is, Dracula thus becomes an empowering vision of the self as Other, as Outsider. When a tradition like the Gothic stands in a parodic relationship to the world, our relationship to it must be analytical or escapist. But as we embrace it as a fable of identity, Dracula passes from fantasy, as does the whole genre, to myth, becoming a fiction that is also a "truth."

But if Dracula can pass into myth, become a new kind of self, why does his opponent fail to do so too? Mina fails because, though she is an androgyne, she does not resolve the problem of pleasure that is the other side of the crisis of the doubled self. Dracula has completely done away with pleasure; he simply redefines it as pain. Though monstrous, he is whole. His success is predicated on his total rejection of the power of pleasure as a means of synthesis and reconciliation. Thus, he is maimed but, at the same time, complete. Mina almost attains the full power of androgyny through her acceptance of pleasure, symbolized in her adult, female sexuality. But in her contact with Dracula we see the failure of her androgyny: Dracula's sadomasochistic sexuality can corrupt Mina, transform her into an "almost" vampire. When the Host touches her forehead, her flesh is seared, for she is, by her own words, "unclean." Yet why should Dracula be able to make the woman who is his equal unclean, while she is unable to transform him at all? She speaks to the men of the necessity of doing what they do to the count out of love, and yet she still must rely on violence, the stake through the heart, to defeat him. Had Mina fully integrated the power of sexuality as pleasure in herself, Dracula could never have corrupted her. Sexual pleasure, except when confined to marriage, remains intrinsically unclean for Mina, and for Stoker. Thus Stoker's heroic androgyne cannot use the most powerful weapon available to her as a defense against the count--the secure knowledge of the purity of her own sexuality---and must rely on traditional masculine violence to do the work of "love."

Stoker's spiritualizing of Mina marks his failure to confront and accept the implications of his own dialectic, one androgyne formed from pain, another from pleasure. Finally, in the last words of the novel, when we see Mina through Jonathan's eyes, she has fallen back into the role of Mother; he sees her now, seven years later, as the woman men defended, not the woman who led men in her own defense. Thus, unlike the count, she is forced back into the unresolved, unacknowledged doubleness that is the usual state of characters in the Gothic. The myth of *Dracula*, then, becomes a myth of the power of pain.

The very fact that it can be used to express this mythology of pain suggests that perhaps the problem with the figure of the androgyne goes deeper than the specific problems of the novel. Stoker's inability to resolve the problem of sexuality and pleasure in relation to individual identify is surely the reason why Mina cannot act directly against Dracula, why she cannot cure him but must kill him. Both Mina and Dracula fail as androgynes because they reflect the corrupted visions of masculine and feminine identity upon which they are based, Dracula in his own nature, Mina in the inescapable images of woman as passive, spiritual Mother that surround her. But can any androgynous vision of identity truly offer a conception of self to which real men and women might adhere? The very idea of the androgyne seems rooted in the notion of differences between masculine and feminine; these two poles must exist before they can be reconciled. We must recall that the Gothic fantasy does not present a critique of the conception of masculine and feminine qualities, but rather of the distortion of those qualities and the definition of the relationship between the two poles of identity as sadomasochistic. This critique is rooted in the cultural values and necessities of the nineteenth and twentieth centuries, not in an eternal vision of an abstract, ideal identity.

Perhaps, then, the androgyne is, not an alternative vision of identity at all, but an idealization, a fantasy that sharpens and focuses our sense of what is wrong with our perceptions of masculine and feminine. The pursuit of the androgyne, in this sense, is indeed the pursuit of an illusion, an illusion that transforms itself into something monstrous. But if the characters in the Gothic fantasy always encounter this monster, in our experience of their encounter, we can obtain a new sense of what the ideals of masculine and feminine might mean and what their relation to living men and women might be. Because men and women cannot escape the biological fact of difference, the androgyne must remain a creature of the imagination, like the unicorn. Dracula's success in transforming himself from man into monster is directly proportional to his achievement of monstrous androgyny; and paradoxically, Mina's failure to retain her androgynous state may point toward the real, rather than the fantasy, alternative to horror. If her reversion to Mother is unsatisfying, particularly for a modern audience, we may take it as a sign that she remains an actual woman, a living human being, not a creature out of nightmare or fantasy. The vision of androgyny that leads Van Helsing to say Mina has a man's brain and a woman's heart is still distorted; these words of praise reveal a deep attachment to the deadly opposition that has made Dracula what he is. Just as he was wrong to think Mina could be kept out of the battle, Van Helsing is wrong about the real nature of her best qualities: it should be, not man's brain, woman's heart, but woman's brain and woman's heart that make Mina who she is. We may also hope for a man's heart to go with a man's brain in some new image of male identity.

JOHN L. GREENWAY, "SEWARD'S FOLLY: *DRACULA* AS
A CRITIQUE OF 'NORMAL SCIENCE,'" *STANFORD
LITERATURE REVIEW* 3 (FALL 1986), 213-30.

Given Bram Stoker's fondness for describing female vampires as "voluptuous,"
the sexuality in *Dracula* (1897) has received considerable critical attention.[9]
While the expressed and repressed libidos do indeed tell us a great deal about the
novel, we will subordinate this side of the story to focus upon one of its minor
characters: Dr. John Seward. While we join in the attempt to discover what
elevates Stoker's novel above its Gothic predecessors and subsequent pastiches,
our commentary will not be psychoanalytic but historical. Beneath the novel's
Gothic trappings and the sexual anxieties, Stoker depicts Seward with a subtle
irony to comment upon the science of his day and the way it was practiced.

The terminology of Thomas S. Kuhn will be of use in this analysis.[10]
We do not intend to join the debate concerning his *The Structure of Scientific
Revolutions*.[11] The book has been strongly criticized by historians of science,
but Stoker (who graduated with Honors in Science from Trinity)[12] seems to
have anticipated some of Kuhn's views, and I suggest that medical history can
illuminate Stoker's attitude toward science in the novel and provide a lens for a
critical approach.

Briefly, Kuhn asserts that science is done in communities. These
communities do research regulated by "paradigms": untested assumptions which
organize results and give directions for future research. Scientists engaged in
what Kuhn calls "normal science" essentially work at "puzzle-solving" within
the context of the communal paradigm. Work done in one paradigm is
incommensurable with that done in another, Kuhn argues, because different
communities operate with different assumptions or alternative explanations. As
an example, Kuhn cites Relativistic and Newtonian mechanics. To approach the
view of "normal science" in *Dracula*, we need to recognize that histories of
science tend to be histories of present science, and often dismiss or ignore
explanations of subsequently rendered obsolete, though plausible in this own
time. In the 1890s, explanations of mental activity in physiological terms had
considerable power, and appear in the novel to bring out the irony in Dr. Seward.

Dr. Seward is the only male pursuer of Dracula to have nuance to his
character. The pseudo-dialect of Abraham Van Helsing, the other scientist,
renders him unintentionally comic; as we will see, it is important that he not be
from England. We find out that Seward is older than Quincey Morris, Jonathan
Harker, and Arthur (Lord Godalming), and, unlike them, is given to some
introspection. Collectively, the male stalwarts form an emblem of Victorian
establishment: Seward, the scientist; Harker, the lawyer; Arthur, the aristocrat;
and Quincey, the expendable American adventurer. As the scientist, however,
Seward's failure to make inferences he should have made contributes to the
growing power of Dracula, and implies an ironic attitude toward him on Stoker's
part. Two principal passages--one by Seward, one by Van Helsing--bring out
these points. They contain topical references to theories plausible at the time but
since forgotten or ignored. These topical references are easily passed over, but a

contemporary reader would see them as establishing Seward's view of himself and Stoker's view of what Seward does.

The first passage concerns Seward and Renfield. Seward's patient Renfield has been eating flies, spiders, birds, and finally announces he would like a cat. A detailed look at Seward's response in his journal reveals a good bit about him:

> . . . what he desires is to absorb as many lives as he can, and he has laid himself out to achieve it in a cumulative way. . . .What would have been his later steps? It would almost be worth while to complete the experiment. Men sneered at vivisection, and yet look at its results to-day! Why not advance science in its most difficult and vital aspect--the knowledge of the brain? Had I even the secret of one such mind--did I hold the key to the fancy of even one lunatic--I might advance my own branch of science to a pitch compared with which Burdon-Sanderson's physiology or Ferrier's brain-knowledge would be as nothing. If only there were a sufficient cause! [13]

Stoker has Seward portray himself here as radically modern. He keeps his notes on a phonograph, an innovation physicians first adopted in 1890.[14] As a physician, he treats madness as a medical problem, seeing Renfield as a "patient." Treating madness by physicians had only begun in mid-century, and came as a response to a growing sense of urgency. [15] The Commissioners in Lunacy Annual Reports showed a marked increase in insanity in the late century (16.49/10,000 in 1850 vs. 29.26/10,000 in 1890), so Seward's field is quite topical.[16]

Seward's use of "experiment" also establishes him as modern, and shows him involved in the still-controversial issue of vivisection. In his *Introduction to the Study of Experimental Medicine* (1865), Claude Bernard distinguished between the physician (a passive observer) and the physiologist, a scientist who intervened in the metabolic process to understand it. We see the physiologists' excitement in their method (as well as their arrogance) in E. Cyon's *Methodik der physiologischen Experimente und Vivisectionen*: "Soll die Medicin ernst eine streng wissenschaftliche Basis in allen ihren Zweigen erhalten, so muss sie dieselbe in erster Linie von der Physiologie erwarten."[17]

Bernard's establishing of medicine as "experimental" ran counter to the traditional view of medicine as observational and diagnostic. Conservatives viewed illness as a punishment, a consequent of sin and folly. As the novelist Mona Caird put it, "There can be no offense more shocking and no act more dastardly than this of trying to shift the natural punishment of our own sins and vices and stupidities, on to the shoulders of those who are powerless to resist us." [18] Seward's willingness to "complete the experiment" would appall readers who suspected that physiologists were conducting vivisection on humans.[19]

Seward, who in this passage considers himself bridging the gap between the laboratory and the hospital--a radical act in itself--also sees himself in the same methodological school as John Burdon Sanderson and David Ferrier. Stoker gives Seward a further nuance of character in mentioning these physicians: Seward's role-models scandalized conservative physicians and antivivisectionists. Burdon Sanderson helped bring the physiological method to England from

France and Germany in the 1870s. His *Handbook for the Physiological Laboratory* (2 vols., London, 1873), intended for beginners, made public the methods of vivisection. By not specifying the use of anesthetics, Burdon Sanderson became the focus of considerable pamphlet literature, which described "A new moral contagion" introduced into England. [20]

Similarly, Ferrier's experiments with cerebral locations in monkeys led to another scandal. In 1881, Ferrier became the second scientist prosecuted under the Cruelty to Animals Act of 1876 by the Victorian Street Society. His acquittal proved crucial for the acceptance of the experimental method.[21]

Renfield's experimenting upon himself tempts Seward. Some truly adventurous physiologists had recently done just this. Endocrinology had little theoretical base when the seventy-two year old Edouard Brown-Sequard reported to the Biological Society in 1889 that he had injected himself with testosterone from dogs and guinea pigs, claiming "dynamogenic" results. In his later publications he extended these experiments to women, claiming rejuvenation and remissions of cancer.[22] He died in 1894.

Seward's medical interests extend to the dynamics of the unconscious: "unconscious cerebration" he twice calls it (71,238). Here, too, he is on relatively new ground, a field which had but recently asserted itself as normal science. Thomas Laycock, for instance, drawing upon the recently discovered law of conservation of energy, puts mental energy under this law, and in his *Mind and Brain* (1869) says he will construct a science of mind founded upon a philosophical physiology of the brain. "Mental science," he declares, "is the chemistry of human nature."[23] By 1889, Jules Hericourt could assume unconscious mental activity as a fact, and concluded that the unconscious directs conscious actions; in extreme form the unconscious expresses itself as Mesmerism, hysteria, and other abnormal states.[24]

Seward considers himself radical, but Stoker does not. Actually, Seward (for all his ostensible progressiveness) is quite conventional, and herein lies the irony governing Stoker's portrayal of him. Seward sees science in terms of the past: he is excited to have a new label for Renfield's aberration "zoophagy"--but he cannot understand Renfield's importance to his own life. If we recall the above passage, Seward sees the significance of his work in social terms: as making Burdon Sanderston and Ferrier obsolete. He is, as Kuhn would say, engaged in "puzzle-solving." He continually responds to crises by admonishing himself to "Work! Work!" but his science accomplishes nothing, save that his unwillingness to synthesize the data to which he has access comes close to precipitating disaster for everyone.

Seward does not let his own "unconscious cerebration" figure out three key chains of evidence, and these lapses form the nucleus of the irony governing his character. First, we see from the above passage that Seward senses the significance of Renfield's experiment in the food-chain. Renfield's experiment fascinates him, but he is content to label it "zoophagy" and not pursue its logic. Physiologists (most notably Huxley) agreed that one acquires the energy of what one consumes.[25] Van Helsing notes that Dracula now has the energy of the four who gave transfusions to Mina (183): Stoker means for Seward to know the theory, for Seward comments that the band has acquired the "animal heat" of their supper (272), but he does not use the theory to link Renfield with Dracula.

Second, Seward has evidence linking Renfield's activity and that of Dracula. His failure to make this connection allows Dracula to enter the hospital through Renfield and prey upon Mina. For the men, defending "their" women is tantamount to defending civilization, but Dracula can now say "Your girls that you all love are mine already" (271). Harker notes with unusual language that Seward is coming close: Seward says "in a dreamy kind of way" that "he seems so mixed up with the Count in an indexy kind of way" (220). Even though Van Helsing has told them in the previous chapter that "he can only change himself at sunrise or sunset," the clinician Seward cannot make the connection between Renfield's moments of derangement and Dracula's times of change.

Third, Mina links Dracula with "the criminal type": "Nordau and Lombroso would so classify him, and qua criminal he is of imperfectly formed mind" (300). Cesare Lombroso's and Max Nordau's descriptions of the physiological traits of criminals was considered normal science at the end of the century.[26] Stoker took some care to describe Dracula and the female vampires as having criminal features. [27] Given Harker's penchant for uncritically recording data, after reading his journal, Seward as a scientist should have done what Mina did unconsciously: recognize Dracula (and vampirism in general) as an atavism, an evolutionary regression to a primordial past (Laycock would agree about their behavior, 2:486). Stoker emphasized these details in his narrative, and it is at least curious that the representatives of the Victorian scientific establishment will not let himself draw inferences from the data familiar to the normal science of his time. Harker, earlier in the novel, established an ironic pattern by uncritically recording data; Seward, too, sees details without allowing them to be significant. Instead, he continually insists that "there must be a rational explanation." There was an explanation, but not one congenial to Seward's puzzle-solving mentality.

Seward does not allow himself to complete the above inferences, for to do so would require questioning the social assumptions regulating his scientific method. His search for a "rational explanation" is a search for one which will reinforce his sentimental view of society. If he followed out the logic of Renfield's experiment, he would realize that we are not at the top of the food-chain: Dracula is. Seward would also have to realize that there is not that much difference between Renfield and himself. As Gattegno points out, the content of their investigations differs, but they proceed the same way.[28] Seward has to fall back on social distinctions to keep the psychological barrier between them. When Renfield, trying to warn the group, attempts to break down the barrier by speaking not only sanely but elegantly, Seward breaks the scene off, saying that it had become "too comically grave" (218). As Seward pursues these connections, he repeatedly fears he is going mad. When he finds out (too late) that the Count lives next door, he realizes that "we had enough clues from the conduct of the patient Renfield." Knowing Lucy's life was the price of this failure, he does not continue: "Stop; that way madness lies!" (201).

Had Seward allowed his "unconscious cerebration" to work, he would have found out a great deal--not just about himself, but about science in general.

The paradigms regulating Seward's science are quite conventional, particularly the assumptions regarding women, and reflect the simple moral world of Seward and the other characters. Here we must see Stoker's depiction of Seward in a larger context. Concerning women, Mosedale generalizes that while most of the nineteenth-century biologists "operated in blissful ignorance of their prejudices, their own socially conditioned feelings about their subject guided the application of the scientific theories."[29] Kuhn points out that scientists operating within a given paradigm see only what they are trained to see and precisely this irony governs Seward's character. Stoker gives Seward enough information to contribute to the solving of the mystery, but his "unconscious cerebration" is inhibited by his assumption that Lucy's "natural state" is one of "sweet purity" (192).

Stoker's narrative strategy does not let Seward find out that he doesn't know Lucy as well as he thinks he does. Even when she was "pure," Lucy did not consider polyandry scandalous. Had he known that Lucy asked Mina "Why can't they let a girl marry three men, or as many as want her, and save all this trouble?" (62), he would not have been startled to find out that in a sense she got her wish. When Seward mentions Arthur's comment that, having given blood to Lucy, he is in a sense married to her after all. Van Helsing senses the shallowness of sentimental metaphors governing relationships: "'But there was a difficulty, friend John. If so that, then what about the others? Ho, ho! Then this so sweet maid is a polyandrist, and me, with my poor wife dead to me, but alive by Church's law, though no wits, all gone--even I, who am faithful husband to this now-no wife, am bigamist" (159). Seward is not amused at this.

Seward's "normal science" expresses a world of sentimental conventions: social theory informs his scientific views, with the reverse being true as well. As physicians, he and Van Helsing decide to exclude Mina from their plans for "We are men, and are able to bear" (215). In the novel, this turns out to be a catastrophically bad decision, but the irony stems from the decision's medical soundness. Although Van Helsing exclaims several times about Mina's intelligence and her "man's brain" (209), conventional medical wisdom dictated that women be shielded from emotional strain. Within the paradigm, the argument was sound, but as Kuhn points out, each paradigm is based upon unquestioned assumptions. In this case, scientists assumed that, since neural energy and electrical energy were similar (a logical inference from Galvani's experiments with frog legs in the 1790s), the nervous system was like a battery or Leyden Jar. [30] Men possess greater neural reserves than women due to their generally larger physiques. Assuming that a given situation exacts the same amount of stress on a man as on a woman, a woman will be proportionally more depleted by the stress than her male counterpart. While Van Helsing can assert that Mina has a "man's brain" qualitatively, physicians generally argued that, as women's cranial capacities were smaller than those of men, one ought not expect the same mental output. [31] Seward concurs.

The proof advanced for this deduction was alleged to lie in history: where are the female geniuses? We may consider Laycock's argument as typical. As progressive as he considers his "mental science" to be, his innovations occur within the conventional paradigm informing the judgment of Seward and Van

Helsing. Having shown the difference in "vital force" between men and women
(2:313), he argues that while a woman is in one sense an imperfectly developed
man, she is perfect in the sense of being adapted to her position (2:314). The
difference in brain-weights renders the woman more neurally susceptible to strain
than the man. Laycock's bland, pedantic style leads one at first glance to infer
that his science is independent of social theory: "Her sedentary habits, and the
less perfect condition of her blood when resident in towns, greatly increases this
natural sensibility or affectibility of her nervous system; and when both are
combined with the erethistic influence of the generative glands on the nerve-
centres, the varied morbid states of the coenasthesis grouped under the term
Hysteria result" (2:317). He concludes that women just do not have the mental
power to compete with men. "Women's excellence over man is not, in truth, in
the manifestation of force of intellect and energy of will, but in the sphere of
wisdom, and love, and moral power" (2:483). In contrast to the "speculative
philosophy" of Mill, Laycock advocates his "more cautious conclusions of an
inductive mental science, founded on the widest and deepest observation of the
order and laws of nature" (2:494).

These sentimental assumptions lead Seward and all the characters to
assume that Lucy falls victim to something alien, but the vampires catalyze a
sexuality latent in all the characters (all, that is, except Dracula and Morris).
Normal science agreed with William Acton, the leading physician in sexuality of
the 1870s, that "the majority of women (happily for society) are not very much
troubled with sexual feeling of any kind."[32] Lucy seems to find a release from
her empty life in vampirism. No longer restrained by convention, she can violate
the assumed "natural" roles for women: wife and mother. She can seduce Arthur,
and as the "Bloofer lady" she preys upon children. Mina, who ends up as both
wife and mother, comments about her encounter with Dracula that "strangely
enough, I did not want to hinder him" (255).

Among themselves, the characters take pains to explain away any
physical contact as unusual, a spontaneous product of extreme emotion.
Although the male narrators attribute the sensual appeal of the vampires to a
hypnotic power, we find out that the other males (except Seward and Quincey)
share Lucy and Mina's libidinous attraction to vampirism. Harker anticipates the
"kisses" of the vampires in the castle, Arthur has no reservations about kissing
Lucy or sharing her coffin, and even Van Helsing finds the three Draculettes
"voluptuous" before he kills them.

The contrast between Seward and Van Helsing illustrates, first, the
irony governing Seward and, in a larger sense, Stoker's views on science in the
novel. While Seward operates in a scientific paradigm where "rational
explanation" and sentimental social theory reinforce each other, Van Helsing
does not, although they share the "weak woman" paradigm. He gives a lecture to
Seward that bears analyzing:

Ah, it is the fault of our science that it wants to explain all; and if it explain not, then
it says there is nothing to explain. But yet we see around us every day the growth of
new beliefs, which think themselves new; and which are yet but the old, which
pretend to be young--like the fine ladies at the opera. I suppose you do not believe in

corporeal transference. No? Nor in materialisation. No? Nor in astral bodies. No? Nor in the reading of thought. No? Nor in hypnotism. . . (172)

Seward breaks in, admitting that "Charcot has proved that pretty well." Van Helsing then asks, "how you accept the hypnotism and reject the thought-reading?" and concludes by saying "There are always mysteries in life" (173). Blinderman, in his otherwise excellent article, dismisses this speech as "superficial and ridiculous,"[33] but I believe he is misled by Van Helsing's strange idiom, for Van Helsing actually raises a fairly subtle issue in philosophy of science and a difficult issue for Seward: how to distinguish between science and pseudoscience.[34] Even though we might not take the topics Van Helsing mentions seriously, reputable scientists at the time most certainly did. Our contention is that Van Helsing makes a crucial point.

The reference to Jean-Martin Charcot in this passage gives Stoker an important link between the science of Seward and that of Van Helsing, for with the work of Charcot, Mesmerism was transformed into normal science. Mesmerism had long been outside normal science, dismissed as chicanery and nonsense in spite of some startling cures. After Braid renamed the modified technique "hypnotism" in 1843, it had been given a place as legitimate therapy with the clinical work of Jean-Martin Charcot at the Salpetriere School in the 1870s. [35] Scientists interested in the workings of the unconscious, such as the above-mentioned Hericourt, conjectured that Mesmerism might be an expression of this dark area of the mind.

When Van Helsing refers to the "things that are done to-day in electrical science which would have been deemed unholy by the very men who discovered electricity" (173), Stoker suggests that the distinction between science and pseudoscience often becomes obvious only in retrospect. What scientists dismissed in Mesmerism as pseudoscience was actually "protoscience," and Van Helsing sees the same situation in telepathy. Interestingly, he was not alone in this analogy, and Seward's refusal to follow Van Helsing's logic provides another ironic commentary upon him as a scientist of the '90s. Given the role telepathy plays in the novel--Dracula's initial contacts with Lucy and Renfield are telepathic, while Mina's inventiveness allows Van Helsing to track the Count through hypnotically induced telepathy--Seward's lack of response further compromises his ostensible radicalism.

Although scientists of the stature of Helmholz and Wundt did not believe telepathy could become legitimate science, others were not so sure, given the startling recent discoveries in other areas concerning energy: radio, X-rays, radiation. The articulation by Helmholz of the Law of Conservation of Energy in 1847 combined with the romantic legacy of the unity of nature to lead influential psychologists such as Alexander Bain to suggest in 1867 "that there is a definite equivalence between mental manifestations and physical forces, the same as between the physical forces themselves, is, I think, conformable to all the facts, although liable to peculiar difficulties in the way of decisive proof."[36]

The Society for Psychical Research went further. If Braid's coining of the term "hypnotism" in the '40s partially freed the field from the stigma of Mesmerism, F.W.M. Myers wished to do the same for telepathy. He coined the term in 1882 in the first volume of the *Proceedings of the Society for Psychical Research.*

Seward does not respond to Van Helsing, for had he seen the membership list of the Society he would have had to admit that many of his eminent colleagues took psychic research seriously indeed; Rayleigh and Thomson were scientists of the first rank, but as Wilson shows, they were not isolated examples of the interest by "normal science" in telepathy. Few took telepathy as seriously as did William Crookes, developer of the cathode-ray. That he could assert the legitimacy of the field in his presidential address to the British Association for the Advancement of Science says something of the stature of the still-controversial idea. [37] Indeed, the long-standing belief in ether as a medium for the transmission of energy convinced some that physics and psychic research differed only in degree: Dr. Imoda felt confident in asserting that "Radiations of radium, the cathodic radiation of the Crookes tube, the mediumistic radiations are fundamentally the same."[38] Wilson concludes that "though never accepted by the larger part of the Scientific community, psychic research was certainly not restricted to popular or non-scientific levels for support and sympathy."[39]

In Seward's field, some physiologists found the arguments for telepathy quite tenable. Laycock and Carpenter's studies of "unconscious cerebration" assumed a physiological basis for mental action. Suggestion, then, had to be a transference of mental energy, a domination of a weaker will by a stronger. Consequently, hypnotists preferred women as subjects, as we see in du Maurier's *Trilby* (1894). Van Helsing encounters increasing difficulty in hypnotizing Mina as Dracula's power over her grows greater, "his forehead was covered with great beads of perspiration" (275), and her hypnosis only comes "in obedience to his will" (303).

The physiological explanation of mental energy led some eminent investigators to suspect that hypnotism, somnambulism, and telepathy might be understood as emanations of energy produced by the will, transmitted through the ether, and hence were not abnormal states at all. Dr. William Carpenter, President of the British Association for the Advancement of Science in 1872, discusses "Unconscious Cerebration" in this Context, concluding that we "will be wise in maintaining a 'reserve of possibility' as to phenomena which are not altogether opposed to the Laws of Physics of Physiology, but rather transcend them. . . Looking at Nerve-force as a special form of Physical energy, it may be deemed not altogether incredible that it should exert itself from a distance, so as to bring the Brain of one person into direct dynamical communication with that of another, without the intermediation of verbal language or or movements of expression."[40] William James, one of the founders of modern dynamic psychiatry, essentially agrees with Van Helsing: he argues that mystics and Mesmerists had only "cursorily and ineffectually" presented "the thesis that a communication can take place from mind to mind by some agency not that of the recognized organs of sense." [41]

Richet describes his experiments on "La suggestion mentale et le calcul des probabilités" in the *Revue Philosophique* 18 (1884) 609-73, in a tone similar to Van Helsing's, pointing out that telepathy is but one of the phenomena unintelligible to contemporary science. "La suggestion mentale,"

Richet says, "est l'influence que la pensee d'un individu exerce dans un sens determine, sans phenomene exterieur appreciable a nos sens, sur la pensee d'un individu voisin" (615). Richet offers two-to-one odds that telepathy exists, but points out the problem of explanation before telepathy can become legitimate research.

We find a real-life incarnation of Van Helsing's methodology in Theodore Flournoy, psychologist and friend of William James. He based his methodology upon Laplace's motto: "We ought to examine them with an attention the more scrupulous as the facts appear to us the more incredible."[42] Flournoy (who wrote to James considering the Brown-Sequard injection for himself) [43] approached telepathy much as Charcot approached animal magnetism: by pairing away the spiritualism, he hoped to find a scientific explanation.[44] Flournoy concludes that, just as hypnosis is not a form of hysteria, mediumship is not pathological: it is a rare condition, but not morbid.[45] James and Flournoy agreed that understanding telepathy would be a scientific revolution, but Flournoy was confident that "our natural sciences can be adapted to everything."[46]

Telepathy, then, might well be an intense form of hypnosis. Charcot noted that in a somnambulistic state (such as Lucy's) one is most receptive to suggestion and hence, Myers and others believed, telepathic communication. Myers would find the telepathy in *Dracula* quite plausible, for he went even further than did Flournoy, whose research he cites. In *Human Personality and Its Survival of Bodily Death* (1904), [47] he strongly links hypnosis with telepathic receptivity. Somnambulism frequently indicates telepathy, more frequently clairvoyance (118). We ought not consider telepathy abnormal, Myers contends, but supernormal, perhaps the next stage in evolution (74).

Van Helsing's lecture has a peculiar effect upon Seward. He admits that his "imagination was getting fired" (174), but he loses his orientation in London (178), and in trying to rationalize the absence of Lucy's corpse he realizes, "I was speaking folly, and yet it was the only real cause I could suggest" (179). Van Helsing sighs, "We must have more proof," but Seward can only accept evidence which agrees with normal science. Van Helsing is asking him to accept an incommensurable paradigm, for Seward needs not proof, but a change in assumptions. He feels "that horrid sense of the reality of things, in which any effort of imagination seems out of place" (181). When he sees Lucy in her coffin, he still insists upon conventional explanations, although he feels ashamed at their inadequacy (181).

Rather than admit the reality of vampirism, Seward first suspects Van Helsing (184), then questions his own sanity (all the men do this), and finally drops out of the novel. When he is forced to admit the truth of Van Helsing's explanation, he becomes increasingly passive, and subsequently becomes virtually useless outside London. He is the only one silent at the group's oath to extirpate Dracula; he makes no comment upon Mina's suggestion to use hypnosis/telepathy to pursue the Count, nor upon her insight that Dracula has the criminal physiology characteristic of the atavistic racial degenerate described by Lombroso and Nordau; nor is he in on the killing of Dracula.

Van Helsing's lecture also implies that science does not always validate social truth. As regards the assumptions concerning women, Seward assumes Lucy's natural state to be "purity," but we noted above that she privately flirts with the idea of polyandry (26). As she acquires the "life-force" of the men through transfusions, she becomes in a sense joined to them. Van Helsing points out the social ambiguity of the transfusions (159). Mina, too, finds Dracula appealing. Seward's sentimental assumptions concerning women, however, were contradicted by research outside his normal science. Otto Weininger, whose *Sex and Character* (1903) had gone through twenty-five editions and eight translations by 1923 declared that woman "nichts ist als Sexualit, weil sie die Sexualitat selbst ist."[48] Though Seward is sexless, the other men have libidos as well; as Weininger puts it, "Die Frau is *nur* sexuell, der Mann ist *auch* sexuell" (109).

Indeed, the science Stoker has Seward express was on the verge of being displaced by a more dynamic paradigm. Seward's sentimental psychology (particularly his view of women) fits well into the Victorian literary imagination, but, as Ellenberger puts it, "Literature was unable to express the full horror of individual fates that occurred in reality."[49] Outside the conventional community, where social theory and scientific theory validated each other, medical research current in the '90s would require Seward to accept this incommensurable paradigm. These discoveries extend the irony in the novel beyond the obsolete view of women and to the nature of psychological reality.

The case histories in Richard von Krafft-Ebing's *Psychopathia Sexualis* in 1886 brought the words "sadism" and "masochism" into the language, as well as a motion that he be dropped as an honorary member of the British Medico-Psychological Association.[50] Among many other things, Krafft-Ebing mentions several cases of necrophilia.[51] Dr. Herbert Mayo's *On the Truths Contained in Popular Superstitions with an Account of Mesmerism* had gone through three editions by 1851 and had twenty-one pages devoted to "Vampyrism." Medical case-histories in Stoker's time were lurid even by tabloid standards. As one example, we may take the case of Justine Lafayette and Martin Dummoland, who in 1881 respectively cannibalized and drank the blood of some eighty girls.[52]

Discoveries in physiology provided a new set of metaphors for eminent scientists to describe the nature of life at its lowest level that ran quite counter to Seward's sentimental science, but which would render *Dracula* less incredible to a contemporary microbiologist.[53] Believing that Huxley had discovered the lowest common denominator of life in the *bathybius haeklii*, G.J. Allman, in his Presidential Address to the British Association for the Advancement of Science (1879) described behavior in the Petri dish in graphic but familiar terms:

Let us observe our Amoeba a little closer. Like all living beings, it must be nourished. It cannot grow as a crystal would grow by accumulating on its surface molecule after molecule of matter. It must FEED. It must take into its substance the necessary nutriment; it must assimilate this nutriment, and convert it into the material of which it is itself composed. . . .A stream of protoplasm instantly runs away from the body of the Amoeba towards the destined prey, envelopes it in its current, and then flows back with it to the central protoplasm, where it sinks deeper and deeper into the soft yielding mass, and becomes dissolved, digested, and assimilated in order that it may increase the size and restore the energy of its captor. [54]

Stoker has Van Helsing tell the stalwarts the "rules" under which Dracula must operate (212-13; 159-61). Although films have used these rules with good effect, vampire lore does not substantiate them. In the novel, Stoker invented these rules to make explicit the real conflict in his story: that between the sentimental world of Seward's London civilization and the libidinous, atavistic anarchy of Dracula. The rules establish Dracula's world as being just as real as Seward's; indeed, the London world is the accident, Dracula's being the norm. What we have noted about normal science and discoveries outside that paradigm holds true for the novel as a whole. The farther one travels from London, the more the definition of "normal" changes from one of rational explanation to one regulated by the norms of myth.

Hence, the true conflict is not a Gothic good versus evil, as the characters repeatedly assert, nor of science versus superstition, but one far more subtle. The characters see Dracula as the "other," but as Senf has argued, he actually catalyzes drives within us.[55] The latent sexuality is obvious; in addition, all the stalwarts violate the rules of their system in the name of the common good. [56] Seward falsifies the death certificate of Lucy's mother to avoid the coroner, Arthur uses his heraldic device to mask their daylight breaking and entering, and Harker resorts to bribery. As we have only the narrators' sentiments, we overlook the contrast between their tedious moralizing and the violence of their behavior.

When confronted by Lucy's rejection of the roles of wife and mother (her "voluptuous wantonness" and her preying upon children), even bland Dr. Seward abandons his world of rational explanation for a moment, asserting that he could now kill Lucy not in the name of the common good, but with "savage delight" (189). Symbols of Victorian technology abound (phonographs, telegraphs, telephones, typewriters, Winchesters, steamboats, etc.), but Dracula is finally dispatched with exotic weapons of American and Indian frontiers: Quincey's Bowie knife and Harker's Ghurka knife.

The irony governing Seward extends to the novel as a whole. If Seward's science contributes nothing to understanding Dracula, neither does the sentimental world upon which it is based. Adherence to scientific and social assumptions constantly precipitates disaster. The characters learn nothing from their adventure: Mina, after all she has experienced, describes the Transylvanians' reaction to the scar on her forehead by saying "They are *very, very* superstitious" (316).

The bland, asexual tableau at the end, when the characters return to Transylvania for old times' sake, officially announces the triumph of the Victorian conventions of rationality and progress. At first glance, the Victorian view of history as a conquest of barbarity and superstition seems affirmed in the happy ending. The men, emblems of the establishment as scientist, solicitor, and aristocrat, have become husbands and providers while Mina, who has the best mind of the lot, has become Jonathan's secretary. Their child, Quincey, is more an emblem of group solidarity than a bond between Jonathan and Mina; they end as Harker began--as tourists. The irony in this tableau, however, suggests that these conventions, just as Seward's science, are merely forms of structured ignorance. The novel grows from this irony: not just from the ignorance of the heroes of a world they cannot understand, but the larger irony that the "other" world is more real than their own.

STEPHEN D. ARATA, "THE OCCIDENTAL TOURIST: *DRACULA* AND THE ANXIETY OF REVERSE COLONIZATION," *VICTORIAN STUDIES* 33 (1990), 621-45.

> "Fashions in monsters do change."
> Joseph Conrad

Bram Stoker's *Dracula* (1897) participates in that "modernizing" of Gothic which occurs at the close of the nineteenth century. Like Stevenson's *Dr. Jekyll and Mr. Hyde* (1886) and Wilde's *Picture of Dorian Gray* (1891), Stoker's novel achieves its effects by bringing the terror of the Gothic home. While Gothic novelists had traditionally displaced their stories in time or locale, these later writers root their action firmly in the modern world. Yet critics have until recently ignored the historical context in which these works were written and originally read. Most notably, criticism has persistently undervalued Dracula's extensive and highly visible contracts with a series of cultural issues, particularly those involving race, specific to the 1890s.[57] This neglect has in part resulted from the various psychoanalytic approaches taken by most critics of Gothic. While such approaches have greatly enriched our understanding of *Dracula*, and while nothing in psychoanalytic critical theory precludes a "historicist" reading of literary texts, that theory has in practice been used almost exclusively to demonstrate, as Stoker's most recent critic puts it, that *Dracula* is a "representation of fears that are more universal than a specific focus on the Victorian background would allow."[58] Yet the novel's very attachment to the "Victorian background" . . . is a primary source of Stoker's continuing power. Late-Victorian Gothic in general, and *Dracula* in particular, continually calls our attention to the cultural context surrounding and informing the text, and insists that we take that context into account.

In the case of *Dracula*, the context includes the decline of Britain as a world power at the close of the nineteenth century; or rather, the way the perception of that decline was articulated by contemporary writers. *Dracula* appeared in a Jubilee year, but one marked by considerably more introspection and less self-congratulation than the celebration of a decade earlier. The decay of British global influence, the loss of overseas markets for British goods, the economic and political rise of Germany and the United States, the increasing unrest in British colonies and possessions, the growing domestic uneasiness over the morality of imperialism--all combined to erode Victorian confidence in the inevitability of British progress and hegemony.[59] Late-Victorian fiction in particular is saturated with the sense that the entire nation--as a race of people, as a political and imperial force, as a social and cultural power--was in irretrievable decline. What I will be examining is how that perception is transformed into narrative, into stories which the culture tells itself not only to articulate and account for its troubles, but also to defend against and even to assuage the anxiety attendant upon cultural decay.

I

Dracula enacts the period's most important and pervasive narrative of decline, a narrative of reverse colonization. Versions of this story recur with remarkable frequency in both fiction and nonfiction texts throughout the last decades of the century. In whatever guise, this narrative expresses both fear and guilt. The fear is that what has been represented as the "civilized" world is on the point of being colonized by "primitive" forces. These forces can originate outside the civilized world (in Rider Haggard's *She*, Queen Ayesha plans to sack London and depose Queen Victoria) or they can inhere in the civilized itself (as in Kurtz's emblematic heart of darkness). Fantasies of reverse colonization are particularly prevalent in late-Victorian popular fiction. . . . In each case, a terrifying reversal has occurred: the colonizer finds himself in the position of the colonized, the exploiter becomes exploited, the victimizer victimized. Such fears are linked to a perceived decline--racial, moral, spiritual--which makes the nation vulnerable to attack from more vigorous, "primitive" peoples.

But fantasies of reverse colonization are more than products of geopolitical fears. They are also response to cultural guilt. In the marauding, invasive Other, British culture sees its own imperial practices mirrored back in monstrous forms. . . .Reverse colonization narratives thus contain the potential for powerful critiques of imperialist ideologies, even if that potential usually remains unrealized. As fantasies, these narratives provide an opportunity to atone for imperial sins, since reverse colonization is often represented as deserved punishment. . . .

A concern with questions of empire and colonization can be found in nearly all of Stoker's fiction. His quite extensive body of work shows how imperial issues can permeate and inform disparate types of fiction. Stoker's oeuvre apart from *Dracula* can be roughly divided into two categories in its handling of imperial themes. First, there are works such as "Under the Sunset" (1882), *The Snake's Pass* (1890), *The Mystery of the Sea* (1902), and *The Man* (1905) in which narratives of invasion and colonization, while not central to the plot, intrude continually upon the main action of the story. Legends of French invasions of Ireland in *The Snake's Pass*; attacks by the Children of Death on the Land Under the Sunset in the fairy tales; accounts of the Spanish Armada, Sir Francis Drake, and, in a more contemporary vein, the 1898 Spanish-American War in *The Mystery of the Sea*; allusions to the Norman invasion of Saxon England in *The Man*---in each work, seemingly unrelated narratives of imperial expansion and disruption themselves disrupt the primary story, as if Stoker were grappling with issues he could not wholly articulate through his main plot. And, as his references to the Armada and to Norman and French invasions suggest, Stoker is everywhere concerned with attacks directed specifically against the British Isles.

The second category comprises Stoker's more overtly Gothic fictions: *The Jewel of Seven Stars* (1903), *The Lady of the Shroud* (1909), and *The Lair of the White Worm* (1911). These works fit Brantlinger's paradigm of imperial Gothic[60] with its emphasis on atavism, demonism and the supernatural, and psychic regression. Each of the "heroines" in these novels--Queen Tera, Princess Teuta, Lady Arabella--represents the eruption of archaic and ultimately dangerous forces in modern life. (That Stoker associates these eruptions with women is worth noting; fear of women is never far from the surface of his novels.) Equally important is the fact that each of these Gothic fantasies intersects with narratives of imperial decline and fall: the decay of the Egyptian dynasties in *Jewel*, the defeat of the Turkish empire in *Shroud*, the collapse of the Roman empire in *Lair*. The conjunction of Gothic and empire brings Stoker's later novels thematically close to *Dracula*. If they cannot match *Dracula'* s power and sophistication, this is in part because Stoker became increasingly unwilling or simply unable to address the complex connections between his fictions and the late-Victorian imperial crisis. Only in *Dracula* is Stoker's career-long interest in the decline of empire explicitly an interest in the decline of the *British* empire. Only in this novel does he manage to imbricate Gothic fantasy and contemporary politics. . . .

Stoker maps his story not simply onto the Gothic but also onto a second, equally popular late-Victorian genre, the travel narrative. By examining how and to what extent *Dracula* participates in these two genres, we can illuminate the underlying fear and guilt characteristic of reverse colonization narratives. Like late-century Gothic, the travel narrative clearly displays aspects of imperial ideology. Like Gothic, too, the travel narrative concerns itself with boundaries--both with maintaining and with transgressing them. The blurring of psychic and sexual boundaries that occurs in Gothic is certainly evident in Dracula (and is one reason the novel is so accessible to psychoanalytic interpretation), but for Stoker the collapse of boundaries resonates culturally and politically as well. The Count's transgressions and aggressions are placed in the context, provided by innumerable travel narratives, of late-Victorian forays into the "East." For Stoker, the Gothic and the travel narrative problematize, separately and together, the very boundaries on which British imperial hegemony depended: between civilized and primitive, colonizer and colonized, victimizer (either imperialist or vampire) and victim. By problematizing those boundaries, Stoker probes the heart of the culture's sense of itself, its ways of defining and distinguishing itself from other peoples, other cultures, in its hour of perceived decline.

II

In many respects, *Dracula* represents a break from the Gothic tradition of vampires. It is easy, for instance, to forget that the "natural" association of vampires with Transylvania begins with, rather than predates, *Dracula*. The site of Castle Dracula was in fact not determined until well after Stoker had begun to write. As Joseph Bierman points out, Stoker originally signalled his debt to his countryman LeFanu's *Carmilla* (1872) by locating the castle in "Styria," the scene of the earlier Gothic novella ["The Genesis and Dating of *Dracula* from Bram Stoker's Working Notes"]. In rewriting the novel's opening chapters, however, Stoker moved *his* Gothic story to a place that, for readers in 1897, resonated in ways Styria did not. Transylvania was known primarily as part of the vexed "Eastern Question" that so obsessed British foreign policy in the 1880s and '90s. The region was first and foremost the site, not of superstition and Gothic romance, but of political turbulence and racial strife. Victorian readers knew the Carpathians largely for its endemic cultural upheaval and its fostering of a dizzying succession of empires. By moving Castle Dracula there, Stoker gives distinctly political overtones to his Gothic narrative. In Stoker's version of the myth, vampires are intimately linked to military conquest and to the rise and fall of empires. According to Dr. Van Helsing, the vampire is the unavoidable consequence of any invasion: "He have follow the wake of the berserker Icelander, the devil-begotten Hun, the Slav, the Saxon, the Magyar." [61]

Nowhere else in the Europe of 1897 could provide a more fertile breeding ground for the undead than the Count's homeland. The Western accounts of the region that Stoker consulted invariably stress the ceaseless clash of antagonistic cultures in the Carpathians. The cycle of empire--rise, decay, collapse, displacement--was there displayed in a particularly compressed and vivid manner. . . .The Count himself confirms that his homeland has been the scene of perpetual invasion: "there is hardly a foot of soil in all this region that has not been enriched by the blood of men, patriots or invaders," he tells Harker (p. 3). His subsequent question is thus largely rhetorical: "Is it a wonder that we were a conquering race?" (p. 41).

The "race" in which Dracula claims membership is left ambiguous here. He refers at once to his Szekely warrior past and to his vampire present. The ambiguity underscores the impossibility of untangling the two aspects of Dracula's essential nature, since his vampirism is interwoven with his status as a conqueror and invader. Here Stoker departs significantly from his literary predecessors. Unlike Polidori and Le Fanu, for instance, who depict their vampires as wan and enervated, Stoker makes Dracula vigorous and energetic. Polidori's Count Ruthven and LeFanu's Carmilla represent the aristocrat as decadent aesthete; their vampirism is an extension of the traditional aristocratic vices of sensualism and conspicuous consumption. Dracula represents the nobleman as warrior. His activities after death carry on his activities in life; in both cases he has successfully engaged in forms of conquest and domination.

Racial conquest and domination, we should immediately add. Stoker continues a Western tradition of seeing unrest in Eastern Europe primarily in terms of racial strife. For Stoker, the vampire "race" is simply the most virulent and threatening of the numerous warrior races--Berserker, Hun, Turk, Saxon, Slovak, Magyar, Szekely--inhabiting the area. Nineteenth-century accounts of the Carpathians repeatedly stress its polyracial character. . . .

Transylvania is what Dracula calls the "whirlpool of European races" (p. 41), but within that whirlpool racial interaction usually involved conflict, not accommodation. Racial violence could in fact reach appalling proportions, as in the wholesale massacres, widely reported by the British press, of Armenians by Turks in 1894 and 1896, the years in which *Dracula* was being written. For Western writers and readers, these characteristics--racial heterogeneity combined with racial intolerance considered barbaric in its intensity--defined the area east and south of the Danube, with the Carpathians at the imaginative center of the turmoil.

By situating Dracula in the Carpathians, and by continually blurring the lines between the Count's vampiric and warrior activities, Stoker forges seemingly "natural" links among three of his principal concerns: racial strife, the collapse of empire, and vampirism. It is important too to note the sequence of events. As Van Helsing says, vampires follow "in [the] wake of" imperial decay (p. 286). Vampires are generated by racial enervation and the decline of empire, not vice versa. They are produced, in other words, by the very conditions characterizing late-Victorian Britain.

Stoker thus transforms the materials of the vampire myth, making them bear the weight of the culture's fears over its declining status. The appearance of vampires becomes the sign of profound trouble. With vampirism marking the intersection of racial strife, political upheaval, and the fall of empire, Dracula's move to London indicates that Great Britain, rather than the Carpathians, is now the scene of these connected struggles. The Count has penetrated to the heart of modern Europe's largest empire, and his very presence seems to presage its doom:

This was the being I was helping to transfer to London. . .where, perhaps for centuries to come, he might, amongst its teeming millions, satiate his lust for blood, and create a new and ever widening circle of semi-demons to batten on the helpless. (p. 67)

The late-Victorian nightmare of reverse colonization is expressed succinctly here: Harker envisions semi-demons spreading through the realm, colonizing bodies and land indiscriminately. The Count's "lust for blood" points in both directions: to the vampire's need for its special food, and also to the warrior's desire for conquest. The Count endangers Britain's integrity as a nation at the same time that he imperils the personal integrity of individual citizens.

Harker's lament highlights the double thrust--political and biological--of Dracula's invasion, while at the same time conflating the two into a single threat. Dracula's twin status as vampire and Szekely warrior suggests that for Stoker the Count's aggressions against the body are also aggressions against the body politic. Indeed, the Count can threaten the integrity of the nation precisely because of the nature of his threat to personal integrity. His attacks involve more than an assault on the isolated self, the subversion and loss of one's individual identity. Again unlike Polidori's Count Ruthven or LeFanu's Carmilla (or even Thomas Prest's Sir Francis Varney), Dracula imperils not simply his victims' personal identities, but also their cultural, political, and racial selves. In *Dracula* vampirism designates a kind of colonization of the body. Horror arises not because Dracula destroys bodies, but because he appropriates and transforms them. Having yielded to his assault, one literally "goes native" by becoming a vampire oneself. . . .In turn, they receive a new racial identity, one that marks them as literally "Other." Miscegenation leads, not to the mixing of races, but to the biological and political annihilation of the weaker race by the stronger.

Through the vampire myth, Stoker gothicizes the political threats to Britain caused by the enervation of the Anglo-Saxon "race." These threats also operate independently of the Count's vampirism, however, for the vampire was not considered alone in its ability to deracinate. Stoker learned from Emily Gerard that the Roumanians were themselves notable for the way they could "dissolve" the identities of those they came in contact with:

The Hungarian woman who weds a Roumanian husband will necessarily adopt the dress and manners of his people, and her children will be as good Roumanians as though they had no drop of Magyar blood in their veins; while the Magyar who takes a Roumanian girl for his wife will not only fail to convert her to his ideas, but himself, subdued by her influence, will imperceptibly begin to lose his nationality. This is a fact well known and much lamented by the Hungarians themselves, who live in anticipated apprehension of seeing their people ultimately dissolving into Roumanians.[62]

Gerard's account of the "imperceptible" but inevitable loss of identity--national, cultural, racial--sounds remarkably like the transformations that Lucy and Mina suffer under Dracula's "influence." In life Dracula was a Roumanian (Gerard designates the Szekelys as a branch of the Roumanian race); his ability to deracinate could thus derive as easily from his Roumanian as from his vampire nature.

The "anticipated apprehension" or deracination--of seeing Britons "ultimately dissolving into Roumanians" or vampires or savages--is at the heart of the reverse colonization narrative. For both Gerard and Stoker, the Roumanians' dominance can be traced to a kind of racial puissance that overwhelms its weaker victims. This racial context helps account for what critics routinely note about Dracula: that he is by his very nature vigorous, masterful, energetic, robust. Such attributes are conspicuously absent among the novel's British characters, particularly the men. All the novel's vampires are distinguished by their robust health and their equally robust fertility. The vampire serves, then, to highlight the alarming decline among the British, since the undead are, paradoxically, both "healthier" and more "fertile" than the living. Perversely, a vampiric attack can serve to invigorate its victim. . . .Indeed, after his attack, Lucy's body initially appears stronger, her eyes brighter, her cheeks rosier. The corresponding enervation that marks the British men is most clearly visible in Harker (he is "pale," "weak-looking," "exhausted," "nervous," "a wreck"), but it can be seen in the other male British characters as well. Harker and Dracula in fact switch places during the novel; Harker becomes tired and white-haired as the action proceeds, while Dracula, whose white hair grows progressively darker, becomes more vigorous.

The vampire's vigor is in turn closely connected with its virility, its ability to produce literally endless numbers of offspring. Van Helsing's concern that the earth in Dracula's boxes be "sterilized" . . . underlines the connection between the Count's threat and his fecundity. In marked contrast, the nonvampires in the novel seem unable to reproduce themselves. Fathers in particular are in short supply: most are either dead (Mr. Westenra, Mr. Harker, Mr. Murray, Mr. Canon), dying (Mr. Hawkins, Lord Godalming, Mr. Swales), or missing (Mr. Seward, Mr. Morris), while the younger men, being unmarried, cannot father legitimately. Even Harker, the novel's only married man, is prohibited from touching Mina after she has been made "unclean." In *Dracula's* lexicon, uncleanliness is closely related to fertility, but it is the wrong kind of fertility; Mina, the men fear, is perfectly capable of producing "offspring," but not with Jonathan. The prohibition regarding Mina is linked to the fear of vampiric fecundity, a fecundity that threatens to overwhelm the far less prolific British men. Thus, as many critics have pointed out, the arrival of little Quincey Harker at the story's close signals the final triumph over Dracula, since the Harkers' ability to secure an heir--an heir whose racial credentials are seemingly impeccable--is the surest indication that the vampire's threat has been mastered. Even this triumph is precarious, however. Harker proudly notes that his son is named after each of the men in the novel, making them all figurative fathers . . . yet Quincey's multiple parentage only underscores the original problem. How secure is any racial line when five fathers are needed to produce one son?

    Such racial anxieties are clearest in the case of Lucy Westenra. If Dracula's kiss serves to deracinate Lucy, and by doing so to unleash what the male characters consider her incipiently monstrous sexual appetite, then the only way to counter this process is to "re-racinate" her by reinfusing her with the "proper" blood. But Stoker is careful to establish a strict hierarchy among the potential donors. The men give blood in this order: Holmwood, Seward, Van Helsing, Morris. Arthur Holmwood is first choice ostensibly because he is engaged to Lucy, but also, and perhaps more importantly, because his blood is, in Van Helsing's words, "more good than" Seward's. . . .As the only English aristocrat in the novel, Holmwood possesses a "blood so pure". . . that it can restore Lucy's compromised racial identity. Dr. Seward, whose blood through bourgeois is English nonetheless, comes next in line, followed by the two foreigners, Van Helsing and Morris. We should note that Van Helsing's old, Teutonic blood is still preferred over Morris's young, American blood, for reasons I will take up in a moment. Even foreign blood is better than lower-class blood, however. After Lucy suffers what proves to be the fatal attack by Dracula, Van Helsing, looking for blood donors, rejects the four apparently healthy female servants as unsafe. . . .That Dracula propagates his race solely through the bodies of women suggests an affinity, or even an identity, between vampiric sexuality and female sexuality. Both are represented as primitive and voracious, and both threaten patriarchal hegemony. In the novel's (and Victorian Britain's) sexual economy, female sexuality has only one legitimate function, propagation within the bounds of marriage. Once separated from that function, as Lucy's desire is, female sexuality becomes monstrous. The violence of Lucy's demise is grisly enough, but we should not miss the fact that her subjection and Mina's final fate parallel one another. They differ in degree, not kind. By the novel's close, Mina's sexual energy has been harnessed for purely domestic use. In the end, women serve identical purposes for both Dracula and the Western characters.

If in this novel blood stands for race, then women quite literally become the vehicles of racial propagation. The struggle between the two camps is thus on one level a struggle over access to women's bodies, and Dracula's biological colonization of women becomes a horrific parody of the sanctioned exploitation practiced by the Western male characters.

By considering the parallel fates of Lucy and Mina, moreover, we can see how the fear and guilt characteristic of reverse colonization narratives begin to overlap. The fear generated by the Count's colonization of his victims' bodies--a colonization appropriately designated monstrous--modulates into guilt that his practices simply repeat those of the "good" characters. Dracula's invasion and appropriation of female bodies does not distinguish him from his Western antagonists as much as at first appears. Instead of being uncannily Other, the vampire is here revealed as disquietingly familiar. And since the colonizations of bodies and territory are closely linked, the same blurring of distinctions occurs when we consider more closely the nature of the Count's invasion of Britain. Just as Dracula's vampirism mirrors the domestic practices of Victorian patriarchs, so his invasion of London in order to "batten on the helpless" natives there mirrors British imperial activities abroad.

As a transplanted Irishman, one whose national allegiances were conspicuously split, Stoker was particularly sensitive to the issues raised by British imperial conquest and domination. Britain's subjugation of Ireland was marked by a brutality often exceeding what occurred in the colonies, while the stereotype of the "primitive . . . dirty, vengeful, and violent" Irishman was in most respects identical to that of the most despised "savage."[63] The ill will characterizing Anglo-Irish relations in the late-nineteenth century, exacerbated by the rise of Fenianism and the debate over Home Rule, far surpassed the tensions that arose as a result of British rule elsewhere. When that ill will erupted into violence, as it did in the 1882 Phoenix Park murders, Victorian readers could see, up close and in sharp focus, the potential consequences of imperial domination. For Stoker's audience, Dracula's invasion of Britain would conceivably have aroused seldom dormant fears of an Irish uprising.

The lack of autobiographical materials makes it difficult to determine the extent, if any, to which Stoker consciously felt himself in solidarity with his Irish brethren. On the one hand, his few published essays, particularly one advocating censorship, reveal a deeply conservative outlook in which "duty to the [British] state" outweighs all other considerations, even those a dubious freedom or self-determination. On the other hand, through Stoker's very adherence to what he calls "forms of restraint" runs a deeply anarchic streak. The attraction of forbidden, outlawed, disruptive action is evident enough in *Dracula* as well as in Stoker's other fictions; the same tension between restraint and rebellion may have characterized his relation to the ruling state. It probably also characterized his professional life. Certainly his status as glorified manservant to the autocratic Henry Irving almost uncannily reenacted, on the personal level, the larger cultural pattern of English domination and Irish subservience. Stoker's lifelong passion for Irving had its dark underside: the rumors, persistent in Stoker's lifetime, that Count Dracula was modelled on Irving suggests the deep ambivalence with which the transplanted Irishman regarded his professional benefactor. Like Quincey Morris, Stoker seems finally to stand in alliance with his English companions without ever being entirely of their camp.

    Dracula suggests two equations in relation to English-Irish politics: not just, Dracula is to England as Ireland is to England, but, Dracula is to England as England is to Ireland. In Count Dracula, Victorian readers could recognize their culture's imperial ideology mirrored back as a kind of monstrosity. Dracula's journey from Transylvania to England could be read as a reversal of Britain's imperial exploitations of "weaker" races, including the Irish. This mirroring extends not just to the imperial practices themselves, but to their epistemological underpinnings. Before Dracula successfully invades the spaces of his victims' bodies or land, he first invades the spaces of their knowledge. The Count operates in several distinct registers in the novel. He is both the warrior nobleman, whose prowess dwarfs that of the novel's enfeebled English aristocrat, Lord Godalming, and the primitive savage, whose bestiality, fecundity, and vigor alternately repel and attract. But he is also what we might call an incipient "Occidentalist" scholar. Dracula's physical mastery of his British victims begins with an intellectual appropriation of their culture, which allows him to delve the workings of the "native mind." As Harker discovers, the Count's expertise in "English life and customs and manners" . . . provides the groundwork for his exploitative invasion of Britain. Thus, in Dracula the British characters see their own ideology reflected back as a form of bad faith, since the Count's Occidentalism both mimics and reverses the more familiar Orientalism underwriting Western imperial practices.[64]

III

    To understand fully how the Count's Occidentalism functions, however, we must relate it to the second literary genre visible in *Dracula*, the travel narrative. Jonathan Harker's initial journey to Castle Dracula constitutes a travel narrative in miniature, and the opening entries in his journal reproduce the conventions of this popular Victorian genre. Critics have occasionally noted the travel motifs in *Dracula,* but have not pursued the implications of Stoker's mixing of genres. To be sure, Gothic has always contained a strong travel component. The restless roaming found in many Gothic fictions--Victor Frankenstein's pursuit of his monster, Melmoth's wanderings, Mr. Hyde's perambulations of London--suggests that an affinity between the two genres has always existed. Stoker's use of travel conventions is new, however. Earlier Gothic writers were interested primarily in the psychological dimensions of travel; the landscape traversed by the Gothic protagonist was chiefly psychological. Stoker on the other hand is interested in the ideological dimensions of travel. Harker's early journal entries clearly reveal his Orientalist perspective, which structures what he sees and what he misses as he travels through the Carpathians. This perspective is embedded in the generic conventions that Harker deploys, conventions familiar to late-Victorian readers. Stoker's disruption of Harker's tourist perspective at Castle Dracula also calls into question the entire Orientalist outlook. Stoker thus expresses a telling critique of the Orientalist enterprise through the very structure of his novel.

Early in his stay at Castle Dracula, Harker to his great surprise finds his host stretched upon the library sofa reading . . . an English *Bradshaw's Guide*. (p. 34). We probably share Harker's puzzlement at the Count's choice of reading material, though like Harker we are apt to forget this brief interlude amid ensuing horrors. Why is Dracula interested in English train schedules? The Count's absorption in *Bradshaw's* echoes Harker's own obsessive interest in trains. . . .An obsession with trains--or, as in Harker's case, an obsession with trains running on time--characterizes Victorian narratives of travel in Eastern Europe. . . .Harker immediately invokes a second convention of the travel genre when, having crossed the Danube at Buda-Pesth, he invests the river with symbolic significance. . . . In crossing the Danube, Harker maintains, he leaves "Europe" behind, geographically and imaginatively, and approaches the first outpost of the "Orient."

Harker's first two acts--noting that his train is late, and then traversing a boundary he considers symbolic--function as a kind of shorthand, alerting readers that Harker's journal is to be set against the background of late-Victorian travel narratives. Once the travel genre is established, there is an inevitability about Harker's subsequent gestures. . . . Harker's first three journal entries (chapter 1 of the novel) are so thoroughly conventional as to parody the travel genre. Such conventions constitute what Wolfgang Iser calls the "repertoire of the familiar" that readers can be expected to bring to texts.[65] Indeed, Harker is so adept an imitator of travel narratives in part because he has been such an assiduous reader of them. Like Stoker himself, Harker "had visited the British Museum, and made search among the books and maps in the library regarding Transylvania" in order to gain "some foreknowledge of the country" (p. 9).

This foreknowledge--the textual knowledge gathered before the fact, the same knowledge that any casual reader of contemporary travel narratives would also possess--structures Harker's subsequent experiences. In assuming the role of the Victorian traveller in the East, Harker also assumes the Orientalist perspective that allows him to "make sense" of his experiences there. For Harker, as for most Victorian travel writers, that "sense" begins with the assumption that an unbridgeable gap separates the Western traveller from Eastern peoples. The contrast between British punctuality and Transylvanian tardiness stands, in Harker's view, as a concrete instance of more fundamental and wide-ranging oppositions: between Western progress and Eastern stasis, between Western science and Eastern superstition, between Western reason and Eastern emotion, between Western civilization and Eastern barbarism. . . .As Harker moves further east toward Castle Dracula, he leaves even the railroads behind and is forced to travel by stagecoach. Simultaneously, he leaves Western rationality behind: "I read that every known superstition in the world is gathered into the horsehoe of the Carpathians" (p. 10).

Harker may marvel and wonder at this strange world he has entered, but he does not expect to be disconcerted. He trades extensively on his "foreknowledge," which allows him to retain a comfortable distance from the scene. He views it simply as a diverting spectacle. . . . At first, Harker's descent into the dark heart of the Carpathians serves only to titillate, not to unsettle. His favorite word in this first section is "picturesque," that stock term of the travel genre. Throughout his journey, he is able to reduce everything he encounters to an example of the picturesque or the poetic.

Until he reaches Castle Dracula, that is. There, everything is disrupted. Stoker undermines the conventions of the travel narrative, just as Dracula undermines all the stable oppositions structuring Harker's--and his readers'--foreknowledge of Eastern and Western races. For the fact is, by Harker's own criteria, Dracula is the most "Western" character in the novel. No one is more rational, more intelligent, more organized, or even more punctual than the Count. No one plans more carefully or researches more thoroughly. No one is more learned within his own spheres of expertise or more receptive to new knowledge. A reading that emphasizes only the archaic, anarchic, "primitive" forces embodied by Dracula misses half the point. When Harker arrives at the end of his journey East, he finds, not some epitome of irrationality, but a most accomplished Occidentalist. If Harker has been diligently combining the library stacks, so too has the Count. Harker writes: "In the library I found, to my great delight, a vast number of English books, whole shelves full of them, and bound volumes of magazines and newspapers. . . .The books were of the most varied kind--history, geography, politics, political economy, botany, geology, law--all relating to England and English life and customs and manners." Displaying an epistemophilia to rival Harker's own, Dracula says: "'These friends'--and he laid his hand on some of the books--'have been good friends too, and for some years past, ever since I had the idea of going to London, have given me many, many hours of pleasure. Through them I have come to know your great England'" (p. 31).

The novel thus sets up an equivalence between Harker and Dracula: one can be seen as an Orientalist travelling East, the other--unsettling thought for Stoker's Victorian readers--as an Occidentalist travelling West. Dracula's absorption in *Bradshaw*'s timetables echoes Harker's fetish for punctual trains, just as the Count's posture--reclining comfortably on a sofa--recalls the attitude of the casual Western reader absorbed in a late-Victorian account of the exotic.

But of course Dracula's preoccupation with English culture is not motivated by a disinterested desire for knowledge; instead, his Occidentalism represents the essence of bad faith, since it both promotes and masks the Count's sinister plan to invade and exploit Britain and her people. By insisting on the connections between Dracula's growing knowledge and his power to exploit, Stoker also forces us to acknowledge how Western imperial practices are implicated in certain forms of knowledge. Stoker continually draws our attention to the affinities between Harker and Dracula, as in the oft-cited scene where Harker looks for Dracula's reflection in the mirror and sees only himself. The texts' insistence that these characters are capable of substituting for one another becomes most pressing when Dracula twice dons Harker's clothes to leave the Castle. Since on both occasions the Count's mission is to plunder the town, we are encouraged to see a correspondence between the vampire's actions and those of the travelling Westerner. The equivalence between these two sets of actions is underlined by the reaction of the townspeople, who have no trouble believing that it really is Harker, the visiting Englishman, who is stealing their goods, their money, their children. The peasant woman's anguished cry--"Monster, give me my child!" (p. 60)--is directed at him, not Dracula.

The shock of recognition that overtakes Harker, and presumably the British reader, when he sees Dracula comfortably decked out in Victorian garb is, however, only part of the terror of this scene. The truly disturbing notion is not that Dracula impersonates Harker, but that he does it so well. Here indeed is the nub: Dracula can "pass." To impersonate an Englishman, and to do it convincingly, is the goal of Dracula's painstaking research into "English life and customs and manners," a goal Dracula himself freely, if rather disingenuously, acknowledges. When Harker compliments him on his command of English, Dracula demurs:

> "Well I know that, did I move and speak in your London, none there are who would not know me for a stranger. That is not enough for me. Here I am noble . . . I am master. . . . [In London] I am content if I am like the rest, so that no man stops if he sees me, or pause in his speaking if he hear my words, to say 'Ha, ha! a stranger!' I have been so long master that I would be master still--or at least that none other should be master of me." (p. 31)

To understand fully how disquieting Dracula's talents are, we have only to remember that in Victorian texts non-Western "natives" are seldom--I am tempted to say never, since I have not come up with another example--permitted to "pass" successfully. Those who try, as for instance some of Kipling's natives do, become the occasion for low comedy or ridicule, since Kipling never allows the possibility that their attempts could succeed to be seriously entertained. Grish Chunder De in "The Head of the District" (1890) and Huree Babu, the comic devotee of Herbert Spencer, in *Kim* (1901) are two examples. Kipling voices a common assumption, one that structures British accounts of non-Western cultures from Richard Burton to T.E. Lawrence. The ability to "pass" works in only one direction: Westerners can impersonate Easterners, never vice versa.

Dracula is different, however. A large part of the terror he inspires originates in his ability to stroll, unrecognized and unhindered, through the streets of London. As he tells Harker, his status as "master" resides in this ability. So long as no one recognizes him as a "stranger," he is able to work his will unhampered. Like Richard Burton travelling disguised among the Arabs, or like Kipling's ubiquitous policeman Strickland passing himself off as a Hindu, Dracula gains power, becomes "master," by striving "to know as much about the natives as the natives themselves." [66] The crucial difference is that in this case the natives are English.

Links between knowledge and power are evident enough in Kipling's work; his two great impersonators--Strickland and Kim--both work for the police, and each uses his talents in the service of colonial law and order. Dracula, too, understands how knowledge and power are linked. In this case, however, knowledge leads, not to the stability envisioned by Kipling's characters, but to anarchy: it undermines social structures, disrupts the order of nature, and ends alarmingly in the appropriation and exploitation of bodies. Stoker's text never explicitly acknowledges the continuity between Dracula's actions and British imperial practices, but it continually forces us to see the first as a terrifying parody of the second. In the Gothic mirror that Stoker holds up to late-Victorian culture, that culture, like Harker peering into the glass at Castle Dracula, cannot see, but is nevertheless intensely aware of, its monstrous double peering over its shoulder.

Dracula not only mimics the practices of British imperialists, he rapidly becomes superior to his teachers. The racial threat embodied by the Count is thus intensified: not only is he more vigorous, more fecund, more "primitive" than his Western antagonists, he is also becoming more "advanced." As Van Helsing notes, Dracula's swift development will soon make him invincible. . . . Van Helsing's metaphor of the child growing into manhood is a familiar and homely way to explain Dracula's progress, but the image deflects attention from the notion of racial development that the real source of the vampire's threat. Since Dracula's growth is not bound by a single lifetime, but instead covers potentially limitless generations, the proper analogy for his development is not that of an individual. He is in effect his own species, or his own race, displaying in his person the progress of ages. Dracula can himself stand in for entire races, and through him Stoker articulates fears about the development of those races in relation to the English. . . .the anxieties engendered by Count Dracula do not derive wholly from his vampirism. He is dangerous as the representative or embodiment of a race which, all evidence suggested, was poised to "step forward" and become "masters" of those who had already "spent their strength." Even Dracula's destruction (which, if he stands in for an entire race, becomes a fantasized genocide) cannot entirely erase the "moral" endorsed by the rest of the story: that strong races inevitably weaken and fall, and are in turn displaced by stronger races. The novel provides an extraordinarily long list of once-proud peoples, now vanquished or vanished--not just the Huns, Berserkers, Magyars, and others who have passed through Carpathian history, but the Romans who gave their name, and perhaps their blood, to the modern Roumanians, as well as the Danes and Vikings who, Mina tells us, once occupied Whitby (pp. 80-81)

Do the British evade the fate of Huns, Danes, Vikings, and others, since Dracula is destroyed by novel's end? Critical consensus follows Christopher Craft when he suggests that *Dracula* embodies the "predictable, if variable, triple rhythm" characteristic of Gothic novels: it "first invites or admits a monster, then entertains or is entertained by monstrosity for some extended duration, until in its closing pages it expels or repudiates the monster and all the disruption that he/she/it brings." [67] This triple rhythm also characterizes many narratives of reverse colonization. The mingled anxiety and desire evident in these texts is relieved when the primitive or exotic invader--Haggard's Aeysha, Wells's Martians, Kipling's Silver Man--is at last expelled and order is restored. *Dracula*, however, is finally divided against itself; it strives to contain the threat posed by the Count but cannot do so entirely. The novel in fact ends twice. The narrative proper closes with a fantasy of revitalized English supremacy: his invasion repulsed, the Count is driven back to Transylvania, and destroyed there. . . . But the satisfaction of closure brought about by Dracula's diminishment and death is immediately disrupted by Harker's "Note," which constitutes *Dracula's* second ending.

Dracula, appropriately, is subdued by the weapons of empire. Harker's "great Kukri Knife," symbol of British imperial power in India, and Morris's bowie knife, symbol of American westward expansion, simultaneously vanquish the Count (p. 447), apparently reestablishing the accustomed dominance of Western colonizer over Eastern colonized. The triumph extends even further for the British, since Dracula is not the book's only fatality. The American Quincy Morris dies too. His demise is not simply gratuitous, for the American represents, however, obliquely, a second threat to British power hidden behind Dracula's more overt antagonism. [68] A shadowy figure throughout, Morris is linked with vampires and racial Others from his first appearance. When he courts Lucy, Morris reminds her of Othello. . . .Morris's dangerous hunting expeditions are a modern equivalent to the Count's warrior exploits, and Lucy's fascination with his stories of adventure repeats Harker's initial response to Dracula's tales. Later, it is left to Morris to pronounce the word "vampire" for the first time in the novel, when he compares Lucy's condition to that of a mare on the Pampas "after one of those big bats that they call vampires had got at her in the night" (p. 183). Morris's familiarity with vampirism apparently exceeds even Van Helsing's, since he correctly diagnoses the etiology of Lucy's symptoms the first moment he sees her.

There is even a suggestion that the American is at times leagued with Dracula against the others. Morris leaves, without explanation, the crucial meeting in which Van Helsing first names the Count as their enemy; a moment later he fires his pistol *into* the room where they are seated (pp. 288-289). He quickly explains that he was shooting at a "big bat" sitting on the windowsill, but this very brief and easily missed tableau--Morris standing outside the window in the place vacated by Dracula, looking in on the assembled Westerners who have narrowly escaped his violence--suggests strongly that Stoker wants us to consider the American and the Roumanian together.

Morris thus leads a double life in *Dracula*. He stands with his allies in Anglo-Saxon brotherhood, but he also, as representative of an America about to emerge as the world's foremost imperial power, threatens British superiority as surely as Dracula does. "If America can go on breeding men like that," Seward remarks, "she will be a power in the world indeed." [69] If *Dracula* is about how vigorous races inevitably displace decaying races, then the real danger to Britain in 1897 comes not from the moribund Austro-Hungarian or Ottoman empires, but from the rising American empire. Without at all dismissing the powerful anxiety that the Count produces, we can say that Stoker's attention to Dracula screens his anxiety at the threat represented by Morris and America. . . . It is appropriate, then, that Morris's death, not Dracula's, closes the story proper; appropriate, too, that the confrontation between England and America is displaced to the Balkans, traditionally the arena where Western powers conducted their struggles with one another indirectly, or by proxy.

England's triumph is immediately troubled and qualified, however, by Harker's appended "Note," written seven years later. In announcing the birth of his son Quincey, Harker unwittingly calls attention to the fact that the positions of vampire and victim have been reversed. Now it is Dracula whose blood is appropriated and transformed to nourish a faltering race. As Mark Hennelly has noticed, in Quincy Harker flows the blood not only of Jonathan and Mina, but of Dracula as well. Little Quincey, who is not conceived until after Mina drinks the Count's blood, is, moreover, born on the anniversary of Dracula's and Morris's demise. Through Roumania, the English race invigorates itself by incorporating those racial qualities needed to reverse its own decline. American energy is appropriated as well, since, as Jonathan tells us, Quincey Morris has also contributed to his namesake's racial makeup: "His mother holds, I know, the secret belief that some of our brave friend's spirit has passed into" their son. The "little band of men" can thus rest assured that the threats to English power have been neutralized on both fronts, East and West, through the appropriation of Dracula's blood and Morris's spirit. The cost of such assurance is great, however. Quincey Harker stands as a mute reminder of the violence upon which the stability of the nation, as well as the family, rests.

The remainder of Harker's "Note" is taken up with two related projects: his account of a return visit to Transylvania, and an apology for the "inauthenticity" of the documents comprising the novel. These two projects point back, in different ways, to the two genres--travel and Gothic--in which *Dracula* participates. Harker first relates that he has recently revisited the Carpathians. . . . The text seems to have come full circle and returned securely to its starting point. The conventions of the travel genre are again invoked. Harker's return to Transylvania ostensibly reenacts the trip that opened the novel; or rather, it attempts to reinstate the conditions and attitudes which preceded and, in a sense, enabled that trip. By returning simply as a tourist (this time he has not even the excuse of business to take him there), Harker implicitly asserts that nothing has intervened to make the tourist outlook problematic. The disruption caused by Dracula is entirely erased; the story ends where it began.

But Harker's words are strikingly tentative. In their general movement, his first two sentences assert that things have indeed returned to "normal." The old ground was (but is not now) full of vivid and terrible memories; we once believed (but do no longer) that what we experienced constituted a living truth. Yet each sentence is significantly qualified, and qualified in such a way as to reverse its effects. The ground not only was, but still is, full of terrible memories; the living truths are not impossible to believe, but almost impossible, which means that belief in them is, at bottom, almost inevitable. The overall effect of the sentences is to exacerbate the anxieties they are presumably intended to assuage. The unalloyed confidence and security of the novel's opening pages cannot be recaptured; any return to the beginning is barred.

The linchpin of the passage is Harker's overdetermined assertion, "Every trace of all that had been was blotted out." On the manifest level, Harker means simply that all evidence of the Count's horrific presence is gone from the land. His next comment contradicts this claim, however, since "the castle stood as before." We might see this "blotting out," then in psychological terms, as a repression of the insights, the "living truths," revealed by the narrative as a whole. Alternately (or simply in addition), what has been "blotted out" is precisely that vision of Transylvania--landscape, people, culture--which Harker, as a travelling Westerner secure in his "foreknowledge" of the region, "saw" on his initial visit. The ideological foundations of that vision having been disturbed, Harker can no longer perceive the land or its people in the same way. Significantly, he now sees nothing at all, only "a waste of desolation." The wasteland is the result, not of Dracula's activities--if that were the case, Harker would have noted such a wasteland on his earlier, not his later, visit--but of the desolation that has occurred to Harker's and the Victorian reader's accustomed modes of perception.

Finally, though, both these kinds of erasures, psychological and epistemological, lead to a different kind of obliteration. The "blotting out" of "traces" points to the cancellation of writing, to Harker's (though not necessarily Stoker's) attempt to disavow the Gothic narrative preceding the "Note." When he returns from Transylvania, Harker retrieves the mass of papers comprising the narrative--diaries, journals, letters, memoranda, and so on--which have remained buried and unread in a safe. "We were struck by the fact," he writes in an oft-cited disclaimer, "that, in all the mass of material of which the record is composed, there is hardly one authentic document!"

Such disclaimers are often found in Gothic fictions; in the same way, Harker's "Note" invokes the narrative framing devices that are one of Gothic's distinctive features. But Harker uses this device to *repudiate* parts of his narrative, whereas in Gothic the function of the frame is precisely to *establish* the narrative's authenticity. Indeed, this is the function of the unsigned note that opens *Dracula*: to overcome readerly skepticism "so that a history almost at variance with the possibilities of latter-day belief may stand forth as simple fact". For Harker, however, the inauthenticity of the documents (what would make for authenticity is unclear) casts further doubt on the veracity of portions of the narrative. "We could hardly expect anyone, even did we wish to, to accept these [documents] as proofs of so wild a story" (p. 449). Not only does Harker not expect us to believe the collected accounts, he does not even "wish [us] to."

At the same time that he tries to recapture the comforting tourist outlook, Harker also tries to erase the "wild" or Gothic parts of his "story," to blot out all their traces. The two gestures are complementary. In effect, Harker asserts the story's "truth" up until the moment he enters Castle Dracula; the moment, in other words, when his travel narrative, disrupted by the Count's Occidentalism, becomes a Gothic narrative. The trouble, in Harker's view, starts there. Once the dichotomies on which Harker's (and imperial Britain's) tourist perspective rest are exploded, anything is possible. The "Note" tries to recontain the anxieties generated by that moment of rupture by invalidating what follows, by calling into question its "authenticity" as narrative. The "realism" of the travel narrative gives way to the fantasy constructions of the Gothic, which can be dismissed--as Harker urges us to do--as untrue. "We want no proofs; we ask none to believe us," Van Helsing says in the novel's final moments, and his words sound remarkably like a plea.

NOTES

[1] An indispensable work for the study of this novel is Harry Ludlam, *A Biography of Dracula: The Life Story of Bram Stoker* (London: W. Foulsham & Co., Ltd. for The Fireside Press, 1962). My biographical account of Stoker is based on this source. Other good writings on *Dracula* include Robert E. Dowse and David Palmer, "*Dracula*: the Book of Blood," *The Listener* (7 March 1963), pp. 428-429; the anonymous "'No, But I Saw the Movie'," *The Times Literary Supplement* (8 December 1966), p. 1148; and an ingenious paper by Joseph S. Bierman, "Dracula, Prolonged Childhood Illness, and the Oral Triad," presented to the meeting of the American Psychoanalytic Association in December 1970. I am grateful to Dr. Bierman for sending me a copy of this paper.

[2] This statement will not seem extravagant if one considers the reception given to Polidori's weak tale "The Vampyre" (1819); see E.F. Bleiler's introduction to *The Castle of Otranto . . Vathek . . . The Vampyre . . . Three Gothic Novels*, ed. E.F. Bleiler (new York: Dover Publications, 1966), pp. xxxviii-xl.

[3] All quotations from the novel are from Bram Stoker, *Dracula* (New York: Modern Library, n.d.).

[4] Montague Summers, *The Vampire: His Kith and Kin* (London: Kegan Paul, 1928); Montague Summers, *The Vampire in Europe* (London: Kegan Paul, 1929).

[5] Maurice Richardson, "The Psychoanalysis of Ghost Stories," *The Twentieth Century*, 166 (1959), 427; Grigore Nandris, "The Historical Dracula: The Theme of His Legend in the Western and in the Eastern Literatures of Europe," *Comparative Literature Studies*, 3 (1966), 393.

[6] Richardson, "Psychoanalysis," p. 428. I do not know whether anyone has suggested that Van Helsing may be based on Dr., Hesselius in J.S. LeFanu's story, "Green Tea."

[7] Richardson, "Psychoanalysis," p. 428.

[8] There is, however, an attempt to read Cold War lessons into the novel in Richard Wasson, "The Politics of Dracula," *English Literature in Transition*, 9 (1966), 24-27.

[9] Stephanie Demetrakopoulos, "Feminism, Sex Role Exchanges and Other Subliminal Fantasies in Bram Stoker's *Dracula*," *Frontiers: A Journal of Women Studies* 2 (1977) 104-12; C.F. Bentley, "The Monster in the Bedroom," *Literature and Psychology* 22 (1972) 27-34; Phyllis A. Roth, "Suddenly Sexual Women in Bram Stoker's *Dracula*," *Literature and Psychology* 27 (1977) 113-21. Research for this project was supported by the National Endowment for the Humanities' program in Humanities, Science and Technology.

[10] Steven T. Ryan, "The Importance of Thomas S. Kuhn's Scientific Paradigm Theory to Literary Criticism," *Midwest Quarterly* 19 (1978) 151-59, points to the potential usefulness of Kuhn's work in understanding nineteenth- and twentieth-century narrative, but Ryan is hampered by his uncritical acceptance of Kuhn.

[11] Thomas S. Kuhn, *The Structure of Scientific Revolutions* [rev. ed.; Chicago: University of Chicago Press, 1970.

[12] Harry Ludlam, *A Biography of Dracula: The Life Story of Bram Stoker* (New York: W. Foulsham, 1962) 19.

13 *The Annotated Dracula* (New York: Ballantine Books) 74. Subsequent references to the novel will be from this edition.

14 Wolf, 63.

15 Andrew Scull, *Museums of Madness: The Social Organization of Insanity in Nineteenth-Century England* (New York: St. Martins, 1979) 113.

16 Scull,224.

17 E. Cyon, *Methodik der physiologischen Experimente* (Giessen: J. Rickersche and St. Petersburg, 1876) 8.

18 Mona Caird, *A Sentimental View of Vivisection* (London: Wm. Reeves, 1895) 28.

19 Susan Eyrich Lederer, "Hideo Noguchi's Luetin Experiment and the Antivivisectionists," *Isis* 76 (1985) 33.

20 *Saturday Review* 41 (1876) 773. See Richard D. French, *Antivivisection and Medical Science in the Victorian Society* (Princeton: Princeton University Press, 1975) 42-50.

21 French 200-03.

22 Edouard Brown-Sequard, "Des effets produits chez l'homme par des injections sous-cutanees d'un liquide retire des testicules frais de cobayes et des chiens," *Comptes Rendus Hebdomaires des Seances et Memoires de la Societe de Biologie*, 9th series (1889) 1:415-19.

23 Thomas Laycock, *Mind and Brain*, 2nd ed., 2 vols. (New York: D. Appleton, 1869) 1:3.

24 Jules Hericourt, "L'activite inconsciente de l'espirit," *Revue Scientifique*, 3rd series, 26 (1889) 2:257-68.

25 Huxley, "On the Physical Basis of Life," *Fortnightly Review* 26 (1869) 137; reprinted in William Coleman, ed., *Physiological Programmatics of the Nineteenth Century* (New York: Arno Press, 1981) [n.p.]; see Everett Mendelsohn, *Heat and Life: The Development of the Theory of Animal Heat* (Cambridge: Harvard University Press, 1964).

26 Stephen Jay Gould, *The Mismeasure of Man* (New York: Norton, 1981) 123-35.

27 Wolf 300; Ernest Fontana, "Lombroso's Criminal Man and Stoker's *Dracula*," *Victorian Newsletter* 26 (1984) 25-27.

28 Jean Gattegno, "Folie, croyance, et fantastique dans *Dracula*," *Litterature* 8 (1972) 77.

29 Susan Sleeth Mosedale, "Science Corrupted: Victorian Scientists Consider 'The Woman Question,'" *Journal of the History of Biology* 11 (1978) 54.

30 Alyosio Galvani, *De viribus electrictatis in motu musculari*, ed. Aldini (Modena, 1792) 17.

31 Gould, *Mismeasure of Man*, ch. 3: "Measuring Heads," 73-112: and John S. and Robin Haller, *The Physician and Society in Victorian America* (New York: Norton, 1977) ch. 2: "The Lesser Man," 45-87.

32 William Acton, *The Functions and Disorders of the Reproductive Organs in Childhood, Youth, Adult Age and Advanced Life Considered in Their Physiological, Social and Moral Relations*, 3rd ed. (Philadelphia: Blakiston, 1871) 163.

[33] Charles Blinderman, "Vampurella: Darwin and Count Dracula," *Massachusetts Review* 21 (1980) 414.

[34] See the discussions in *Psychology's Occult Doubles: Psychology and the Problem of Pseudo-science*, ed. Thomas Hardy Leahey and Grace Evans Leahey (Chicago: Nelson-Hall, 1983).

[35] See H.F. Ellenberger, "Charcot and the Salpetriere School," *American Journal of Psychotherapy* 19 (1965) 253-67.

[36] Alexander Bain, "On the Correlation of Force in its Bearing on Mind," *Macmillan's Magazine* 16 (1867) 377. For Helmholz, see Yehuda Elkana, *The Discovery of the Conservation of Energy* (Cambridge: Harvard University Press, 1974) ch. 5: "Die Erhaultung der Kraft," 114-45; on Bain's significance, see Roger Smith, "The Background of Physiological Psychology in Natural Philosophy," *History of Science* 9 (1973) 95.

[37] David B. Wilson, "The Thought of Late Victorian Physicists: Oliver Lodge's Ethereal Body," *Victorian Studies* 15 (1971) 38.

[38] Dr. Imoda, *Annals of Psychical Science* (August-September, 1908) 38.

[39] Wilson 40.

[40] William B. Carpenter, *Principles of Mental Physiology*, 6th ed. (London: Kegan Paul, 1881) 633.

[41] William James, "Frederick Myers' Service to Psychology," *Proceedings of the Society for Psychical Research* 17 (1901) 223.

[42] Theodore Flournoy, *Spiritism and Psychology*, tr. Hereward Carrington (New York and London: 1911) 214.

[43] Oct. 2, 1894: *Letters of William James and Theodore Flournoy*, ed. Robert C. LeClair (Madison: University of Wisconsin Press, 1966) 37.

[44] Flournoy, *Spiritism and Psychology* 211.

[45] Theodore Flournoy, *Des Indes a la planete Mars: etude sur un cas de somnambulisme avec Glossolalie* (Paris and Geneva: Atar, 1900) 41.

[46] *Spiritism and Psychology* 211.

[47] Ed. Susy Smith (New Hyde Park, New York: University Books, 1961) 140-48.

[48] Otto Weininger, *Sex and Character* (London: Heinemann; New York: Putnam, 1903) 110.

[49] Henri Ellenberger, *Discovery of the Unconscious* (New York: Basic Books, 1961), 291.

[50] Ellenberger 299.

[51] *Psychopathia Sexualis, With Especial Reference to the Antipathic Sexual Instinct: A Medico-Forensic Study*, 12th ed., tr. Franklin S. Klaf (New York: Stein and Day, 1965) 408-09.

[52] Anthony Masters, *The Natural History of the Vampire* (New York: Putnams, 1972) 7-8; Montague Summers mentions other cases of nineteenth-century necrophilia in *Vampire: Kith and Kin* (London: Kegan Paul, 1928) 66-70. See the paper by W.A. F. Browne, former Commissioner for Lunacy in Scotland on "Necrophilism," *Journal of Mental Science* (January 1875) 551-66. See also Hans von Hentig, *Der nekrotrope Mensch; vom Totenglauben zur morbiden Totenahe: Beitrage sur Sexual Forschung* 30 (Stuttgart: F. Enke, 1964), and Theodor Spoerri,

Nekrophilie; Strukturanalyze eines Falles. Bibliotheca psychiatrica et neurologia, Fasc. 105 (Basel and New York: S. Karter, 1959).

53 See Gerald L. Geison, "The Protoplasmic Theory of Life and the Vitalist-Mechanist Debate," *Isis* 60 (1969) 273-92.

54 G.J. Allman, "Presidential Address," *Report of the British Association for the Advancement of Science* (1879) pt. 1:7.

55 Carol A. Senf, "*Dracula*: The Unseen Face in the Mirror," *Journal of Narrative Technique* 9 (1979) 160-69.

56 Senf 165.

57 The divorce of Gothic and "history" goes back at least to Walter Scott's famous distinction between the two in the introduction to *Waverly* (1814). By contrast, I take as one of my starting points David Punter's sensible claim, in his *Literature of Terror: A History of Gothic Fictions from 1765 to the Present Day* (London: Longman, 1980), that "within the Gothic we can find a very intense, if displaced, engagement with political and social problems" (p. 62). Recently, critics have begun to place *Dracula* in the context of late-Victorian culture, usefully complementing the traditional psychoanalytic readings of the novel. Carol A. Senf sees Stoker reacting to the phenomenon of the "New Woman" of the 1890s fiction; Charles Blinderman relates Dracula to aspects of Darwinian types of Lombroso's criminal man; Mark M. Hennelly, Jr., argues that the novel's British characters are engaged in a ghostic quest to redeem the late Victorian "wasteland"; Christopher Craft relates the novel's "anxiety over the potential fluidity of gender roles" to late Victorian discourses on sexual "inversion"; and Franco Moretti sees Dracula as a "metaphor" for monopoly capitalism that late-Victorian bourgeois culture refuses to recognize in itself. See Senf, "*Dracula*: Stoker's Response to the New Woman," *Victorian Studies* 26 (1982), 33-49; Blinderman, "Vampurella, Darwin, and Count Dracula," *Massachusetts Review* 21 (1980), 411-428; Fontana, "Lombroso's Criminal Man and Stoker's Dracula," *Victorian Newsletter* 66 (1984), 25-27; Hennelly, "The Gnostic Quest and the Victorian Wasteland," *English Literature in Transition* 20 (1977), 13-26; Craft, "'Kiss Me With Those Red Lips': Gender and Inversion in Bram Stoker's Dracula," *Representations* 8 (1984), 107-133; Moretti, "The Dialectic of Fear," *New Left Review* 136 (1982), 67-85.

58 John Allen Stevenson, "A Vampire in the Mirror: The Sexuality of *Dracula*," *PMLA* 103 (1988), 139-149. Stevenson's remark is somewhat surprising, since his essay convincingly places Dracula in the context of late-centiury thought on marriage, race, and exogamy. Psychoanalytic readings of Dracula include C.F. Bentley, "The Monster in the Bedroom: Sexual Symbolism in Bram Stoker's *Dracula*," *Literature and Psychology* 22 (199972), 27-32; Stephanie Demetrakopoulous, "Feminism, Sex Role Exchanges, and Other Subliminal Fantasies in Bram Stoker's Dracula," *Frontiers* 2 (1977), 104-113; Carrol L. Fry, "Fictional Conventions and Sexuality in *Dracula*," *Victorian Newsletter* 42 (1972), 20-22; Gail Griffin,"'Your Girls That You All Love Are Mine': *Dracula* and the Victorian Male Sexual Imagination," *International Journal of Women's Studies* 3 (1980), 4554-465; Maurice Richardson, "The Psychoanalysis of Ghost Stories," *Twentieth Century* 166 (1959(, 419-431; Phyllis Roth, "Suddenly Sexual Women in Bram Stoker's *Dracula*," *Literature and Psychology* 27 (1977), 113-121. I am not suggesting that there is a single psychoanalytic paradigm that these writers all follow; but each considers psychoanalysis as the critical approach best suited for Stoker's novel.

59 Standard accounts of the late-Victorian crisis of confidence and its relation to the imperial ideal include Elie Halevy, *Imperialism and the Rise of Labour* (1927; rpt. New York: Barnes and Noble, 1961); Eric Hobsbawm, *The Age of Empire 1875-1914* (New York: Vintage, 1989); Ronald Hyam, *Britain's Imperial Century 1815-1914* (New York: Barnes and Noble, 1976); Richard Shannon, *The Crisis of Imperialism* (London: Granada, 1976); and A.P. Thornton, *The Imperial Idea and Its Enemies* (London: MacMillan, 1959).

60 Patrick Brantlinger, *Rule of Darkness: British Literature and Imperialism, 1830-1914* (Ithaca: Cornell UP, 1988).

61 Bram Stoker, *Dracula* (1897; rpt. Hammondsworth: Penguin, 1984), p. 286.

62 Emily Gerard, *The Land Beyond the Forest: Facts, Figures, and Fancies from Transylvania*, 2 vols (Edinburgh and London: William Blackwood and Sons, 1888), I, 304-305.

63 See L.P. Curtis, *Anglo-Saxons and Celts: A Study of Anti-Irish Prejudice in Victorian England* [Bridgeport, CT: Bridgeport UP, 1968].

64 See Edward Said, *Orientalism* [New York: Vintage, 1979].

65 *The Implied Reader: Patterns of Communication in Prose Fiction from Bunyan to Beckett* [Baltimore: Johns Hopkins UP, 1974], p. 334. See also Hans Robert Jauss, *Toward an Aesthetic of Reception*, trans. Timothy Bahti [Minneapolis: U of Minnesota Press, 1982).

66 Kipling, "Miss Youghal's Sais," in *Plain Tales from the Hills* [1886; rpt. Oxford: Oxford UP, 1987], p. 24.

67 Craft, p. 107.

68 Aside from Moretti's essay, little has been written on Morris. Hatlen gives the majority view when he says that Morris's function is to become "an honorary Englishman," whose "reward" is "the privilege of dying to protect England" [p. 83].

69 P. 209. Stoker's ambivalence about America is more visible in his earlier *A Glimpse of America. . . .* Stoker claims a kinship between the two countries, since their citizens spring from the same racial stock, but he also sees America becoming racially different, and he suggests that the countries may become antagonistic in the future. His racial language is drawn straight from late-Victorian evolutionism.

Miss Betty

"REVIEW OF *MISS BETTY*," *PUNCH* 114 (MARCH 5, 1898), 105.

Mr. BRAM STOKER, having lately harried the world, in *Dracula*, with one of the most blood-curdling novels of the age, makes amends by giving us what my Baronite declares is one of the prettiest. *Miss Betty* (Pearson) is a story of the days of WALPOLE. BRAM, in making studies for his background, has happily caught something of the flavour of the literary style of the age. *Miss Betty* is a charming girl, and wins her affianced from evil ways by a device it would not be fair to disclose in anticipation of the safely-promised pleasure of reading the book.

"REVIEW OF *MISS BETTY*," *ATHENAEUM* 111 (MARCH 26, 1898), 401.

Quite pleasantly and unambitiously Mr. Stoker tells his tale of a certain Miss Betty. It is an innocent and simple rather than a powerful love story, greatly to be preferred to an earlier one he wrote concerning vampires and their ghoulish and unpleasant proceedings. The Georgian days and old Chelsea are the epoch and setting for the figures of Miss Betty, her faithful nurse, and one or two more. Some delicacy of touch rather than originality characterizes the story. The Gentlemen of the Road, so popular just now in fiction, are utilized, but only episodically. The "lover true" of the gentle yet spirited lady possesses little of this world's gear, and his offerings by no means represent his wishes. He is soon lured into the broad road leading to eventual destruction; but the temporary possession of valuable objects, his too costly gifts, with other circumstances, awaken the suspicions of the high-minded girl. Not to spoil the interest of readers, we need merely say that a scene follows in which she knowingly endangers her life to save the young man from ruin. Though all ends well, their happiness is not at once restored. An ordeal of absence and danger has to be gone through before the pair are happily united.

"REVIEW OF *MISS BETTY*," *BOOKMAN* 14 (APRIL 1898), 21.

We opened "Miss Betty" quite early in the evening, determined to finish it long before bed-time, for we had a most unpleasant recollection of a *nuit blanche* which followed the reading of "Dracula." True, neither the title nor the gay cover suggested horrors, but the outside of a book is as often as not deceitful above all things, and there was more than a suspicion of uncanniness about the table of contents--"Chapter V. In the Dead Watch of the Night"!--and we shuddered in anticipation. But Mr. Bram Stoker had prepared a delightful surprise. From "Dracula" to "Miss Betty" is such a far cry that it is almost impossible to realise that both novels come from the same pen. "Miss Betty" is exactly the soothing, quiet, "pretty" novel to read after a day spent in the company of the harrowing problematists. It is one of those simply told, idyllic love stories which are now so out of fashion, and which come as a boon and a blessing to restore one's faded faith in fiction. "Miss Betty" is full of an old world charm, and by its publication Mr. Stoker makes his peace with his former readers. Only in future he should take care to issue two books simultaneously--one of them to be labelled, "To be taken immediately after the shock."

The Mystery of the Sea

"REVIEW OF *THE MYSTERY OF THE SEA*," *DIAL* 32 (JUNE 1, 1902), 391.

Like its predecessors from the same hand, Mr. Bram Stoker's "The Mystery of the Sea" (Doubleday, Page & Co.) is a bit of glowing melodrama, with hidden treasure, desperate villains, secret passages in ancient castles, abductions, shipwrecks, Spanish dons, old women with the gift of second-sight, and other unusual elements of interest. It would be hard to get more action, or more kinds of action, between the covers of a book than will be found here; and it can be depended upon to keep one awake o' nights.

'REVIEW OF *THE MYSTERY OF THE SEA*," *PUNCH* 123 (AUGUST 20, 1902), 110.

The Mystery of the Sea (Heinemann) is a rattling story which sometimes recalls *Monte Cristo*, anon *Treasure Island*. Through it all beams the breezy personality of BRAM STOKER. The scene is set by the curved shore of Cruden Bay, Aberdeenshire. The wild scenery by day and night Mr. STOKER describes with loving touch and master hand. The basis of the plot is discovery of hidden treasure information respecting which naturally comes from correspondents in Spain. They are, however, not the shady parties Mr. LABOUCHERE devotes the leisure of a useful life to unmasking. The treasure originally belonged to the POPE, who contributed it to the expenses of the Armada. The *San Cristobal* that was, as the wise say, "conveying" the treasure, sank in Cruden Bay. How Archibald Hunter was led to the discovery of the gold and gems, how he found still greater treasure in the person of a charming American girl, is told with unfailing animation and marvellous skill. Amongst many powerful scenes is that wherein Lauchlane Macleod's desperate attempt to swim ashore, when Lammas Flood swirled round the broken masses of rock known as "The Skares" is vividly described. My Baronite finds in the book the rare quality of adventure that enthralls the boys and pleases their parents.

"REVIEW OF *THE MYSTERY OF THE SEA*," *BOOKMAN* 23 (OCTOBER 1902), 32.

This is one of those weirdly sensational stories that no living author writes better than Mr. Bram Stoker. The hero, Archibald Hunter, is gifted with second sight and is therefore haunted by an uncanny melodramatic old crone, named Gormala who is imperfectly endowed with similar powers and wants him to league with her in attempting to fathom certain mysteries of the unseen. The whole world of the story revolves in its own ghostly atmosphere; wraiths move across it, and spectral processions of drowned men; there are mysterious documents containing a more mysterious cypher from which Archibald learns of a buried treasure belonging to one of the Popes in the days of the Spanish Armada, and sunk now in some blind sea cavern; and the search for this treasure is followed by the appearance of the last descendant of the ancient Spanish family to whom it had been entrusted. Through all this mystery and peril, through much that is ghostly and ghastly and full of horror, the love story of Archibald and sweet American Marjorie develops into one of the most charming of idylls. Altogether a thrilling and absorbing romance, ingeniously constructed and exceedingly well written.

The Jewel of
Seven Stars

"REVIEW OF *THE JEWEL OF SEVEN STARS*," *HARPER'S*
48 (FEBRUARY 20, 1904), 276.

Mr. BRAM STOKER is a born story-teller. He has a knack of engaging your
interest at the very outset and holding it through a series of exciting chapters
until the denouement. Perhaps he has never told a better story than *The Jewel of
Seven Stars*, which has just been published, although his stories always have
something about them that leave an impression, and won't be forgotten. Mr.
Stoker already numbers a large audience of readers, both in this country and in
England, but I feel certain that this latest story of his will greatly increase his
popularity. It is a tale of wonder and mystery, and the reader who is already
acquainted with Mr. Stoker's previous work, knows how well he can mystify his
readers and keep them on tenter hooks of suspense until the end is reached. It is
full of "thrills." There are pages in it which are capable of making the flesh of
the most *blase* reader creep. The story opens with the discovery of an attempted
crime which at first glance might seem to have no further importance than that
of some daily occurrence reported in the newspaper, but the circumstances that
attend the trance into which the victim has fallen after being attacked by some
unknown person become grave and complicated and mysterious. It transpires that
he is a learned scholar and Egyptologist who has been engaged on some great
experiment; the room in which he lies is full of strange Egyptian curios and
mummies which he has collected during his travels in Egypt. The scholar
eventually revives and proceeds immediately with his experiment, which
involves the others who have been brought into association with him through
the strange attack on his life, the nature of which he alone seems to understand.
The experiment concerns the mummy of a queen, buried centuries ago in Egypt,
whose sarcophagus the scholar had discovered under peculiar conditions, and in
which he had also found the mysterious Jewel of Seven Stars. Now the occult
begins to play a weird part in the story when it is learned that the queen had

made secret plans for her own resurrection, and that the Egyptologist coming upon her plans during his investigations, had resolved to make the experiment himself and bring the queen to life from the mummied remains in the sarcophagus. For this purpose the scholar, accompanied by those who have been drawn into his scheme, among whom are his daughter, and the barrister who tells the tale and who is in love with Margaret, seek a lonely castle in Cornwall to make the great experiment. What takes place there must be held as a surprise for the reader. The result of the experiment is most astounding, and is worked out with great ingenuity and unexpectedness. All through the story the reader is bewildered and tantalized by the strange and bewildering turn of events which cannot even be hinted at in a brief notice of Mr. Stoker's extraordinary story. For example, to mention only one instance, there is the peculiar psychological relation of Margaret, the beautiful daughter of the Egyptologist and her Persian cat, to the mummy of the queen and the mummy of a cat, which, like Margaret's feline companion, presents the strange phenomenon of a paw with seven claws. The effect of Margaret's personality, as her mood changes under the varying influences of her surroundings, is felt by the young barrister to whom she is attached. It should be noted also that Mr. Stoker has very successfully surrounded his story with an atmosphere that impresses the mind and warms the imagination of the reader to the unusual and extraordinary character of the tale he is telling. Mr. Stoker has undoubtedly written a very clever and masterly story of thrilling interest which is likely to command a popular audience.

NINA AUERBACH, *WOMAN AND THE DEMON: THE LIFE OF A VICTORIAN MYTH.* CAMBRIDGE: HARVARD, 1982, 24-25.

The implicit primacy of women in *Dracula* becomes explicit in Stoker's later romances: *The Lady of the Shroud* (1909), *The Lair of the White Worm* (1911), and *The Jewel of Seven Stars* (1912).[1] These are sketchy and desultory repetitions of the myth that in *Dracula* was painstakingly and elaborately documented, but in all of them, the Dracula-figure is missing: like a vestigial organ of waning patriarchal divinities, he is displaced in centrality by a larger-than-life woman of a "strange dual nature." In *The Lady of the Shroud*, Stoker's one Radcliffian denial of the supernatural, the brave daughter of a Voivode nationalist disguises herself as an Undead. Before she reveals her mortal nature the hero, obsessed with her as a lamialike vision, marries her in a secret ceremony. In this slight story a woman takes over Dracula's role as Voivode nationalist with the powers of the Undead to transform and possess, but the rationalistic political context alchemizes male demonism into female heroism.

In contrast, *The Lair of the White Worm* is Stoker's darkest myth of womanhood. The book's Dracula-figure, Lady Arabella March of Diana's Grove, is in her true self a giant white worm older than mankind, living at the bottom of a deep and fetid well that crawls with the repulsive vitality of vermin, insects, and worms. From the mythic associations of her estate to the vaginal potency of her true lair, Lady Arabella's metamorphic power seems darkly intrinsic to womanhood itself. Lilla, the pure heroine, is so passive and susceptible as to be virtually nonexistent. She is recurrently mesmerized, but she has no capacity for transformation, suggesting that Lucy and Mina's powers are being divided: here, the acceptable womanly woman has renounced access to the powers of womanhood. *Dracula's* women were poised between angelic service and vampiristic mutation; here, the lovable domestic woman loses her strength, while the dark outcast woman alone is equated with primal, self-transforming truth.

   The Jewel of Seven Stars is a still more blatantly unresolved allegory of female power. Its Dracula-figure is the ancient Egyptian Queen Tera, passionate and intellectual as Rider Haggard's mighty She-Who-Must-Be-Obeyed (1887). We see Queen Tera only through mysterious signs indicating that she is about to be reincarnated in our strapping heroine, Margaret Trelawny. The story builds ominously toward Margaret's amalgamation with her potent and ancient double, but at the designated moment the Queen fails to appear: Stoker can no longer accommodate his noble Victorian wives-to-be with his vision of primordial transfigured womanhood. Reigning without need of Dracula's catalyzing powers, Stoker's later magi-women hover without the gates, but they are blocked from invading modern London. Efficient contemporaneity may defeat an immortal foreign Count, but it could not withstand the assault of these dark and brilliant women.

PHYLLIS A. ROTH, "*THE JEWEL OF SEVEN STARS*," *BRAM STOKER*. BOSTON: TWAYNE, 1982, 66-74.

None of the novels written subsequently is as good as *Dracula*, though several are fascinating in their own ways, especially *The Jewel of Seven Stars*, written during 1902. Moreover, Stoker's talents as a researcher and his skill in employing the fruits of his research serve him well in creating the uncanniness of his tale. In *Jewel* Stoker has taken great pains not only to describe Egyptian objects and metaphysics in full detail and with considerable accuracy, but also to provide such a wealth of detail about the mysterious Queen Tera, her plans, and her tomb that reader credulity is readily enlisted, especially that of the reader who recognizes the names of Wallis Budge and other Egyptologists, the names of Hathor, Ptah-Seker-Ausar, and other Egyptian deities, as well as the analysis of the "several parts of a human being. . . the Ka or Double, the Ba (the soul of Ka), the Khu (spirit), the Sekhem (power), the Kaibit (shadow), the Ren (name), the Khat (physical body), and the Ab (heart)" quoted from Budge. Clearly, Stoker has done his research, and *Jewel* is a novel with which he took some pains.

In *Jewel*, Stoker duplicates the romance of the endangered woman rescued by a small group of men, both older and younger, which he first employed in *Dracula*. As in *Dracula*, the plot of *Jewel* is complicated by the doubling of the female protagonist and by ambivalence toward her. The ending in particular expresses this ambivalence clearly and is less satisfactory, though as interesting as the ending of *Dracula*. The narrative technique of *Jewel* is far simpler than the journal-letter format Stoker employs in *Dracula* and elsewhere, though the innocent-I account of Malcolm Ross is highly effective in building and sustaining suspense.

The novel opens as Malcolm is summoned from his sleep by a persistent and ominous knocking at his door. Called to the home of a beautiful woman he has met only twice before, Margaret Trelawny, Ross discovers that she hopes for his help in discovering the cause of a mysterious attack on her father which has left him with a bizarre wound on the same wrist on which he wears a key soldered to a bracelet. Discovered in a pool of blood beside an iron safe in his bedroom, Trelawny is in a cataleptic trance from which he cannot be roused for four days. During those four days, the mystery deepens as the attacks on Mr. Trelawny are repeated, as the doctor observes that the slashes on Trelawny's wrist are made by a seven-clawed creature, as Scotland Yard is called in, and as Malcolm observes his own increasing fascination both with the ancient Egyptian objects in Trelawny's house and with Margaret herself. By the time Mr. Trelawny awakens, the mysteries are absolutely obscure. Malcolm and Margaret have tacitly understood their mutual affection. Both the detective and the doctor have separately voiced to Malcolm suspicions of Margaret's complicity in the attacks on her father, and Malcolm is torn between his love for her and the force of the evidence (he is a lawyer): Margaret is the first one to find her father after the attacks, she appears at inconvenient moments, and she has a pet to whom she is devoted, a seven-toed cat, which makes a frenzied assault on an ancient cat mummy every time it is allowed into Mr. Trelawny's bedroom. Moreover, a Mr. Corbeck, an associate of Mr. Trelawny, comes on the scene announcing that he has located, after many years of effort, seven lamps in search of which Mr. Trelawny had sent him. These lamps have mysteriously disappeared from Corbeck's hotel room, but they reappear, equally mysteriously, in Margaret's sitting room.

The complexity of the mystery, and its uncanniness, is heightened by the nature of Mr. Trelawny's and Corbeck's studies and experiences as well as by the nature of the objects in Trelawny's bedroom. The lamps are the final equipment Trelawny has needed to fulfill his great experiment, one which the reader learns of as Margaret, Malcolm, and Dr. Winchester do. The rest of the necessary objects have already been collected and placed in the bedroom, including the jewel of seven stars--an enormous ruby carved like a scarab and containing seven stars in the exact contemporary position of the stars in the constellation of the Plough--a great stone sarcophagus and "Magic Coffer," sharing similar hieroglyphics, carved gaps, and protuberances, and most ghastly, both the mummy of a great Egyptian queen and the severed hand of the mummy, a beautiful, dusky white, perfectly preserved hand--with seven digits! The mummy and hand are those of "Tera, Queen of the Egypts, daughter of Antef.

Monarch of the North and South, Daughter of the Sun. Queen of the Diadems,"
a remarkable "historical" figure who was adept, not only in statecraft, but in
ancient magic and ritual and all the Egyptian sciences. Locked in a battle with
the priests of her day and representing the powers existing before the gods, Tera
determined to suspend herself in time, making all preparations necessary for her
resurrection centuries later. The time has come for her project to be fulfilled, and
this is the great experiment in which Mr. Trelawny is engaged.

The mystery does not end here, however, for while Trelawny's discovery
of Tera's tomb hidden in the "Valley of the Sorcerers" was not the first, it was
intimately bound up with his own life. Leaving his young and pregnant wife at
home, Trelawny had set off for the tomb and, while he was in the burial chamber
itself, his wife died in childbirth, their daughter being delivered from her dead
body. Margaret does not, we are told, resemble her mother; rather, she looks
strikingly like the portraits of Queen Tera; moreover, for birthmark she has a
jagged scar across one wrist, though she has only the normal number of fingers.
Gradually, Malcolm must come to terms with the realization that Margaret's
body is inhabited both by her own spirit and by that of Queen Tera as well and,
as the time determined for the great experiment approaches, she is less and less
his and more and more the queen's.

Central to the conception and the mystery of the novel is a complex of
familiar motifs: the ambivalence toward the female and the mergings or
doublings of identity. Here, too, *Jewel* manages these elements adeptly.
Margaret's involvement with the attacks on her father is skillfully done: we must
suspect her a little but suspicion must not lead too quickly to a recognition of
her identity with Queen Tera, nor must either Tera or Margaret be viewed as
essentially dangerous and threatening until the right moment. Stoker handles this
problem both by the involved narrator and by establishing Margaret's ignorance
of her father's life and studies: she has only recently come to live with him.
Thus, Stoker is able to maintain Margaret's essential innocence at the same time
that he prepares for her doubling with the powerful, numinous Queen Tera, and
for the resolution which, in effect, purifies the woman.

Perhaps even more subtly, Stoker employs the archetype of the journey
into the realm of the fantastic, the realm of dreams, nightmares, and encounters
with doubles, by use of foil characters and magical spaces. As the novel opens,
the narrator is in his own home and asleep, recapitulating in his dreams his brief
meetings with Margaret Trelawny. The first paragraph itself establishes the
dream-memory as a shadowing forth of the resurrection motif: "It all seemed so
real that I could hardly imagine that it had ever occurred before; and yet each
episode came, not as a fresh step in the logic of things, but as something
expected. It is in such wise that memory plays its pranks for good or ill. . . .It
is thus that life is bittersweet, and that which has been done becomes eternal".
. . . Malcolm continues significantly: "For it is in the arcana of dreams that
existences merge and renew themselves, change and yet keep the same--like the
soul of a musician in a fugue. And so memory swooned, again and again, in
sleep". . . . The threshold crossing into the world of dreams is repeated in the
threshold crossing into the Trelawny household where Malcolm, as it were,
rejoins his dreams in a magical space. The sacredness of the space is reinforced

and reaffirmed through a series of events, including the expelling of the uninitiated and the inward movement toward an even more sanctified arena: the labyrinthine path the mystery figuratively traces is literally acted out in the characters' movement through space in the novel.

Two significant though minor characters function further to demarcate the magical space of the dream world in *Jewel*. Most obvious is the world-renowned medical authority called in for a consultation about Trelawny by Margaret. This older male authority recalls *Dracula*'s Van Helsing but, unlike the latter, Sir James Frere, as he is significantly named, voices the skeptical views of modern science, and is willing to take the case only on the condition that the magical space be violated. Either Trelawny or the Egyptian artifacts must be moved from his room. This, of course, is precisely the tabooed act, prohibited by Trelawny in a letter written prior to the first attack on him. Frere is denied his condition and ejected from the magical space. However, the attending physician, a Dr. Winchester, agrees not only to stay but to see it to the end, thus maintaining the circle of initiates.

Similarly, the character of Nurse Kennedy, originally brought in to attend Trelawny, is also removed from the inner circle. During her first night watching by the bedside, Nurse Kennedy is sent into a trance resembling Trelawny's. This bit of business seems, on the whole, gratuitous, except for the fact that Nurse Kennedy, too, embodies rationality and common sense. Moreover, she is introduced in a crucial passage in which she is described in vivid detail as a foil to Margaret and Margaret's type of beauty. The significance of the contrast is heightened both by the detail in which it is described by the narrator and by its location at the very beginning of the third chapter:

By comparison of the two I seemed somehow to gain a new knowledge of Miss Trelawny. Certainly, the two women made a good contrast. Miss Trelawny was of fine figure; dark, straight-featured. She had marvellous eyes; great, wide-open, and as black and soft as velvet, with a mysterious depth. To look in them was like gazing at a black mirror such as Doctor Dee used in his wizard rites. . . . The eyebrows were typical. Finely arched and rich in long curling hair, they seemed like the proper architectural environment of the deep, splendid eyes. Her hair was black also, but was as fine as silk. Generally black hair is a type of animal strength and seems as if some strong expression of the forces of a strong nature; but in this case there could be no such thought. There were refinement and high breeding; and though there was no suggestion of weakness, any sense of power there was, was rather spiritual than animal. The whole harmony of her being seemed complete. Carriage, figure, hair, eyes; the mobile full mouth, whose scarlet lips and white teeth seemed to light up the lower part of the fact--as the eyes did the upper; the wide sweep of the jaw from chin to ear; the long, fine fingers; the hand which seemed to move from the wrist as though it had a sentience of its own. All these perfections went to make up a personality that dominated either by its grace, its sweetness, its beauty, or its charm.

Nurse Kennedy, on the other hand, was rather under than over a woman's average height. She was firm and thickset, with full limbs and broad, strong, capable hands. Her colour was in the general effect that of an autumn leaf. The yellow-brown hair was thick and long, and the golden-brown eyes sparkled from the freckled, sunburnt skin. Her rosy cheeks gave a general idea of rich brown. The red lips and white teeth did not alter the colour scheme, but only emphasised it. She had a snub nose--there was no possible doubt about it; but like such noses in general it showed a nature generous, untiring, and full of good-nature. Her broad white forehead, which even the freckles had spared, was full of forceful thought and reason.

Nurse Kennedy is nothing if not the antithesis of mystery and uncanniness, the rejection of purely "animal" spirits and power, and she, too, is removed from the magical space.

During the rest of the novel others are ejected, singly and in groups: namely, Sergeant Daw from Scotland Yard and most of the servants. Finally, the circle of the initiated moves to Trelawny's secret castle, through winding passages into an enormous cave by the sea to perform the great experiment. This circle includes, of course, Margaret, Trelawny and Malcolm Ross, and Dr. Winchester and Mr. Corbeck as well. Thus, we have a configuration similar to that of *Dracula* though without the marked Oedipal and sibling rivalry of the earlier novel, in which a band of men, led by a father figure (here actually the father), dedicate themselves to saving the woman.

Mr. Trelawny's preparations for the experiment are fascinating and elaborate. Equally compelling is the suspense Stoker builds as the time for the consummation of Tera's and Trelawny's dream approaches. The first-person narration is exceptionally effective, for Malcolm more than anyone else is attuned to the changes in Margaret and therefore to the presence of the spirit of Queen Tera. The personality alterations Margaret undergoes are, to him, uncanny and terribly distressing as he recognizes the possibility that, should Tera arise, she might not be submissively grateful for the assistance she has received. Indeed, the chances are that she will not be, for, in unguarded moments, as her spirit dominates Margaret's, Malcolm has seen Margaret fall "into a positive fury of passion. Her eyes blazed, and her mouth took on a hard, cruel tension which was new to me". . . . And this, in response to her own cat's attack on Tera's familiar, the cat mummy.

How then, is this doubling, and the novel, to be resolved? As in the case of *Dracula,* the solution is the destruction of the violent woman. The alternations Margaret manifests closely resemble those of Lucy Westenra; the spirit of the vampire, with all its seductive force, is that of Queen Tera, the other side of the submissive, loving wife. Moreover, the similarity extends to the questioning of the animation of the entombed body and to the sexuality of the "dead" woman: in *Jewel,* Margaret recognizes this sexuality when she objects to the striptease Tera is forced to provide as her body is robbed of its wrappings. As in *Dracula,* the undead and sexually threatening woman is destroyed. While Trelawny's surmises are accurate and the spirit of Tera returns to her flesh as she begins to rise, mysteriously the resurrection is aborted: all that remains of Tera is a handful of dust.[2]

The rather lame ending seems weak in part because of the rest of the novel. From the very first the mysteriousness, the uncanniness is unremitting; all details are revealed in their place, not before, all seem essential, and all build toward the one climax. The reader is led to credit it all by the sheer force of the detail Stoker provides, based both on his own research and on stories of Egypt and Egyptology heard at the table of Sir William Wilde, Oscar Wilde's father.

Enhanced by identification with the narrator who learns as we learn and who has human doubts and anxieties, reader assent in the fantasy is optimal. Moreover, our desire for the consummation of the great experiment is strong: only that will resolve the novel. But, through Malcolm's distress, we are also concerned about the potential destructiveness of the terrible Tera, so we alternately wish for failure, or at least, escape.

Not surprisingly, however, the final paragraphs, reasserting the romance component of the story, are anticlimactic. Moreover, they hark back to the weakest section of the novel, the section in which, as if in a trance, Margaret pours forth her convictions about Tera's motivation for arranging her resurrection.

"I can see her in her loneliness and in the silence of her mighty pride, dreaming her own dream of things far different from those around her. . . . A land of wholesome greenery, far, far away. Where were no scheming and malignant priesthood; whose ideas were to lead to power through gloomy temples and more gloomy caverns of the dead, through an endless ritual of death! A land where love was not base, but a divine possession of the soul! Where there might be some one kindred spirit which could speak to hers through mortal lips like her own; whose being could merge with hers in a sweet communion of soul to soul, even as their breaths could mingle in the ambient air! . . .

Margaret is clearly projecting, here, saying that she knows what Tera dreamed of now that such a love has come into her own life; moreover, the imagery suggests that Tera's motivation is to move from the heated passion and violence of the desert to the purified, spiritualized, Edenic innocence of a Northern love, such a migration reflecting the novel's transformation of Margaret as well. Transcending the personal level of romance, the care and effort taken both by Tera and by Trelawny in executing the great experiment seem to warrant a more universally significant motivation, just as the genius and power of the woman requires greater scope than that afforded by the quest for a Prince Charming. Indeed, toward the climax of the novel, Mr. Trelawny remarks, "What is a woman's life in the scale of what we hope for! . . . Imagine what it will be for the world of thought--the true world of human progress--. . . if there can come back to us out of the unknown past one who can yield to us the lore stored in the great Library of Alexandria . . . we can be placed on the road to the knowledge of lost arts, lost learning, lost sciences". . . .

We see again, then, that Stoker's power lies with the mysterious and uncanny and that his novels succeed to the degree that the romance components are subordinated to those of the fantastic. Further, we recognize the basic plot pattern employed in *Jewel* and in Stoker's other tales of terror: ostensibly directed toward saving the female, in this case almost giving birth to her, the journey in *Jewel* has as its underlying function the need to come to terms with ambiguous female nature. As in *Dracula*, the confrontation entails the destruction of the dangerous dimension of the woman. As Tera dies, so too does her spirit in Margaret, and the novel ends with Margaret's and Malcolm's marriage and with a return to the daylight. Margaret's last words bring us out of the dream, out of the magical space in which we confront the double and our fears and desires about the female which the novel has portrayed: "Do not grieve for her! Who knows, but she may have found the joy she sought? Love and patience are all that make for happiness in this world; or in the world of the past or of the future; of the living or the dead. She dreamed her dream; that is all that any of us can ask!"

NOTES

[1] Auerbach is apparently referring to the abridged and amended version originally published by Rider in 1912. According to Dalby, "This and all subsequent British editions (Rider, Jarrolds, and Arrow) have the abridged, amended text. Besides the rewritten 'happy' ending, the original chapter XVI, "Powers--Old and New," was entirely omitted." (p. 43). Oddly, this chapter deals most directly, as the title might suggest, with the relationship between the past and the present.

[2] Like Auerbach, Roth is apparently not using the first edition of the novel.

The Man

"REVIEW OF *THE MAN*," *PUNCH* 129 (SEPTEMBER 27, 1905), 234.

As *Dogberry* has his losses, so Mr. BRAM STOKER, reckoned as a novelist, has had his successes. But his earlier works, popular as they remain, do not approach the level of *The Man* (HEINEMANN). My Baronite recognizes its place among the best half-dozen novels of the year. It starts on a note of originality rare in days when novels are turned out by the hundred. The heroine, a beautiful, high-spirited girl, conceives the idea that, woman being at least the equal of man, there is no logical reason why he should have the monopoly of selecting a partner for life. She accordingly proposes to her childhood's friend, *Leonard Everard*, who, exercising the equal right of man, declines the proffered hand. This is a fantasy that would bore if carried too far. Mr. BRAM STOKER skilfully uses it as the basis of his plot, and for the development of the character of his chief *dramatis personae*. The story is full of episodes that hold the reader at breathless attention. He will think nothing could be finer than the account of the saving of a child swept off the decks of a steamer in mid-Atlantic, till he comes to the story of the shipwreck on the English coast. This need not shrink from comparison with DICKENS'S classic narrative of the wreck off Yarmouth to which *Peggoty* went to the rescue of *Steerforth*. It may be added that *Miss Norman* and *Harold* are the kind of woman and man with whom THACKERAY occasionally made us acquainted. Admirably written, vivid in narrative, rich in character, pure in tone, absorbing in interest, *The Man* will be found well worth knowing.

"REVIEW OF *THE MAN*," *BOOKMAN* (OCTOBER 1905), 38-39.

Miss Stephen Norman is the only child of a wealthy English squire who had set his heart upon a son. Foiled in this ambition, he gives his daughter a man's name, and, as her mother dies at her birth, educates her in a much more free manner than is common among English girls. One result of this early training is to foster in the girl a romantic and dangerous belief in the equality of the sexes, which actually leads the young heiress, after her father's death, to propose marriage to a fascinating and worthless scamp in the neighbourhood. How she gets out of this entanglement, and how the true lover comes eventually to his own, is Mr. Stoker's secret, and to his pages the reader must turn for the solution. He or she will not turn without being rewarded. The characters of Miss Norman, her aunt, and her two lovers, are vividly conceived and drawn. Mr. Stoker is a master of the dramatic in fiction. And he has specially excelled in depicting this pure, delicately minded girl's nature in a situation which would make most women seem unmaidenly. There is a thrilling description of a rescue in mid-Atlantic, also, and a fine shipwreck. The book at first tends to be a trifle heavy with psychological reflections. But the author works through to a swifter vein as the story unfolds; if the end is obvious, the stages to it are versatile enough to please the most exacting taste. The one weak sentence in the book is the last.

"A GIRL BY THE NAME OF STEPHEN," *NEW YORK TIMES* 13 (AUGUST 15, 1908), 448.

There are novelty and variety in Bram Stoker's novel, "The Gates of Life." The heroine is named Stephen after her father. The worthy English gentleman's heart was set on having a son and heir, and he was greatly disappointed when his wife presented him a girl. He thinks to conquer fate, however, by bringing up the latter as a boy.

The baby grew into a very beautiful woman, but she got some rather advanced notions into her head with respect to the relations between man and woman, and presently she invited a young man she thought she loved to marry her--proposed to him, as a man would propose to a woman and stoutly urged her suit, even going so far as to promise to pay the young fellow's debts.

Her proposal was summarily rejected.

"What a girl you are, Stephen!" remarked the young man. "You are always doing something or other to put a chap in the wrong and make him ridiculous. Upon my soul I don't know what I've done that you should fix on me."

But the rejection was due to the suddenness of the proposal: there had been no preliminary lovemaking. The next day the young man was of a different mind and hunted up Stephen and told her so. But she too had changed; she undertook to pay the young man's bills amounting to something over 4,000, but she no longer wanted him for a husband.

That same day her time came to reject a suitor--a youthful giant of six foot four, whom she had known all her life--and dearly loved, although she didn't know it. She was so harsh in her treatment of the giant that he fled broken-hearted to Alaska, distinguishing himself on the way by leaping into the ocean after a child who had been washed overboard in a storm.

Of course, the young man came back from Alaska and of course he picks up any number of adventures along the way. With similar inevitableness he and Stephen come to a mutual understanding--all of which should be, if it is not, quite satisfactory and entertaining to the reader.

"REVIEW OF *THE GATES OF LIFE*," *NATION* 87 (AUGUST 20, 1908), 163.

Stephen Norman, in her fourteenth year, had a firm-set jaw, square chin, flame-colored hair, full crimson lips, and purple-black eyes. These traits were "Saxon through Norman," with a dash of mediaeval Saracen. From that time to the end of her story, she always wore a scarlet riding-habit, and the intensity of her feelings matched her color-scheme. Harold An Wolf (Gothic through Dutch) had nothing very remarkable about him, except his six feet four inches and the propensity, common to all the characters in this book, to behave as nobody in his senses would do. In short, Mr. Stoker has written a blatant melodrama, all the trashier for the grandiloquent moralizings--in which the word "sex" is unpleasantly frequent--which punctuate the surprising actions of his characters.

"REVIEW OF *THE GATES OF LIFE*," *BOOKMAN* 28 (SEPTEMBER 1908), 69.

The Gates of Life, by Bram Stoker, needs only a passing comment, lest any one, recalling the uncanny strength of that author's *Dracula*, of a few seasons ago, should mistake this new volume for another attempt along the same weird line. On the contrary, *The Gates of Life* deliberately avoids the least hint of the supernatural and aims to be a straightforward, rational tale of modern English life, the central motive being the mortification of a young girl, who having imbibed the doctrine of equality of the sexes proposes to a man who does not love her, and meets with a blunt rejection. The resultant volume simply goes to prove how much harder it sometimes is to picture the actualities of life than the wildest visions of a disordered brain. Surely Mr. Stoker is still capable of better things. It takes something akin to genius to produce such a nightmare horror as *Dracula.*

PHYLLIS A. ROTH, *"THE MAN," BRAM STOKER.* BOSTON: TWAYNE, 1982, 38-51.

The Man, published in 1905, is Stoker's most leisurely and sophisticated romance; indeed, with regard to characterization, it is his most painstaking and satisfying novel. None of his other novels entails the time and detail devoted to the examination of complex motivation as does this one. Moreover, it is also the most direct and lengthy analysis of female sexuality and behavior Stoker undertook and, although his conclusions typify Victorian era confusions and stereotypes as well as Stoker's own ambivalences, the strengths of the female protagonist are given a good deal of liberty. *The Man* is also a bizarre book, playing on a clearly defined question of sexual identity: the female hero is named Stephen Norman after her father who very much desired a son from his only marriage, one made late in his life. Since from the outset Stephen both tries to be her father's son and questions conventional sex roles, the reader assumes that "the Man" refers to Stephen. Stoker is not writing *Orlando*, however; late in the book one discovers that the title refers explicitly to Harold An Wolf, clearly the male protagonist but just as clearly secondary to Stephen in interest and attention paid to him. This rather belated revelation parallels and sets forth the final disposition of sex roles in the novel: while Stoker allows Stephen considerable latitude in her behavioral experimentation when she is a girl and a young woman, she finally learns what it "really" means, according to Stoker, to be a woman. "She was all woman now; all patient, and all submissive. She waited [for] the man; and the man was coming!" When she learns the lesson of womanhood, she also learns the identity of her true love; the reader discovers that Harold is "the Man" and that Stephen Norman is no man.

　　　The plot of *The Man* is not much more complicated than those of the other romances. The major characters include Stephen, her father, Harold An Wolf, another boy Stephen grows up with named Leonard Everard, and Stephen's great-aunt Laetitia Rowly, who raised Stephen's mother and who becomes Stehen's surrogate mother after her own dies in giving birth to Stephen. As is true in many Victorian novels in addition to Stoker's, most characters grow up without mothers, a device allowing the characters to explore behaviors and make mistakes against which their mothers presumably would have warned them. In Stephen's case, the lack of a mother is even more crucial, for Stephen has no model of the proper Victorian wife; no woman Stephen knows is married. Additionally, in the course of the novel, both Stephen and Harold lose their fathers, forcing them into positions both of premature responsibility and of misunderstanding. Stephen's difficulties are very much obviated, more or less in the nick of time, by the assistance first of Aunt Laetitia and then, when she dies, of a strange "Silver Lady" who doubles for the aunt. One of Stoker's typical difficulties is the introduction of gratuitous characters or, viewed another way, the employment of characters about whom we are not told enough to see them function successfully as foils or in a subplot, the Silver Lady being such a character.

As the small number of characters indicates, the plot of *The Man* is clear and unfolds in a single chronological dimension, although the author occasionally returns to an earlier point in time to be able to inform the reader what another character has been doing in the meanwhile. Growing up without a mother and indulged by a father to whom she is a son, Stephen Norman begins to question conventional restrictions on female behavior. Raised, however, both in the lap of luxury and out of society on a large estate in a place called Normanstand, Stephen finds little opportunity to develop "masculine" skills or even to imagine possible behaviors. For example, one of her most gleeful moments as a young girl occurred when her uncle Gilbert put his fez on her head and penciled in a moustache and thickened the eyebrows on her face. As Stephen gets a bit older, however, and even before her father dies, she wishes to assume her role in the country and among "their people" with as much vigor as he. This she does, to the extent at any rate of fulfilling the rather feudal obligations of the lady Victorian aristocrat, visiting and aiding the poor, and so forth. Additionally, much to the dismay of her proper aunt, she expresses a wish to attend the Petty Sessions Court with her father to improve her knowledge of the difficulties and evils of the lives of her people.

Stephen feels, moreover, that she needs further to test her theory that women should be allowed rights and privileges equal to those men enjoy and, consequently, determines to propose marriage to Leonard Everard. The complication of the novel's plot lies in this determination which is, not surprisingly, a hideous mistake. First of all, Leonard is clearly the wrong man; from what we know of him, though Stephen does not, he is an unbounded egotist, caring for no one and nothing but his own pleasure and dominance. Interestingly, in terms of the novel's final stand on proper sex role behavior which stresses the dominance of the man, it is Leonard's desire to dominate which both attracts Stephen and deceives her about him. Further, Leonard is a profligate, deep in debt, and, possibly, responsible for the pregnancy of a young peasant woman less fortunate than Stephen. Finally, Leonard is a coward, a fact demonstrated to the reader on an occasion when Stephen willfully ignores the advice of Harold and, with Leonard, enters the old church crypt where her mother is entombed. Distraught by the discovery of her mother's coffin, Stephen faints away in the darkness of the crypt. Harold arrives just in time to discover the cowardly Leonard rushing out alone into the daylight and fresh air. While Harold rescues Stephen, Leonard hangs around and it is the latter's face Stephen sees first, leading her to the conclusion that he carried her from the crypt. A sensitive, self-effacing sort, Harold does not correct her and neither does the mean and craven Leonard. In consequence, an animosity is born between the men and a misapprehension regarding Leonard is nourished in Stephen's heart. The reader knows that Leonard is not the man; he is far beyond the reclaiming Rafe Otwell enjoys from the good graces of Miss Betty.

Moreover, the reader knows that Harold is the man. From the moment of their first meeting as the children of two close friends, their fathers, Harold and Stephen have loved and trusted each other. Their lives have had meaning by virtue of shared experiences and, when Harold's father dies, neither wishes for anything more than the fulfillment of their childhood dream that Harold would come and live at Normanstand and be Stephen's father's other son. This dream is fulfilled with the effect of strengthening the ties between Stephen and Harold as well as initiating Harold into all the affairs of the Normans. Harold is on the scene of Stephen's father's accident and, before the elder man dies, he entrusts Stephen to Harold, saying it is his dearest hope that Harold and Stephen should someday marry but that Harold should give Stephen time and her own choice. This advice becomes for Harold not only law but both his temporary downfall and his ultimate triumph, for it indicates to him his duty with regard to Stephen. Believing that Stephen is too young for thoughts of marital love, Harold suppresses his desires for her and, indeed, avoids her.

For her part, Stephen is as young as Harold surmises but not too young to try out her theories of woman's equality. Limited by her narrow field of activity, Stephen concludes, not so much that she wishes to *marry* Leonard, whom she has not seen for some time and whose true character she has never gauged, but that she wishes to *propose* to him. Since Harold puts himself "outside practical range" and since Stoker claims that while "a man loves a woman and seeks that woman's love, a woman seeks love" regardless, apparently, of the man, Stephen "naturally" turns to the one other man of her acquaintance. Step by step Stephen's determination grows into an obsession which has so compelling a hold on her imagination and pride that she thinks of nothing else. In this lengthy middle section of the novel Stoker is at his best, allowing time and detail fully to explore the minds and personalities of the three major characters. His rendering of Stephen's mingled pride, determination and diffidence is superb, enabling the reader to sympathize with her sense of mission and her strength of will while recognizing the error of her judgment if not of her theory. Little in Stoker's work is as excruciatingly painful as the proposal scene in which Stephen is forced by Leonard's callous unconsciousness into greater explicitness than even she intended or as the following days in which Stephen excoriates herself with self-loathing and shame which assault her "wave upon wave." Unable to share her humiliation and pain with anyone, hiding her anguish from her Aunt Laetitia, and attempting to fulfill her daily obligations, Stephen cannot find comfort even in the temporary solace of tears, the tears available only to real women, as later becomes apparent.

Having brutally refused Stephen's proposal although he wants her to pay his debts as she has offered, Leonard begins to recognize his stupidity--his only saving grace in the reader's eyes for, had he accepted Stephen, she would have married him despite subsequent revelations regarding his character. Characteristically, his response is to get drunk and to brag of his conquest of Stephen to none other than Harold. At first incredulous, Harold is forced to believe that Stephen has proposed when he sees her letter to Leonard asking for a meeting and when he hears the ring of truth in Leonard's voice. Devastated by his loss, Harold spends a sleepless night trying to understand Stephen. Knowing her as he does, he correctly concludes that she does not love Leonard; rather, he surmises she has been testing a theory. Moreover, he understands her humiliation and determines to offer himself up as a sacrifice to her pride, deciding to propose so she can have the sense of superiority gained by turning him down. This psychology, however, is somewhat facile, as Harold discovers, for his proposal meets with horror, outrage, contempt, Stephen comprehending instantly that Harold knows all. Tortured by her profound mortification, Stephen strikes out at the one person who could provide the comfort she needs. And Harold is forced by his generosity and naivete to listen to the woman he adores tell him she wishes she never met him and would never see him again.

At this point the complication of the novel is wrought to its greatest degree, marking also the beginning of the resolution. The first element to be resolved is Leonard, who poses a threat to Stephen by knowing of her shame, but who also sorely needs his debts paid, debts of which his father cannot and will not relieve him. Stephen has agreed to pay these debts and, in a series of brilliant scenes narrated primarily from within Leonard's selfish perspective, Stephen gains the upper hand and evades his simultaneous blackmailing and lovemaking. A rather lengthy quotation from the text serves to indicate the mastery of motivation and narration Stoker achieves here, employing dialogue which distinguishes characters, tones both comic and ominous, and the narrative technique of *erlebte rede*, or free indirect speech, in which the narrator moves in and out of the character's thought patterns:

> As he spoke, his words seemed, even to him, to be out of place. He felt that it would be necessary to throw more fervour into the proceedings. . . .
> "Oh, Stephen, don't you know that I love you? You are so beautiful! I love you! Won't you be my wife?"
> This was getting to much too close quarters. Stephen said in a calm, business like way:
> "My dear Leonard, one thing at a time! I came out here you know, to speak of your debts; and until that is done, I really won't go into any other matter. Of course if you'd rather not. . . . " Leonard really could not afford this; matters were too pressing with him. . . .
> "All right! Stephen. Whatever you wish I will do; you are the Queen of my heart, you know!"
> "How much is the total amount?" asked Stephen.
> . . . He had come prepared to allow Stephen to fall into his arms, fortune and all. But now, although he had practical assurance that the weight of his debts would be taken from him, he was going away with his [tail] between his legs. He had not even been accepted as a suitor, he who had himself been wooed only a day before. His proposal of marriage had not been accepted, had not even been considered by the woman who had so lately broken iron-clad convention to propose marriage to him. . . . He had even been treated like a bad boy. . . . And all the time he dare not say anything lest the thing shouldn't come off at all. Stephen had such an infernally masterly way with her! . . . . He would have to put up with it, till he had got rid of his debts! He never even considered the debt which he must still owe to her. When that time came he would. . . . Well he would deal with some people and some things in a different way from that which he had to do now!

Stephen has shared some of her shameful secret with her aunt Laetitia who, also knowing Leonard, deems it advisable to pay Leonard's debts in her own name and with her own money. Together the two women outwit and outmaneuver the now pathetic Leonard.

The major element to be resolved is, of course, the relationship between Stephen and Harold, but Harold takes Stephen at her word and goes directly from his last meeting with her to London and from there ships out to Alaska on a symbolically named cargo vessel, the *Scoriac*. The balance of the story shifts here from Stephen to Harold as Stoker narrates his version of the quest myth in which the hero seeks his fortune in the typical forms, first, of a treasure of gold and, then, of the princess. Before making his fortune in the Alaskan goldfields, however, Harold wins the undying affection and gratitude of the Stonehouses, husband and wife and their tiny daughter Pearl (doubtless influenced by Hawthorne's Pearl), when during a tremendous storm Pearl is washed overboard and Harold rescues her. Little Pearl is, of course, a delightful child and reminds Harold of the girl Stephen was when he first met her. Upon saving Pearl, Harold, traveling under the name John Robinson, is dubbed "the Man" by the child, and the reader has little doubt that this rescue is prophetic. (In a rather bizarre scene, Pearl spends the night in bed with Harold, since she only feels safe when she's with him. Stoker is rather obsessively fastidious about informing his readers when and where Harold puts on his pyjamas and takes off his robe.) The next two years of Harold's self-imposed exile are summarized rapidly as, refusing Mr. Stonehouse's offer to become a partner and, echoically, the son the Stonehouses never had, Harold makes his fortune founding Robinson City in Alaska. At the end of that time, Harold boards a ship to return to England via a northern route.

The two years have passed less eventfully for Stephen, though she has had to face the implications of what she describes as her murder of Harold. Shortly after ridding herself of Leonard, Stephen realized her behavior toward her best friend and advisor was far more shameful than that toward Leonard. "Sadly she turned over in her bed, and with shut eyes put her burning face on the pillow, to hide, as it were, from herself her abject depth of shame." Around the same time, Stephen is informed she has become the countess of Launoy (or Lannoy--the text has it both ways) and therefore owner of prodigious estates on the north coast of England. Aunt Laetitia, Stephen's beloved friend, dies at this time, after predicting that Stephen will find happiness at her new estate. Subsequently, Stephen decides to travel north and view her new land where her warmth and generosity make her beloved, where she takes long rides on her white mare, feeling happier--and more "feminine"--than she has in years, and where she meets and is befriended by the "Silver Lady," a Quaker who dresses all in silver grey. Becoming Stephen's counselor and comforter, the Silver Lady enables Stephen finally to find relief in tears.

Riding out one day as a storm threatens, Stephen sees a ship rushing perilously toward the rock-studded shore. Assisting in the rescue operations, she sees a large, athletic, bearded man save the ship by swimming toward port with the line tied to his waist. Although the ship is secured, the swimmer must return seaward or be dashed on the rocks. After considerable suspense and heroism on the part of many, Harold, for of course it is he, is brought ashore, alive but apparently blind. With the others rescued from the ship, he is brought to the Castle of the countess de Launoy where he recognizes Stephen's voice. She, however, does not recognize Harold under beard and bandages on the one occasion when she is allowed to see him, and Harold does not want her pity. Taking the doctor into his confidence, Harold forestalls for three weeks Stephen's desire to talk with him. At the end of this time, the Stonehouses arrive on the scene, Pearl having insisted that the great hero of the shipwreck was "the Man." The subsequent revelation scene includes Stephen fainting as she did once before when Harold saved her, as well as the discovery that Harold has regained his sight (shades of Jane Eyre and Rochester). But now that they are reunited, one further barrier needs to be overcome. Recalling once more the promise he made to Stephen's father, Harold wants Stephen to make her own choice; but mindful of her earlier folly--and now a real woman at long last able to weep tears-- Stephen waits for the man to speak first. Just as Aunt Laetitia helped Stephen with Leonard, so now the Silver Lady helps with Harold, and the two lovers are finally united.

Like *Miss Betty*, *The Man* is a novel with a message, a dominant idea but, unlike the earlier novel, the idea in *The Man* is both more problematic for Stoker and more interesting to his readers. While both novels can be read as extended parables, based on a just universe presided over by a benevolent divinity and informed throughout by a judicious natural order, *The Man* complicates plot through a detailed rendering of human emotion rather than reducing it to a mechanical unwinding. Moreover, students of Stoker's work as a whole will be fascinated by the direct examination of the nature and role of women which is a sustained though more or less disguised concern of the other fiction. *The Man*, then, provides explicit evidence of Stoker's ambivalence toward women. Clearly fascinated by strong, intelligent, willful women--some of the finest scenes are those in which Stephen bests Leonard--and by the feminist concerns of his day, Stoker is determined to demonstrate the natural inferiority of Woman. Indeed, a contributing factor to the contradictions in his portrayal of women is his effort to force into the mold of Women the individual human being whom his imagination recognizes as more distinctive than his wishes or his message would like to allow. . . . Stoker seems conscious of difficulties in fitting the individual to the mold for, in the prologue to *The Man*, during a proleptic debate between Stephen and Harold regarding woman's ability to be just . . . Stoker comments: "But sex is sex all through. It is not, like whiskers or a wedding ring, a garnishment or maturity. Each little item of humanity gurgling in the cradle, or crowing when tossed in brawny arms, has a method of its own. For one sex there are thumpings, for the other, tears and such like blandishments. Not that either sex has an absolute monopoly of these means of accomplishing a wished-for end. But averages rule life". . . . In *The Man* Stoker attempts to demonstrate this axiom by portraying the evil attendant upon Stephen's behaving "like a man," specifically in proposing to Leonard. In a limited sense, Stoker provides a precis of the whole novel when he editorializes, "The punishment of her arrogant unwomanliness had, she felt, indeed begun". . . . It is precisely this sort of commentary which mars the novel's dramatic achievements. Elsewhere, Stoker describes Stephen's beauty as follows: "The hair, growing well down over the eyebrows, took away that look of barrenness which is often in a woman attendant on intellectually [*sic*]. . . . This view of the incompatibility of intelligence and sexual fertility in women is a standard Victorian conviction and is also demonstrated vividly in the character of Mina Harker in *Dracula* who has a "male mind" and no female sexuality.

Yet, the book is both richer and more complicated than this. Stoker takes pains to indicate the greatest problem lies with Stephen's mistaking Leonard and acting on theory rather than affection and respect. Indeed, and paradoxically given the moral of the story, Stephen's attraction to Leonard is based on her misapprehension of him as a real man, resulting from his unique opposition to her when they were children: Stephen "thought that this was a real boy who was masterful. Every fibre in her little feminine body realized the fact". . . . Stephen mistakes selfishness for manliness. Only later does she recognize Harold's self-sacrifice for her as true virility--a rather unexpected conclusion for a novelist who seems to wish to reinforce stereotypes. Moreover, although the painful distance between Harold and Stephen at the end of the novel is a result of her newly found womanliness, their final understanding is dependent upon the intervention of a surrogate mother, as was Stephen's earlier liberation from Leonard's plotting. Finally, Stephen's attractiveness lies in her strengths, her ability to initiate, to dominate, and to act, not just in her knowledge of when to submit. Her money and social position as well as her childhood encouragement to behave like a man, to be her father's son, confer power upon her, a power and a strength of will which help her save Harold from the sea at the end of the novel. Stephen's "masculine" behavior in fact both defines her and is the source of delight to the men. Little Pearl resembles her in nothing so much as in a sort of imperious dominance.

Thus, *The Man* is a fascinating novel for students of Stoker's fiction, and indeed of Victorian fiction, revealing as it does Stoker's concern with the role of women, their power, their sources of attraction, and their nature. Moreover, Stoker has come some distance since *Dracula* in which Mina Harker, the perfect Victorian woman, reviles those of her sex who, in putting themselves forward, might even someday dare to propose to men! By 1905 Stoker is not so unsympathetic as Mina. In a series of discussions between Stephen and her aunt Laetitia, Stephen avers the equal responsibility of men for pregnancies, even when they are unwanted. Moreover, she is horrified by the behavior of the women she sees at Oxford, both the proper women and the immoral, and she delivers a speech reminiscent of Hawthorne at the end of *The Scarlet Letter*: "Some day women must learn their own strength, as well as they have learned their own weakness. . . . It is bad women who seem to know men best, and to be able to influence them most. . . . Why should good women leave power to such as they? Why should good women's lives be wrecked for a convention? . . . The time will come when women will not be afraid to speak to men, as they should speak, as free and equal". . . .

While the moral of the book may seem to belie the import of these questions, they seem nevertheless to be sincere on Stoker's part as well as on Stephen's. Moreover, Stoker himself appears to ridicule women's education and role in Victorian society by using a conservative Aunt Laetitia as a negative role model, a woman who lost the love of her life as a result of not being able to speak out. Treating her satirically as the representative of proper Victorian society, the narrator comments, "In Miss Rowly's young days Political Economy was not a subject which ladies were supposed to understand. . . . As to physiology, it was simply a word in use amongst scientific men, and associated in ordinary minds with lint and scalpels and that new creation of man's mind 'anesthetic'--whatever it may mean. . . . 'Sex' or 'sexual' were not words which could be used lightly. . . . Why, in certain select circles, it was not becoming to even mention the word 'leg,' anything below the belt was spoken of as 'foot,' or 'feet'". . . . Stoker strikes a final blow against this manifestation of Victorianism when Stephen complains of her ignorance and Aunt Laetitia responds indignantly, "Ignorant! Of course you were ignorant. . . . Isn't it what we have all been devoting ourselves to effect ever since you were born". . . .

Again Stoker's major achievement in *The Man* is a richness of characterization which belies the facile moralizing, a depth apparent in the fact that, despite these repressive elements in her character, Laetitia Rowly is a shrewd and heroic woman whose protective and loving relationship with her niece is rendered in most moving terms. This complexity is rendered down to the least significant of relationships as well. In a discussion of one of Stephen's governesses, Miss Howard, the narrator comments that, while Stephen in her childish ignorance scorns the woman and therefore proposes to learn all she can the better to maintain her contempt of Miss Howard, she learns rather to respect and pity her.

The Man is strengthened also by Stoker's characteristically vivid rendering of natural scenes and of suspense. The scenes of rescue, both of Pearl and of Harold, through ripe for melodrama, are instead noteworthy for dramatic depictions of the natural forces, enlisting our hopes and sympathies for the characters as we await with our breath caught in our throats despite our awareness of the inevitable happy endings. It is worth pointing out with regard to the rescue scene, not only that it is a motif often found in Stoker's novels and linked to his own attempted rescue from the Thames of a suicide, but that Stoker's transatlantic travels were frequently besieged by terrific storms and that he almost lost his wife and son in a shipwreck. The autobiographical element in the novel is, indeed, strong, for the descriptions of Harold An Wolf, especially as the bearded giant, match those of Stoker. Like Stoker, too, Harold graduates from Trinity (Cambridge, though, not Dublin) with honors both in academics and athletics. Stoker's projection of himself into Harold may be most obvious in a rather bitter comment directed against the charming, debonair young man Leonard has grown into, the type of man who avoids the awkward stage of "men made in a large pattern." *The Man* enacts a sibling rivalry resolved by the triumph and rewarding of the heroic, self-sacrificing and virtuous brother who is the true man and who, consequently, wins the esteem and love of--ultimately--a womanly woman. Despite the simple plot, the heavy-handed and contradictory moralizing, and the occasional overtelling, *The Man* is a strongly rendered story. Its greatest strength being its characterizations, it is unique among Stoker's novels which typically depend on the mysterious or horrifying elements of their plots to exert their fascination. Stoker is capable of being an astute psychologist, especially perceptive regarding unconscious workings of the psyche: "The mind of an earnest man works quickly when once it has been set in motion. It is as though 'unconscious cerebration' were perpetually tilling the whole estate of one's mind ready for some possible harvest. Data hitherto almost unnoticed comes in on every side. Facts half remembered, half forgotten loom up large. Deductions leading to a definite end follow memories which had themselves seemed final". . . . While many of Stoker's most general speculations about the cosmos and human history and destiny are animistic and naive or just plain silly some are fascinating, as in the foreshadowing of the work of Claude Levi-Strauss: "Morals require heat of some kind. They are hardly indigenous to the animal, natural man; but rather to the civilized man. Man does not progress on raw food. The heat of cooking food may be the first propulsive force toward the Nirvana."

Despite the roughness, then, and the contradictions, or perhaps partially because of the latter, *The Man* is a compelling and rewarding novel, most fascinating among Stoker's romances and explicit in its representation of his preoccupations, especially the nature of women and the blurring of identity.

DANIEL PICK, "'TERRORS OF THE NIGHT': *DRACULA* AND 'DEGENERATION' IN THE LATE NINETEENTH CENTURY," *CRITICAL QUARTERLY* 30 (WINTER 1988), 84-85.

Where *Dracula* had turned on the vision of degeneration and corruption, Stoker's new novel, entitled *The Man* (1905), was a kind of 'positive eugenic' homily, the saga of the struggle to get good stock together, in order to achieve female beauty, pride and self-reliance (p. 3) and male strength, intelligence, bravery and determination (p. 4). Although petrified in an interminable, hackneyed romance, the text uttered prosaically and routinely the words 'sex' and 'sexuality', for as we are reminded, 'sex is sex all through. It is not, like whiskers or a wedding-ring, a garnishment of maturity' (p. 19). The very perception of sex and childhood had changed, it was suggested, from an ill-informed past where the infant was treated by adults as a kind of neuter object without feelings--'the baby was "it" to a man' (p. 18)--and, one might add, the representation of fear, desire and subjectivity had shifted in Stoker's own writing from the earlier novel where the vampire had constituted an ambiguous, threatening third person: 'I saw It--Him': 'He--It!' (*Dracula*, p. 85); 'It--like a man' (p. 84).

The coincidence of timing was again striking: 1905 was the year of Freud's *Three Essays on the Theory of Sexuality*. Stoker no doubt knew little or nothing of this, but he too charted masculinity, femininity and their discontents, through the destiny of the daughter of Stephen Norman, who has been brought up as a 'tom boy' and indeed christened Stephen herself, at the instigation of her dying mother ('let her be indeed our son! Call her by the name we both love!' p.

16), in order to console the father for his bitter disappointment at the gender of his child.

In *The Man* women are still shown to be constantly in danger not only from 'a certain [male] resentment' (p. 20) but also from themselves. Stephen's very physiognomy, we are told, suggests the prospect of 'some trouble which might shadow her whole after life' (p. 3); moreover her description is strangely reminiscent of the female vampires in the earlier text; she too has a trace of Eastern blood and a seductive mouth 'the voluptuous curves of the full, crimson lips' (p. 3), albeit no sharp, deadly teeth. The total effect is declared to be 'admirable', emblematic of a fine lineage: 'In her the various elements of her race seemed to have cropped out' (p. 3). She has a 'wide, fine forehead', 'black eyes', 'raven eyebrows', 'acquiline nose', a face which 'marked the high descent from Saxon through Norman'. The dangers are all internal, there are no monsters: the only 'wolf' in the story is not 'the wicked wolf that for half a day had paralysed London' (*Dracula*, p. 140), but in fact her saviour: Harold An Wolf. The crisis stems from Stephen's wilfulness and forwardness: she comes close to disaster in usurping the male role and proposing marriage to a worthless man only to be rejected and humiliated.

A hint of the new story had certainly been there in *Dracula* when Mina Murray speaks scathingly of the 'New Woman' writers who 'will some day start an idea that men and women should be allowed to see each other asleep before proposing or accepting' and even speculates that 'the New Woman won't condescend in future to accept; she will do the proposing herself' (p. 89), but in *The Man*, a certain style of indirectness and displacement has gone, as though the author is insisting that the veil of the vampire can now be seen through, leaving in place of the Count's castle and its surrounding wolves, only the occasional necessary sexual euphemism where total frankness still remained out of the question. We are presented with knock-about adventure, patriotism, long descriptions of the true qualities of fine men and women amongst the superior races, and various 'matter of fact' comments on the distance still to be traversed to dispel all remaining sexual mystery: 'Perhaps some day, when Science has grappled successfully with the unseen, the mysteries of sex will be open to men. . . . ' (p. 103). Through hundreds of pages, the protagonists battle with those enduring mysteries of sexuality, caught up in a drama of profound misunderstanding, a personal 'trial' culminating in shipwreck and temporary blindness. Before their final union, the hero and the heroine are to be overwhelmed by emotional frustration, remorse and the most painful confusions of identity.

Thus in 1905 *Dracula* was banished and replaced with a melodrama of psychological suffering, neurosis, cruelty and redemption, full of 'longings and outpourings of heart and soul and mind' (p. 104). Of course, vampires have returned in innumerable guises in cinema, theatre and writing since then. But at that moment for Stoker, there were no psychotic, 'undead' blood-sucking creatures needed. For the lovely, impetuous Stephen and the lovesick Harold there were only long and lonely private mental torments--'the tortures and terrors of the night' (p. 104).

Personal Reminiscences of Henry Irving

"TWO ACTORS," *ACADEMY AND LITERATURE* 71
(OCTOBER 13, 1906), 369-70.

MR. BRAM STOKER'S book on Sir Henry Irving has been eagerly expected. High hopes were entertained of it. It was known not only that the author was a close personal friend of the great actor, intimately associated with him during the whole of his career and so better able than any other living man to give an account of him in public and in private life, but that he was one who, if business matters claimed the most of his time and ability, was also an author with a fine gift of telling a story and impressing a picture on the mind. An ideal biographer, one would have imagined, possessing at once the knowledge of his subject, the power of expressing it and (if we may say so without offence) just that touch of Boswell about his admiration that is of such value in these cases. And the reminiscences, now we have them, prove anticipation to have been right in everything but the one point of the workmanship. This is not a book at all; it is a congeries, a collection, a scrap-album. It contains a mass of the very things which we hoped it would omit--pieces of gossip, records of people whom Irving met, of suppers and speeches. The only thing it spares us is press-notices, and those not entirely. Gossip is good, when it is Boswellian gossip and when the subject of the memoir has the tongue of a Johnson. Mr. Stoker's Boswellianism is of the wrong sort; it remembers and records trivial things which do not bring out the characteristics or the genius of his subject. And Sir Henry had not the tongue of a Johnson. His genius lay in other fields, in fields that cannot be covered by chronicles of small beer.

Had Mr. Stoker been content to cut out one half of his work--we refer especially to some uninteresting reminiscences of other people than Irving in vol. ii.--the remainder would have been a fitting monument of a great friendship with a great man. For when he comes to the point, so to speak, when he tells us what he alone could tell, the financial history of Sir Henry's management, the relations between Irving and Tennyson, Irving's attitude towards the modern dramatist, he is extremely interesting; and when he comes to tell of his own feelings for his chief, of the "turn of the tide" through accident and illness, of the last years and the death, he rises to what we expected of him. It is impossible to read unmoved. So just, so strong, so manly, so wise a tribute has never yet been paid to Sir Henry, and never will be again. Here, at last, the man lives for us in the pages of his friend; here, at last, we catch the sense of his greatness, which makes all the gossip and chatter seem dustier and dryer than before.

Three things in the book are of importance: the account of Sir Henry's views on his art; the financial history of his management and his attitude towards the contemporary dramatist. To take the last first. It was often said that Irving did nothing for the modern drama. Mr. Stoker shows that, besides the plays by living authors which he produced, he accepted and paid for more than twenty. If it be objected that none of these plays were really representative of modern movements in drama, there are two pertinent replies possible. In the first place, there was in Sir Henry's prime no modern movement worth forwarding; in the second, he could no more be blamed for not forwarding it than a Porson could be blamed for not writing a novel. It was not there that his genius lay; and what his genius did for the stage we need not now point out. The financial side of the story will clear up many doubtful points and dissipate many calumnies, and Mr. Stoker's chapter on the philosophy of acting and other references to Sir Henry's views make it plain that he was not on the side of Diderot in the great dispute. We should have liked, by the way, to have seen more emphasis laid on a side of his work which entitled Sir Henry, quite as much as his acting, to the name of artist--his productions. Charles Kean had done something in that direction. It remained for Irving to establish once for all that the play was the thing; that it must be regarded as a whole; that every line and every movement, even the smallest, of every character, must be subordinated to the single effect. In this he showed himself indeed a great artist. All the Royal Academy assistance in the world would not have availed him much, had he not owned the master-mind to throw all into scale together.

We have taken objection to some of Mr. Stoker's gossip, and feel it only fair to add that the rest of it is very interesting gossip. Tennyson, according to Mr. Stoker, who is generous in his admirations, had in him all the elements of a great dramatist, and only needed technical knowledge of the stage. Irving was always asking him for new plays, and on one occasion suggested a play on Dante. "A fine subject!" replied Tennyson. "But where is the Dante to write it?" Had Sir Henry laid that reply to heart, what disappointment he and all of us would have been spared a few years later! We hear, too, all about Sir Henry's own adaptation of *Becket* for the stage; and the admiration of poet and actor each for the other appears to have been very great. The visits to Freshwater must have been amongst the pleasantest of recollections. We find Tennyson reading aloud, and Irving telling him he would have made a fine actor; Tennyson telling stories, and opening his mind to Mr. Stoker in a way which few have enjoyed. Mr. Stoker quotes something that Tennyson said to him not long before his death:

You know I don't believe in an eternal hell, with an All-merciful God. I believe in the All-merciful God! It would be better otherwise that men should believe they are only ephemera!

There are good stories, too, not a few--of the stuffed horse in the railway horse-box; of Mr. Stoker's reply to a happy father who offered the use of his own child for the baby in *Henry VIII*, which concluded:

As the play will probably run for a considerable time, your baby would grow. It might, therefore, be necessary to provide another baby. To this you and your wife might object--at short notice.

"IRVING AS MAN AND ACTOR," *NATION* 83 (OCTOBER 18, 1906), 334-35.

"For my own part the work which I have undertaken in this book is to show future minds something of Henry Irving, as he was to me." So says Bram Stoker, in his preface to these two bulky volumes of personal reminiscences, and no one, after reading them, can deny that to this extent at least he has fully and ably accomplished his purpose. Of Irving, as man and manager--a personality potent, intellectual, indomitable, ambitious, honorable, tender, imperious, picturesque, and fascinating--he gives a most attractive and vital portrait; a portrait, moreover, whose truthfulness is not attested solely by the manifest sincerity of his own enthusiastic affection and somewhat perfervid Celtic oratory, but by the plain record of indisputable facts, the wonderful sum of Irving's labors and accomplishments, the extraordinary position which he won for himself in the highest literary, artistic, and social worlds, the steadfastness with which he pursued high ideals, and the esteem and reverence in which he was held in the hearts of his friends and subordinates. In these respects the book is full, accurate, and interesting almost from the first page to the last, in spite of much matter that is not new or strictly relevant; but it will bring disappointment to all those who try to find in it any illuminating details of Irving's growth and development as an actor, any definition of the methods of the new school of acting which he is said, somewhat arbitrarily, to have originated. . . any reference to his peculiar histrionic limitations, or the notorious defects and mannerisms of his style, or any attempt to discriminate between the comparative excellence of his different impersonations. With Mr. Stoker each new character is but an illustration of a new perfection. So many parts, so many masterpieces.

The attitude of Mr. Stoker, indeed, towards his chief is always that of a worshipper, although never that of a sycophant. A strong and clever man himself, good scholar, and noted athlete, he was dominated by Irving as by an hypnotic spell. He tells how, in the days of their first acquaintance, Irving's recital of Hood's "Eugene Aram"--an interpretation of weird and thrilling power--made him hysterical and demonstrated a bond of emotional sympathy between him and the actor, which ripened quickly into an intimate and lifelong friendship, of which this book is a monument, equally honorable to both. Rarely has a magnanimous chief had more loving or faithful service or any executive officer more justly earned the title of right-hand man.

Unquestionably Irving had genius--if not of the highest order--but he had in much larger measure that quality which is said to be allied to it--the infinite capacity for taking pains. Mr. Stoker's volumes are packed with instances of his indefatigable attention to even the minutest details of his comprehensive art. No labor was too excessive for him, no cost too great, in the execution of his plans. Although he had a large and capable staff, nothing was done without his personal supervision. Before undertaking a classic play he studied the principal authorities bearing upon the subject, and then formulated in his own mind the scene plan which he required. In preparing "Romeo and Juliet," after having employed the best available authority to design the costumes, he rejected them all, and supplied others, which he had himself collected from ancient books and prints. He consulted an army surgeon concerning the proper way of lifting wounded or dead men. He practised various poses at odd moments with personal friends. Days and nights he spent in drilling the supers for the frays between the factions of the Capulets and Montagus. When no satisfactory music could be procured he engaged Sir Julius Benedict to write it for him. All stage groupings were in accordance with his personal directions. In the famous church scene of "Much Ado"--which was never seen in its full perfection in New York--he went for inspiration to the cathedrals of Seville and Burgos, both for architecture and costumes; and in order that all might be correct, and no religious prejudice offended, he asked an eminent Roman Catholic prelate to supervise the accessories. It was during a visit to Morocco and the Levant that he studied effects for his Shylock, saying afterwards that he had never had any clear notion of what the Jew merchant ought to be until he saw him in his own habitat. Long before this he had begun to study from the life. His Digby Gant in "Two Roses," one of his earliest great successes, was a reproduction of that picturesque adventurer, the Chevalier Wikoff, well known in his day on both sides of the Atlantic. The mimetic ability which Irving showed in this impersonation was remarkable.

How comprehensive was his conception of any general effect is shown in an incident which occurred during an early rehearsal of "Macbeth." Sir Arthur Sullivan had written the incidental music and was present to lead the orchestra. In an important scene Irving stopped him. "It is fine as music," he said, "but for our purpose no good at all." Then he proceeded by means of swaying gestures, motions of the hands and arms, and queer vocal sounds to indicate the rhythmical effect that he needed. Sir Arthur, greatly to his credit, caught the idea, and there and then made the needed alterations. Again in preparing his spectacle of "Faust" he thought out the whole color scheme of the wonderful Bocken scene, in reference to the dominant note of his own scarlet custome, before putting the artists to work upon it, and he was the practical inventor of the striking tableau of poised angels in the last act. Another instance of his minute care and almost limitless ingenuity may be found in the devices by which he made his tall, gaunt figure assume the semblance of the short and stout Napoleon in Sardou's flashy

"Madame Sans Gene." The details are too long to print. Suffice it to say that all kinds of tailor trickery were employed, that the furniture was built out of its proper proportions, and the tallest performers brought into contrast with the Emperor. All this, of course, has nothing to do with acting, but is significant as an illustration of skilful and conscientious stage management. . . . It is lamentable to think that the almost priceless accumulation of scenery and costumes, representing a quarter of a century of munificent and artistic management, was swept away by fire almost in an instant. This blow was the turning point in Irving's fortunes, and indirectly led to the anxieties and labors which shortened his life.

More than half of Mr. Stoker's work is devoted to the social side of Irving's life, and this part might have been shortened with advantage. A man may be known by his friends, but not necessarily by his acquaintance. But it is a fact that the social position of Irving is unique in the history of the stage. Neither Garrick nor Macready ever stood on such terms with so many leaders in politics, literature, science, and the arts. . . . He elevated the stage not only as an art but as a profession. Prime ministers and archbishops, diplomats and professors, princes and potentates, poets, painters, sculptors, and authors of high degree, were proud to be in his company. Mr. Gladstone had his special corner on his stage, Browning loved to discuss Shakespere with him. . . Tennyson held him in so much reverence that he gave him a free hand in relation to his noble "Becket." Queen Victoria honored him, Lady Burdett Coutts loved him, and Presidents of the United States entertained him. All this and much more may be learned in Mr. Stoker's facile and interesting gossip.

But perhaps, with all his successes and glories, nothing so much became him in life as the manner of leaving it. Mr. Stoker tells, very pathetically, how, when shattered in health and strength and almost overcome by cruel mishaps and still more cruel mistakes, he, dying by inches, yet struggled on valiantly to recover fortune, serving the public literally with his last breath. . . . Very pretty, too, are the stories of his life-long love for the comedian Toole and the fraternal friendship between him and Ellen Terry. Mr. Stoker has indeed paid a tribute to his dead friend which is likely to keep him long in remembrance as the greatest manager and one of the most impressive actors of his time, a splendid host, a charming companion, and most virile man, one who not only achieved success, but deserved it.

"THE DRAMA: MR. STOKER'S IRVING," *TIMES* 5 (OCTOBER 19, 1906), 353.

It has been somewhat churlishly said that in Mr. Bram Stoker's "Personal Reminiscences of Henry Irving". . . there is a little too much of Mr. Bram Stoker. Nobody says that in Boswell's Johnson there is too much Boswell. The friendship between Boswell and Johnson was neither so close nor so prolonged as the friendship between Mr. Stoker and Irving. Nor was Boswell anything like so notable a figure in the great world as Mr. Stoker, who at one time or another must have known pretty well everybody worth knowing in the United Kingdom, to say nothing of the United States. Why, Mr. Stoker once turned a Grand Duke off the premises! Is there another man in London who can boast of such an achievement as that? "His diction charmed me," says Mr. Stoker, but nevertheless his Serene Highness--if the vulgar expression may be pardoned--was "chucked." Mr. Stoker's own diction was fully up to the Grand Ducal level. "I trust you will pardon me, Sir, in case my request to leave the stage may have seemed too imperative or in any way wanting in courtesy." The whole conversation reads like one of the more ornate pages of Landor. . . . Soon afterwards Irving took the Lyceum on his own account, and Mr. Stoker became his acting manager and remained his close friend, confidential adviser, factotum, and watchdog, for nearly thirty years. They had a great time together. The theatre became not only an artistic force but a social rendezvous such as had never before been known in the history of the English or any other stage. Of the artistic side of the matter Mr. Stoker has naturally much to say, but little that is new or valuable. For that side of the matter we of this generation have all been able to observe and appraise for ourselves. From Mr. Stoker impartial criticism of Irving as an actor was not to be expected. His temperament no less than the peculiarity of his position forbid it. Indeed, his excursions into criticism are the weakest part of his book. It seems that he began his career in Dublin as--among other things--a dramatic critic. The extracts which he prints from his "notices" are not likely to inspire readers with any poignant regret for his early abandonment of that calling. He is at some pains to expound his idol's theory of the actor's art--which is mainly the familiar theory of "dual consciousness"--and the exposition makes anything but illuminating or even lively reading. After all, if Mr. Stoker had been, what he quite obviously is not, a born critic, he would never have become the excellent acting manager that he was. In treating of his proper business, the commercial and social side of the Lyceum, he is always interesting. A poor critic may be an invaluable bookkeeper and an admirable majordomo. And it is for the information which Mr. Stoker supplies in these two capacities that most readers, we fancy, will turn eagerly to his book.

"It must be remembered," he says, "that a theatre, and especially a popular one, is a centre of great curiosity. Every one wants to know all about it, and curiosity-mongers if they cannot discover facts invent them." Mr. Stoker is the one man who can give the facts, and he gives them in an abundance which ought to satisfy the most curious. He tells you exactly how many pounds sterling the Lyceum held at this and that date. It is the history of an enormous business undertaking, laid bare in all its details. . . . At the end came a financial crash, and Mr. Stoker gives you all the figures of that, too. (You remember that he got honours at Dublin in Pure Mathematics.) But the enormous social vogue of the Lyceum was the great thing, the unprecedented thing. In the late eighties, Irving desired to give a garden party to all his friends, and bade Mr. Stoker make out a list. He had to stop--halfway through--at five thousand. Mr. Stoker prints a thousand names as a mere selection of those who used to be invited to Lyceum entertainment behind the scenes. He tells of banquets and convivial suppers by the score. It reads sometimes like an account of one of the later Roman Emperors--like one long panorama of gorgeous display. The viands are of the choicest, the band is always playing, and the crowd is always cheering without. Occasionally Mr. Stoker would snatch a moment to quote poetry to Tennyson or to discuss Home Rule with Gladstone, or to hobnob with Roosevelt. "The Chief," of course, was not far off. It was a dazzling time for both. Then came Irving's closing years, years of discouragement, ill-health, stoic endurance--a most pathetic story as Mr. Stoker tells it. Many readers, however, will hardly regret getting away from the blaze of glory to the more intimate and human interest of the last chapters, which in our judgment are Mr. Stoker's best chapters. His sincere and manly nature--which includes, in the best sense, something of the childlike--here shines forth, his writing drops all traces of the prize for Oratory and the Grand Ducal conversations and becomes simple, strong, and moving. The book may often enough provoke a good-humoured smile, but it is of first-rate interest for the light it throws on one who was, in his line, a great man, and none the less welcome because it incidentally records the entirely honourable career of that man's faithful friend.

"SIR HENRY IRVING," *BLACKWOOD'S MAGAZINE* 180 (NOVEMBER 1906), 613-21.

Mr Bram Stoker's two volumes, appropriately and copiously illustrated, contain not a little that is interesting. The glimpses given behind the scenes, for example, will fascinate many who may have failed to realise the amount of labour and ingenuity required for the production of a play in the last quarter of the nineteenth century. But, upon the whole, we are afraid that he has missed his chance. For many years he was Sir Henry Irving's acting manager and right-hand man, both on and off the stage. He was the recipient of his confidences, his accomplice in policy, the constant and ever-present witness of his failures and his triumphs. And if his privileges were exceptional, so also was the personality of his hero; for upon a strongly marked personality depended the whole of Irving's art and the whole of his conception of that art. Perhaps Mr Stoker stood too close to his subject to see him in a true perspective--perhaps he may have taken pen in hand a little too soon after the actor's death. But, whatever the explanation, the fact remains that a great opportunity has been lost. Mr Stoker has failed to endow his sketch with life. The outline is conventional where it is not vague, and the filling in shows a decided want of the sense of proportion. "The veil which covers the mystery of individual nature" (the phrase is Mr Stoker's own) has not been lifted. And thus the result must be pronounced disappointing, even granting that expectation soared a little too high.

There are, in truth, many blemishes in the book with which a critic might find fault and yet come short of a Rhadamanthine standard of justice. It is too long by far, and contains much that is barely germane to the matter. We may cite as an instance of irrelevancy the narrative of the author's juvenile adventures among the works of Walt Whitman, and his subsequent correspondence and intercourse with that bard: all very interesting, no doubt, in its proper place, but entirely beside the purpose here. We are occasionally, indeed, driven to ask ourselves who, after all, is the chief personage in the story, and to speculate whether Sir Henry Irving's 'Personal Reminiscences of Bram Stoker,' if written on the principles on which this work is constructed, would not, in all probability, have told us considerably more about Sir Henry Irving than at the present moment we can profess to know.

Nor is this diffuseness atoned for by any charms or graces of style. Mr Stoker's vocabulary is not particularly well-found, and the epithets "subtle" and "masterly" appear to mark the high-tide of his efforts to express admiration. Strange bastard adjectives, like "basic," "pivotal," and "typal," drop every now and then from his pen; and the abuse to which the innocent little word "such" is subjected might move a fiend to tears. "I was thus able," he writes. . . "to direct public attention, so far as my paper could effect it, where in my mind such was required." This is but one out of at least a dozen instances of a usage dear to the soul of the country reporter. . . .

Again, Mr Stoker's incidental reflections upon life and art are neither very profound nor very original. Print and paper were not needed to certify us that "hissing hurts [an actor's] self-esteem," that, to be sure being an organ notoriously susceptible of much less overt injury. Irving himself only read expurgated criticisms: criticisms "filtered through the judgment of his friends," as Mr Stoker puts it. In a rather laboured and obscure disquisition of the philosophy of acting, Mr Stoker remarks that "the wasp and the viper, the cuttle-fish and the stinging ray work to different ends from the sheep and the sole, the pheasant and the turtle. . . .

But, for all his excursions into the obvious, we are not sure that we do not prefer Mr Stoker as a philosopher to Mr Stoker as a *raconteur*. Some of his "yarns" are amusing, but most of the stories which help to pad out the work (including, we think, all the Scotch ones) are neither new nor entertaining. No joke is too well worn for Mr Stoker; his is the enviable secret of perpetual youth. That is why, perhaps, he seems to believe in the "progress" of the arts and of everything else. He hints that a knowledge of the "influence of worms on the outer layer of the structure of the world" has materially modified the public taste in acting. He is nothing if not up to date--never more than a day and a half behind the fair. He compliments Mr Whistler on having been "before his time--long before it. He did fine work and created a new public taste." Purblind and obstinate reactionaries, like ourselves, who cling to the view (for which there is high authority) that the thing which was is the thing which shall be, and that there is no new thing under the sun, have naturally some difficulty in understanding this frame of mind. We are not in the habit of summarising our opinion of artists or works of art in terms of chronology. We do not read into the label which bears their date a connotation disparaging or the reverse in proportion to their priority in time. "Medieval" has never commended itself to us as a term of withering contempt any more than of exaggerated and indiscriminate eulogy. But if we were to adopt this shorthand method of classification, we should set down Mr Stoker's general mental attitude, without the slightest hesitation, not as early-Victorian, but as pre-Noachian. And that, possibly, is why immense popularity is assured both for his jests and for his philosophy at any "large and fashionable luncheon-party" in Chicago.

The force of these and similar animadversions is undeniable, yet we own that Mr Stoker's work has exercised a species of fascination over us, and that we would willingly pardon a thousand faults more heinous than any to be discovered in its pages. It is not only that, as we have indicated, there are many passages of undoubted interest to the ordinary reader. The secret of its spell lies in the unstudied fidelity with which it reproduced the atmosphere of thought and feeling characteristic of the microcosm with which it is concerned--that singular region, so remote, so secluded, so far aloof from the common herd of men. There for close on thirty years has Mr Stoker lived and moved and had his being; he has snuffed its exhilarating breezes; he has revelled in its distinctive exhalations. Is it wonderful that his book should smell, not of the lamp but of "the lamps"? Is it wonderful if he is so steeped in its mysterious influences that for him the universe outside has to all intents and purposes ceased to exist?

It is a region of stupendous and amazing vanity, a region in which we count the world well lost so that our name be printed in large capital letters. It is a region in which success is anxiously desired and laboriously pursued, but in which success turns to Dead Sea fruit unless accompanied by an intangible something known as "recognition."

It is a region in which we speak (half pompously, half facetiously) of the King as His Most Gracious Majesty King Edward VII., R. and I. (a reminiscence this, surely, of the gas-lustre); in which we cannot mention the Rt. Hon. William Ewart Gladstone without calling him "that great Englishman"; and in which, if we have occasion to refer to a self-made man, we immediately ejaculate, "all honour to him." It is a region in which we habitually keep late hours long after we are old enough to know better. It is a region in which we take Mr Caine (the popular novelist) quite seriously, and sympathetically note that when he has finished a novel he is as exhausted as a woman after childbirth.

It is a region in which, when we have recited "The Dream of Eugene Aram," immensely strong men--men who had played for years in the University football team--men who had edited a newspaper and had exercised their spare time in many ways--men who represented in their own persons something of that aim of University education, *mens sana in corpore sano*--burst out into something like a violent fit of hysterics. It is a region in which we thereupon present them with our photograph dated, signed, and inscribed "My dear friend So-and-so. God bless you! God bless you!!" It is a region in which, if our playhouse prospers, it becomes celebrated as a national asset, and in which, if we entertain distinguished foreigners to supper, we are said to aid the popularity of our country among the nations of the world.

It is a region of heartfelt *au revoirs,* of pent-up enthusiasm bursting forth like a storm, of roars of applause, of cheers, detonating cheers, full-throated Anglo-Saxon cheers, or else cheers which somewhat resemble a May shower, for they are sudden, fierce, and short. It is a region of many public banquets and multitudinous entertainments in our honour; a region in which, if the drama is ignored in the toast-list, something of a *faux pas* is felt to have been committed and is much commented on.

It is a region of addresses: of addresses presented by our fellow-actors in beautiful caskets of gold and crystal; of addresses presented by vice-chancellors in delightful and carefully worded speeches. It is a region in which a public address (no ordinary one) is presented to us signed by all the great public officials both of the city and of the country. . . . It is a region where, throughout that ceremony, the Lord-Lieutenant makes a point of remaining in his box, so that he may be seen to be present.

It is a region in which we are always receiving honours "at the hands of" some public or quasi-public body, whereby our calling is elevated in the eyes of the world. It is a region in which we deliver lectures or receive honorary degrees at ancient seats of learning, and in which a weird figure called "Dr" Jowett, alleged to be a supreme authority on Plato, flits across the bewildering scene. It is a region in which a mayor, or vice-chancellor, or provost seems ever to brood over us, extending a cordial welcome on behalf of the community, while Leading Citizens hang respectfully on his every word.

It is a region of which inane and dismal practical jokes form the principal diversion: the region whose abstract and far from brief chronicle is the theatrical gossip page of 'The Era': the region whose perpetual and immortal sovereign is Vincent Crummles: in a word, it is the stage.

And it is this region and no other (as Mr Barrie would say) which Mr Stoker has displayed to our sympathetic and admiring gaze with a native simplicity and a total want of humour possible only to an Irishman.

Mr Stoker, as we have hinted, is perhaps at his weakest and least convincing when he discourses of the art of acting and would fain elucidate the player's mystery. Such quasi-psychological discussions are almost always unsatisfactory. Every man must reach the goal in his own way. Irving refused to accept Diderot's Paradox, as he had a perfect right to do; but the fragments of his own theory here presented on a string of exposition by Mr Stoker are not particularly illuminating. All theorists would agree that intelligence, study, forethought, preparation, are indispensable to good acting, which is not composed of a series of "happy thoughts"; and we doubt if Irving's phrase about "passing a character through one's own mind" means anything more. The fact of "dual consciousness," on which Mr Stoker dwells, is not the rare or novel phenomenon he seems to suppose, being familiar enough to any one with the least practice in public speaking. But we are not to invite the reader into this trackless maze. Our purpose is to glance at the characteristics which distinguished Irving as an actor, and to trace what services, if any, he rendered to the British stage during an arduous and in many respects brilliant career. In this investigation, we fear, we can expect little or no assistance from our author.

One thing must be sorrowfully confessed, and that is that Irving did more than any man of his time to foster and indulge the depraved taste of the British public for "realism" and spectacle. If he did not descend a sulphur mine at the risk of his life to make sure that his audience got the "real thing," it was merely because a sulphur mine did not happen to fit into any of his plays. No one, of course, will maintain that Macbeth should be arrayed in a suit of tweeds, or the uniform of a Highland regiment. But a point is reached at which archaeology becomes irrelevant, for the minutest attention to accuracy will never make the average "super" less absurd than he intrinsically is, any more than a coat of black paint all over will assist the most conscientious of tragedians to exhibit his conception of Othello. The point at which sumptuousness of decoration becomes merely distracting is reached much earlier. These boundary-marks Irving systematically overstepped. He paused not to consider whether a drama may not be overloaded by the accumulation of unessential accessories; and, paradoxical as it sounds, he probably did more to expel the Shakespearean drama from the British theatre by his gorgeous revivals than he did to prolong or renew its languishing existence.

When he entered upon the management of the Lyceum, nothing would serve him but to replace the equipment found sufficient for "Hamlet" five years before with costly new scenery and dresses. "The taste of the public had so improved and their education so progressed," is Mr Stoker's explanation. But the appetite for senseless show, once pampered, grows like others by what it feeds on, so that a few seasons later unparalleled lime-light effects, and real broken heads among the rival factions of Capulet and Montague, were invoked to carry off a grotesque Romeo, a mature Juliet, and a robust Mercutio whose voice (it has been said) possessed all the delicacy and charm of a brass band. Then came "Much Ado about Nothing," in many ways a pleasing and memorable performance. The Lyceum cult was in its zenith. Not to fall down and worship was to be set down as a sort of offender against grace. You went to the theatre in much the same spirit in which you were supposed to go to church, and you went to see *inter alia* a representation of the interior of a church on the stage. When you got there, you found Shakespeare transposed and adorned with a tag of the manager's devising--for, as Mr Stoker euphemistically has it, "modern conditions" (whatever that may mean) "necessitate now and again the concentration of ideas, the emphasis of purposes." Sir Henry Irving had just as much and just as little scruple in cutting and carving upon Shakespeare to suit his own ends as Colley Cibber or any other actor-manager.

The quality of the play in hand made no difference. Its goodness or badness afforded an equally valid pretext for lavish decoration. "The story of Juliet and her Romeo," says Mr Stoker, "is one which not only lends itself to, but demands, picturesque setting." "'Macbeth,'" he remarks again, "is a play that really requires the aid of artistic completeness. Its diction is so lordly, so poetical, so searching in its introspective power, that it lifts the mind to an altitude which requires and expects some corresponding elevation of the senses." On the other hand, an indifferent piece like "Ravenswood" required something to set it off, and Irving looked upon it as "needing all the help it could get." The craze for elaborate mounting culminated in the extravaganza of "Faust," with its Brocken scene and its childish apparition of pantomime angels, of which Mr Stoker declares that "never was seen so complete, so subtle, so divine a vision on the stage." "Faust" was a great success both in London and in the provinces, but it exercised, we think, a baleful influence alike on the ideals and on the fortunes of the manager. We believe him to have been strong enough, had he had the will, to lead public taste along a nobler and safer path. Yet he never dispensed even with the ridiculous vision of the sledge in the snow in "The Bells." That he "helped his audience to think," may or may not be true. Certain it is that he would leave nothing to their imagination.

And this was one of the defects in his acting--a defect which the lapse of time did nought to remedy. All the i's must be dotted, all the t's crossed. "Business" was the very breath of his nostrils. What matter though it were irrelevant and inappropriate so long as it was "clever"? To describe his acting as "natural," in contradistinction to the style and method of the old school, seems to us a curious misuse of words. He was invariably stagey, and he was "always Irving." So much did he rely upon his own individuality that he took no pains (on the boards, at all events) to pronounce his native language with even moderate propriety or correctness. The words of "Macbeth" are tolerably familiar to all playgoers; but, on the last occasion on which we saw him represent that hero, some years ago, his utterance resembled an inarticulate sort of bellow, and it was with difficulty that we followed his speeches. These characteristics told against him more in some pieces than in others. In melodrama, and in all parts where there was scope for the portrayal of some decided eccentricity or of a grim sardonic humour, he was excellent. In "The Bells" he was powerful, or at least used once to be; in "The Lyons Mail" he found his true element; and we believe he was admirable in "Jingle" and "Macaire." His method also well suited that glorified melodrama, "Richard III." All the grimacing and winking and leering were in harmony with the part of the hunchback, as they were with that of his brother monarch "Louis XI." His "Hamlet," too, had many striking qualities, and some of the earlier extravagances (such as the scribbling on his "tables" raised above his head and supported on the wall of the castle) were judiciously dropped. True, "Hamlet" is perhaps the best of all "acting plays," and the Prince of Denmark is a character with so many aspects and patient of so many different interpretations, that only a dullard can fail in it completely. But Irving is probably entitled to the distinction of having been the best--shall we say, the only?--Hamlet of his generation in England.

What he really lacked as an actor was repose and reticence--the power of self-suppression. To say with Mr Stoker, in his own grandiloquent way, that "the Irving school of acting" became "a part of the nation's glory," is merely to talk nonsense: there was no "Irving school" of acting, and there never could be. For with all his great gifts he did but succeed in perpetuating the restless tradition of the British stage, in obedience to which the comic-countryman makes believe to catch a blue-bottle during Mrs Crummles's heroics, so as to attract the notice of the London manager. Mr Stoker admits that as Napoleon in "Madame Sans-Gene," Irving was too big for the play, and was "out of the picture," as the expression goes. He blames the playwrights, rather unfairly perhaps, for he has omitted to blame the author of "Cymbeline" in offering an identical criticism on Irving's Iachimo. Whatever share of censure may justly be allotted to the dramatist, the player must always take the larger proportion on his own shoulders. If he cannot sufficiently divest himself of a dominating personality, if he cannot reduce himself at need to insignificance, if he cannot withdraw into his shell, the less actor he. Innocent as we are of a sound convention in the matter, and destitute of anything in the shape of a "school" of acting at all, it is not easy to see how this elementary truth is to be inculcated in the members of "the profession" in this country. From a municipal theatre we hope nothing; for a municipal theatre would merely wallow in pathos, jobbery, and the ratepayers' money to an extent that even Poplar and West Ham, in their most inspired and fortunate moments, have not yet been able to attain to.

We set eyes on Sir Henry Irving for the last time in the precincts of a venerable Court of Justice, where he was about to give evidence. There was the tall, stooping, emaciated figure in the short black coat; there were the fine though care-worn features set in a frame of long grizzled hair, and surmounted by a black silk hat with a prodigiously broad flat brim and a prodigiously tall cylindrical crown. As he stalked to and fro among the mob of clients and solicitors and members of the bar, he seemed, in a once familiar phrase, to bring the very scent of the Strand--of the heart of the old theatrical Bohemia--over the footlights. He made an admirable witness--clear, logical, and self-possessed; his manner was perfect, and he was always ready with the right answer under cross-examination, though much too wise to indulge in sharp retort or pert recrimination. Very rarely indeed has a man of his abilities and intellectual power adorned the British stage. The glories of the Lyceum--the entertainments, the banquets, the receptions, the supper-parties, chronicles by Mr Stoker with a particularity which would be pathetic were it not monotonous--have long since departed; but the adversity that dogged his later years developed a latent fortitude and resolution of soul which might well have been sapped by a series of prosperity and adulation. Truly, if the successful actor is the petted child of fortune, the goddess balances her favours with cruel blows. Irving was not immune from the weaknesses and foibles apparently inseparable from the calling of his choice. But, having selected his walk in life, he was the soul of loyalty to his brethren from the greatest to the least. He was never a hanger-on of "society," though some members of "society" were eager to hang on to him; and he would have instinctively revolted from that last meanness which besets the histrionic mind--the trading professionally upon the practice of the domestic virtues in private life. He could wish no higher praise than that, in his own peculiar line, he was a great actor; and it will probably be long before his true niche in our theatre is filled.

F.G. BETTANY, "REMINISCENCES OF IRVING," *BOOKMAN* 31 (NOVEMBER 1906), 92-94.

It is a curious feature of Mr. Bram Stoker's "Personal Reminiscence of Henry Irving," a book the chief charm of which depends on its wealth of anecdote, that the best stories it contains are concerned, not with the actor himself, but with distinguished members of his circle of acquaintance and friends. Scattered through the pages of these two volumes with generous profusion are tales of Gladstone,

Disraeli, Tennyson, Whitman, Burton, Toole, and a host of painters, composers, actors, men of letters and men of affairs who delighted in doing honour to the acknowledged head of the theatrical profession; but for any memorable *bon mot* of Irving's own, any instance of his caustic humour, any anecdote throwing light on the less obvious traits of his character, or revealing such foibles as make even great men human and therefore loveable, readers of Mr. Stoker's memoirs will search very nearly in vain. Henry Irving, indeed, throughout his old comrade's record is uniformly made to figure as public man, and is scarcely ever allowed to show himself in undress. Of Irving the most strenuous of histrionic artists, the most conscientious of theatrical *entrepreneurs*, the most princely of entertainers, we are given as complete a description as could well be desired; but on the man as he unbosomed himself to his intimates, or his conversation during those midnight suppers and those long talks till dawn, which he persisted in keeping up till the very last years of his life, on the little weaknesses and eccentricities and perversities which must have helped to constitute his individuality, the friend who could have told us most preserves an obstinate and almost unbroken silence.

Mr. Bram Stoker's opportunities for observing and knowing his "chief" were well nigh unlimited; for thirty years he held the post of Irving's acting-manager. He saw the famous player daily, he sat up with him nightly, he was consulted on every question of policy; he knew, till the syndicate took over the Lyceum, every detail of the actor-manager's business--he was, in fact, entirely in Irving's confidence; and yet, now that he has come to set down his impressions, he fails somehow to bring us into close contact with the object of his lifelong admiration. In part, no doubt, the blurred outlines of Mr. Stoker's portrait of his friend may be accounted for by the very ardour of his devotion. So anxious has he been to give no offence or pain to the living friends and relatives of the dead, so eager to avoid the faintest suspicion of disloyalty, that he has confined himself to giving a merely external view of his hero, and has adopted towards him a tone of what becomes, in the end, too persistent and unwearied eulogy. A morbid dread, that is to say, of committing any possible indiscretion has prevented him from adding those little personal touches which would have given colour and contrast to his "appreciation." But there is another explanation of the more disappointing side of Mr. Stoker's reminiscences. Quite unconsciously he is for ever insisting on sharing the stage with his chief; "we" is his favourite pronoun, and a malicious critic might discover some amusement in counting up the number of times in which the phrase "Irving and I" occurs in this narrative. It is the natural fault of an acting-manger who identifies himself with his "governor," and is the more excusable in this instance, inasmuch as Mr. Stoker's chaotic notes seem obviously to have been expanded from his private diary; but, at the same time, it illustrates clearly enough the limitations of his biographical method. Debarred by a surely too fastidious scrupulousness from divulging the more confidential portions of Irving's table-talk, the alternative left to Mr. Stoker was to fall back upon the official life he shared with the great actor. So it is that the only stories, as a rule, in which Irving has his part treat of humorous happenings at rehearsals, misadventures behind the scenes, or the perils of touring--the commonplaces of every player's experience. So it is that the only secrets here published, apart from certain distressing details of the actor's physical state in later life, affect the finances or the stage-management of the Lyceum. So it is that Mr. Stoker in this book of his shows us only that side of Irving which he "faced the world with," not the other that he reserved for his friends.

How wonderfully Irving appealed to the imagination of his contemporaries, posterity will easily gather from the mere list of notable persons whom Mr. Stoker is able to mention as staunch supporters of his chief. Among those names stands first, perhaps, that of Tennyson. There are no more interesting pages in Mr. Stoker's reminiscences than those in which he describes the delicate and tactful way in which Irving soothed the poet's susceptibilities over the re-arrangement and "cutting" of the text of his plays. Tennyson gave his adapter *carte blanche*, and one of his last remarks as he lay dying expressed full confidence in Irving. . . .

One of the strangest characteristics of Mr. Stoker's reminiscences is the omission of nearly all reference to Irving's chief stage-supporters. Miss Genevieve Ward, whose finest impersonation, that of Volumnia in "Coriolanus," was curiously enough, not presented in Irving's own revival, obtains adequate mention. . . . Ellen Terry, of course, that perfect embodiment of the very spirit of gaiety, never quite happily matched with Irving's flamboyant and rather macabre genius, obtains the notice that is her due. Irving was not always her admirer, but once he was converted, his enthusiasm for her was unbounded. . . . Ellen Terry was Irving's greatest, perhaps his only woman friend--it was to her he carried first the news of his knighthood; but there was another friend whom he loved with an affection almost passing the love of woman--John Lawrence Toole. Of Toole it is happier to think in his merry, unstricken days, and of those Mr. Stoker has a most delightful and surely new tale. . . .

Happy stories indeed abound in these volumes, especially in the chapters which give some account of Irving's lavish hospitality. So vivid are Mr. Stoker's sketches of the more famous of his "governor's" guests that he almost calls up before our eyes and ears Sarah Bernhardt railing at stage tradition and hurling out over the supper-table "A bas la tradition!" Barnay getting worried over the term "fluffy," and saying in piteous tones,"Flof! fluoof-fluff! Alas, I know him not"; Gounod sobbing aloud over the last verse of his favourite song, "O that we two were maying!" and replying to a question, "Whom do you think the best composer?" with "Mendelssohn! Mendelssohn is the best!" yet, then adding after a pause, "But there is only one Mozart". . . .

These were the days of the zenith of Irving's career; the black days were to follow. There were several causes of the change. First, though Mr. Stoker does not even hint as much, a loss of managerial judgment. Next, a stroke of sheer ill-luck in the accident which cut short on its very first night the run of the revival of "Richard III." Third, that cruel disaster, the burning of all the Lyceum's stored scenery. And worst of all, the deadliest scourge of actors, illness. On the conditions under which Sir Henry worked during the final years of his life, Mr. Bram Stoker makes some rather startling revelations. It appears that for more than six years before his death Irving was "coughing up pus from an unhealed lung," and the virulence of his disease may be judged from the fact that he used "five hundred pocket handkerchiefs a week." There is much to extol in Henry Irving's career--his consistent dignity, his loyalty to his art, his generosity to his fellow-players, his absolutely royal munificence. There are performances of his--his Shylock and his Hamlet, his Louis XI. and his Corporal Brewster in "Waterloo," his Becket and his Wolsey, his Charles I. and his Mathias in "The Bells," his Richard III. and his Dubose in "The Lyons Mail," which for playgoers who witnessed them are imperishable memories. But in many ways, the noblest of all his achievements must seem to all who have read Mr. Stoker's reminiscences to be the losing fight which he waged against not a little public apathy, against a pitiless series of misfortunes, and finally, against a disease which must have given him hourly torture. No wonder, as Mr. Stoker remarks, Irving shrank into himself during the closing years of his life; no wonder he evinced a certain protesting bitterness against Fate. The marvel is that he held on stoically till the end.

INGRAM A. PYLE, "THE INTIMATE LIFE OF SIR HENRY IRVING," *DIAL*   41 (NOVEMBER 1, 1906), 276-79.

As Johnson had his Boswell, so it may well be said in years to come that Irving had his Stoker. And in justice to the gentleman last named, we may add that the statement is made from a literary point of view, with due consideration of the art of biographical portraiture: to exaggerate Boswell's weaknesses is perhaps impossible, but the talents mingled with them have sometimes been underrated, and a paradoxical antithesis has been set up between the folly of the man and the greatness of his book.

For upwards of thirty years the author of these Reminiscences was an intimate friend of Sir Henry Irving, in certain ways the most intimate friend of his life; and it is truly said that he knew him as well as it is given to any man to know another. In a prefatory note Mr. Stoker points out that the fame of an actor is won in minutes, not in years, the latter being only helpful in the recurrence of opportunities; that it is not practicable to record adequately the progress of his work, for that in its perfection cannot be recorded, as words can convey but faint suggestions of awakened emotion. . . .

Forty years ago, provincial playgoers did not have much opportunity to see great acting, except in star parts. It was the day of stock companies. Mr. Stoker first saw Irving as Captain Absolute in "The Rivals," at the Theatre Royal, Dublin, on the evening of August 28, 1867. It was nine years before, as dramatic critic on the "Dublin Mail," he met the actor. Their friendship began at a dinner, after which Irving asked permission to recite Thomas Hood's poem, "The Dream of Eugene Aram." Stoker sat spellbound. Irving had found an understanding and appreciative friend; and the friendship thus begun continued till the end of Irving's life.

In the present work the author has aimed not so much at a formal biography as to present a picture of his subject's life by showing him amongst his friends and explaining who those friends were, by affording glimpses of his inner life and mind as gained by intimate association. To trace Irving's career for several years after their first meeting is only to follow him from one scene of triumph to another. During these years his one ambition was to have a theatre to himself where he would be sole master, an ambition which was realized when he took the management of the Lyceum and made Mr. Stoker his acting manager. During Irving's personal management of the Lyceum he produced over forty plays, making an average of two plays each year from 1878 to 1898. The memorable series of Shakespearean plays were a part of these. Never before had such scrupulous attention been given to the details of stage-production. Irving was always careful not to offend the feelings of the public, especially in religious matters. For instance, when the church scene of "Much Ado about Nothing" was set for the marriage of Claudio and Nero, he got a Catholic priest to supervise it, who pointed out that the white cloth spread in front of the Tabernacle on the High Altar meant that the Host was within, whereupon Irving ordered a cloth of gold; when the red lamp hung over the Altar-rail by his direction, for purely scenic effect, was pronounced a sacramental sign, he replaced it by others to destroy the significance. But not so when, as Becket, he put on the pall to go into the cathedral, where the murderous huddle of knights awaited him. There were no feelings to be offended them, though the occasion was in itself a sacrament--the greatest of all sacraments, martyrdom. All sensitiveness regarding ritual was merged in pity and the grandeur of the noble readiness, "I go to meet my King."

Perhaps no successful play ever had so little done for it as "The Bells" on its production. When Irving took the management of the Lyceum, this play was one of its assets. The original choice of the play is an object-lesson of the special art-sense of an actor regarding his own work. As Mr. Stoker points out, it would be difficult for an actor to explain in what this art-sense consists, or how it brings conviction to those whose gift it is. . . . This chapter on "Irving's Philosophy of his Art" is one of the most interesting in the entire book.

Irving's first visit to America, in 1883, was a matter of considerable importance. At that time the great body of the British people did not know much about America, and did not care a great deal, according to the present author.

The welcome which Irving received on that night of October 29, 1883, lasted for more than twenty years--until that night of March 25, 1904, when at the Harlem Opera House he said 'Good-bye' to his American friends--forever! Go where he would, from Maine to Louisiana, from the Eastern to the Western sea, there was always the same story of loving greeting; of appreciative and encouraging understanding; of heartfelt *au revoirs*, in which gratitude had no little part. As Americans of the United States have no princes of their own, they make princes of whom they love. And after eight long winters spent with Henry Irving, amongst them I can say that no more golden hospitality or affectionate belief, no greater understanding of purpose or enthusiasm regarding personality or work, has ever been the lot of any artist--any visitor--in any nation. Irving was only putting into fervent words the feeling of his own true heart, when in his parting he said: 'I go with only one feeling on my lips and in my heart--God bless America!'"

In the closing chapter of the book, Mr. Stoker explains the cause of Irving's illness during the last seven years of his life. Here we learn for the first time the details of his patient suffering. Little wonder that, when the 13th of October, 1905, came around, he was tired, tired out. The actual cause of his death was physical weakness; and the last words he spoke on the stage were Becket's last words in the play: "Into Thy hands, O Lord! Into Thy hands."

That Sir Henry Irving had many rare and winning gifts of mind and soul; that his impulses were right and noble; that most of those who knew him best seem also to have loved him most dearly; that his ambition, large as it was and growing with what it fed on, seldom if ever outran his honesty of purpose, or turned his proud self-reliance into uncharity and self-conceit; that he had his dramatic principles and never sacrificed them to a greed for worldly advancement; that he had a fine scorn for hypocritical pretenses of every kind, and a fine sense of honor for himself, are convictions which are confirmed by Mr. Stoker's book. His candid Reminiscences have opened the actor's life and character to the public. The wit, the wisdom, the anecdote, the talk by famous men and about them, the strangeness and vivacity of many of the incidents and eminence of many of the characters, combine to render the work fascinating and instructive. It is in two handsome volumes, adequately illustrated.

"FOUR BIOGRAPHIES," *OUTLOOK* 84 (NOVEMBER 24, 1906), 713-14.

(Also reviewed in the original essay but not included in this volume of criticism are *Garrick and His Circle* by Mrs. Clement Parsons, *Moliere: A Biography* by H.C. Chatfield-Taylor, and *Charles Dickens* by G.K. Chesterton.)

In assigning biographers to the men whose lives are here to be considered, fate, though it has delivered them all into the hands of their friends, has not treated all with equal kindness. It will be convenient, in considering these four new books, to speak first of the three "theatrical" biographies, and of these first of the Irving, concerning which there is naturally a present curiosity.

The reader, as he makes his way through Mr. Stoker's two handsome and generously illustrated volumes, will now and again incline to the opinion that "Personal Reminiscences of Henry Irving" might with equal propriety have been entitled "Autobiographical Sketches of Bram Stoker." The author takes the stage-center in the Preface, and throughout is more in the limelight than the biographical proprieties permit. So much is this the case that at times Irving slips into the middle distance, fades into the far distance, or quite vanishes over the horizon. But if Mr. Stoker has sometimes found it impossible duly to suppress himself, the reader will forgive him, for, if not a prince of biographers, he is still a stanch friend, who put at the service of the man he worshiped a cultivated mind and a good heart, and has here recorded a friendship honorable both to Irving and himself.

These reminiscences make no pretense of being, and are not, a formal biography. Of Irving's parentage, of his early struggles, of his private life, or of the inner life of his mind, we hear little. What we do get here is a full chronicle of his career as an actor from 1878, when Mr. Stoker became his acting manager, until his death. There are sketches of his associates--the pages given to Ellen Terry are especially pleasant reading--and circumstantial accounts, detailed to the last degree, of his stage triumphs, and of his wrestling with the difficult problems that confronted him in striving to perfect the rich and elaborate realistic stage-settings for which he was famous--this last, in the opinion of many, largely a misplaced effort, since it tended to distract the audience from the business of the play, and to set it agape at the ingenuity of stage-carpenters, scene-painters, and upholsterers.

Another striking feature of this book is the picture it presents of the social side of Irving's career, a phase of his subject upon which Mr. Stoker never tires of enlarging. Indeed, the reader would be content with less talk of the titled and distinguished acquaintances who, whatever Irving may have been to them, were little or nothing to Irving. And when he has read all that Mr. Stoker has thought it worth while to set down on this head, he will be tempted to exclaim with Artemus Ward, "This is 2 mutch." Pages and pages that might have done better service are given to mere lists of men and women of name and fame, from Queen Victoria, King Edward, and Presidents of the United States down, who have either been entertained by Irving in the Beefsteak Room or on the stage of the Lyceum, or who have themselves entertained him. No other actor, not even Garrick, has been so honored socially. Chiefs in every line of endeavor--poets, painters, sculptors, prime ministers, archbishops, and authors--graced his entertainments, and returned in kind his generous hospitality.

Besides chronicling Irving's histrionic achievements and recording his social triumphs, the "Reminiscences" aims to make us intimately acquainted with Irving the man. In this the author has but imperfectly succeeded. He lacks the gift of the creative biographer who can bare to us the heart of his hero and make him live in the pages of his book. From Mr. Stoker we do get, however, a very clear conception of the group of qualities which we are accustomed to associate with Irving's name, and which made him loved and respected beyond any other English actor of his generation. We see in him a masterly man, a man of fine grain, with a clear, strong mind and a kind heart; a man who strained every nerve for the honor of his art, and was steadfast in the pursuit of his ideals; one, too, who was affectionate to his friends, and considerate to even the humblest of his fellow-workers. Other shortcomings there are in these volumes besides the failure to make known to us the real Irving--Irving the man, as distinguished from Irving the actor. We get from them little idea of the development of his art, of his histrionic limitations, or of the relative excellence of his impersonations. But, after all is said, this is a book to be grateful for, a book that will be of deep interest to gentlemen of "the profession," and an important contribution to the history of the English stage.

I. RANKEN TOWES, "BRAM STOKER'S IRVING," *BOOKMAN* 24 (DECEMBER 1906), 367-371.

Mr. Bram Stoker's book is singularly interesting on account of the intimate view which it affords of the fascinating personality of a very remarkable man, who played a prominent part for nearly a third of a century in the artistic and social world. Readers who expect to find in it an illuminating account of the making of a great actor, any critical or comparative review of his capacities or an impartial estimate of his actual achievements, will be disappointed, but they will learn some of the secrets of his extraordinary success and still more extraordinary popularity. Incidentally too, they will learn a great deal about the energetic, loyal and enthusiastic character of Mr. Stoker himself, who, in the discharge of his function as a modern Boswell, throws the fullest light upon the extent of his own able, indefatigable and loving service. His amiable and quite unconscious egotism only serves to emphasise an affection highly honourable to both men.

From the very first the clever Irishman, who had already won recognition as a scholar and athlete at Dublin University, was dominated by Irving's masterful individuality. He tells how he was made hysterical by the weird power of the actor's recitation of Hood's "Eugene Aram," and how the manifestation of sensibility won Irving's heart and cemented a friendship only to be ended by death. Thenceforward Irving was to him a paragon, and it is not surprising, perhaps, that he can only speak of him in terms of eulogy, in which, however, there is no trace of subserviency. But his indomitable enthusiasm, scorning all reservation or qualification, deprives his opinions on the subject of Irving's acting of all weight. To him each new impersonation was but the signal for a new rhapsody. The actor's mannerisms and physical limitations, so conspicuous to all unprejudiced observers, were for him practically non-existent. Apparently he deemed his glorified chief's Othello, Lear, Macbeth and Romeo, only to mention a few instances, to be on the same place of excellence with his Mathias, Louis XI, Malvolio and Iago. But if his opinions are misleading, his facts are most interesting and instructive. Nobody can read his account of the golden period of the London Lyceum, with its wealth of official detail, without realising that Irving was a man of the rarest nervous force, most resolute will and great intellectuality as well as phenomenal executive ability. This last quality displayed itself in the judgment which he displayed in the selection of his executive staff, but Mr. Stoker makes it quite plain that he was not only the soul of that vast establishment, with its army of actors, scene-painters, mechanics and supernumeraries, but that he actually superintended and directed everything, from the music in the orchestra to the painting of the scenes and the management of the stage. In some cases he was known to discard the costumes prepared by the experts whom he had engaged in favour of others which he had copied from rare prints of the designated period. More than once during the preparation of some greater spectacle he helped famous artists to solve problems in colour or arrangement by which they had been baffled. Although he had not ear for music, he was able to give Sir Arthur Sullivan hints as to the nature of the accompaniment which he desired when that eminent composer had failed to meet his requirements. He got the inspiration for his wonderful production of *The Merchant of Venice* from Morocco, and took his scene painters to Nuremberg to get local colour for his *Faust*. No pains or expense was too great, no detail too small, for his attention when a new piece was in hand, and it was by this conscientious labour, backed by a comprehensive intelligence and the keenest theatrical instinct, that he secured the harmonious effects so characteristic of his representations. The amount of money that he spent habitually on scenery, furniture and costumes sounds almost fabulous. But Mr. Stoker is precise in his figures. In one instance, at least, a sum of $75,000 was expended before the curtain was raised. When particular dresses were required, the London shops would be ransacked for the most suitable material, and sometimes after all the costumes had been completed and found unsatisfactory a new set was ordered. In preparing for a stage picture, cost was the last thing taken into consideration. Whether this sumptuous adornment was always in accordance with the highest principles of dramatic art is a question that is open to debate, but it is impossible not to admire the zeal that dictated it. . . .

Mr. Stoker gives an eloquent and pathetic account of the actor's last days, his gallant endurance of the sudden and repeated shocks of ill-fortune, his final collapse and his burial in Westminster Abbey. There can be little doubt that his death occurred for him at a happy time, while his fame was still fresh and his state fairly prosperous. This tribute of love and admiration which his sorrowing lieutenant lays upon his tomb is not the least of his honours.

"REVIEW OF PERSONAL REMINISCENCES OF HENRY IRVING," *PUTNAM'S* 1 (DECEMBER 1906), 382.

Mr. Stoker, as was to be expected, gives free rein to the hero-worship that was the ruling passion of his life. Yet, Boswelian though he was and remains, in his attitude towards the great English actor and his memory, these two sizable and handsome volumes are not Boswelian in treatment or scope. They do not contain a biography, or anything but what their title indicates--"personal reminiscences". . . . Within the limitations laid down for himself by the author, however, the work is brimful of interest as a contribution not only to the history of the technical advance of the stage during half a century, but to that of its social rise as well. . . .

Of most interest are the chapters devoted by Mr. Stoker to Irving's preparation for his productions, and to his resourcefulness and originality as a stage manager who had the eye of a painter for large effects, and at the same time the ingenuity of a mechanic in the inventing of simple devices for the carrying out of his illusions. These chapters will be valuable to all actors and stage managers; their perusal will enhance the pleasure of all playgoers to whom something else besides the play is the thing. Irving planning the scene on the Brocken in "Faust" is hardly more interesting than is the earlier Irving who created a wonderful winter stage picture in the "Corsican Brothers" with the aid of bags of common kitchen salt. Mr. Stoker tells plenty of good anecdotes of the interesting circle that knew and honored Irving personally, friends and admirers, English, American, and continental. Americans are, indeed, numerous in these pages--presidents, authors, artists, actors, diplomatists. Ellen Terry smiles upon us from many a page, in text as well as picture. Mr. Stoker presents a series of portraits of Irving, of course, the most interesting of them being the frontispiece reproduction of Bernard Partridge's pastel of 1905, the last picture of the English actor painted.

ELLEN TERRY, *THE STORY OF MY LIFE*. LONDON: HUTCHINSON AND CO., 1908, 166.

Bram Stoker, whose recently published "Reminiscences of Irving" have told, as well as it ever *can* be told, the history of the Lyceum Theatre under Irving's direction, was as good a servant in the front of the theatre as Loveday was on the stage. Like a true Irishman, he has given me some lovely blarney in his book. He has told *all* the stories that I might have told, and described every one connected with the Lyceum except himself. I can fill *that* deficiency to a certain extent by saying that he is one of the most kind and tender-hearted of men. He filled a difficult position with great tact, and was not so universally abused as most business managers, because he was always straight with the company, and never took a mean advantage of them.

"OBITUARY: MR. BRAM STOKER," *TIMES* (APRIL 22, 1912), 15d.

After Irving's death it was not unnatural that Stoker should write his biography; and this task Mr. Stoker performed with his customary enthusiasm. A fluent and flamboyant writer, with a manner and mannerisms which faithfully reflected the mind which moved the pen, Stoker managed to find time, amid much arduous and distracting work, to write a good deal. He was the master of a particularly lurid and creepy kind of fiction, represented by "Dracula" and other novels; he had also essayed musical comedy, and had of late years resumed his old connexion with journalism. But his chief literary memorial will be his Reminiscences of Irving, a book which with all its extravagances and shortcomings--Mr. Stoker was no very acute critic of his chief as an actor--cannot but remain a valuable record of the workings of genius as they appeared to his devoted associate and admirer.

The Lady of the Shroud

W.F.P., "BRAM STOKER'S LATEST NOVEL," *BOOKMAN* 37 (JANUARY 1910), 194.

Mr. Bram Stoker in "The Lady of the Shroud" is prodigious. He presents us with a huge prophetic melodrama of the Near East: he creates in outline at least that Balkan Federation, which may or may not be feasible, but certainly seems essential to the curbing of Austrian ambitions on the one hand and Turkish pretensions on the other. And that is not all. He gives us a great Ruritanian romance in the manner of Anthony Hope, or rather perhaps we should say in the fashion of Stanley Weyman, palpitating with passion, full of high colour, breathless in movement. But this romantic melodrama is tinged with the scientific spirit of H.G. Wells on the one side and the influence of the Psychical Research revival on the other. As if this were not enough and sufficiently varied matter for a single novel, we are treated to a long legal or pseudo-legal introduction, with an old-style reading of the will; the modern touch here consisting the possession by the testator of a fortune of over one hundred millions sterling. The result is a remarkably interesting volume, which contains some of the best work Mr. Bram Stoker has done: that is to say, very fine and individual work indeed.

One fear besets us in commending this story alike to the reader for mere sensation and the reader who asks more than emotional disturbance in his fiction. An extract from the "Journal of Occultism" which opens the story tells us of the midnight appearance off the Land of the Blue Mountains of "a tiny white figure of a woman drifting on some strange current in a small boat, on the prow of which rested a faint light (like a corpse candle)." The boat turned out to be a coffin, whose midnight passenger vanished through the moonlight "just as mist or smoke disappears under a breeze." This whets our appetite. But lo and behold, Mr. Stoker fends us off from his most excellent courses for a long time: too long a time some of his readers may think, with a rather complicated "record" concerning the will of Roger Melton, the millionaire merchant and international financier, made by a most incredible bounder (the word is Mr. Stoker's) named Ernest Roger Halbard Melton, law student of the Inner Temple.

When we come to the entry of Rupert Sent Leger, giant, explorer, man of arms and science, upon his inheritance as chief legatee under the will of his uncle Roger, matters soon develop briskly. Among the trusts left to young Rupert are the Fort or Castle of Vissarion in the Land of the Blue Mountains, where he is to reside, carving out for himself and the people of the region, by means of his personality and his wealth, a dazzling future. To him in his lonely chamber one night arrives the ghostly but moving figure of a lady from the sea, dressed in a dripping shroud. Gradually love for the unhappy virgin, or vampire or whatever she may be, wells up in the heart of Rupert. He marries her secretly in an old church and in semi-darkness after the uncanny experience of discovering her in a glass-topped tomb in a mysterious crypt. Of course, she proves very woman--the centre of an astounding patriotic deception--and the daughter of the chief of the Blue Mountaineers. She is seized by Turks and rescued by Rupert, who thereafter is made king of her people; she bears him a child, and this child, or his father at the close, bids fair to become to the Balkan States what Bismarck was to Germany. Of the second-sight possessed by the MacKelpie, of the opera-bouffe old Scottish soldier, of the ex-piratical Admiral Rooke, we have no room to speak. Suffice it to say that Mr. Bram Stoker's latest is a most readable book, full of creeps and thrills, as well as many quaint touches of character and phrase.

CAROL A. SENF, *"THE LADY OF THE SHROUD: STOKER'S SUCCESSOR TO DRACULA," ESSAYS IN ARTS AND SCIENCES* (1990), 82-96.

(This excerpt is edited to eliminate summary material and lengthy quotations. Page numbers in the essay refer to the Arrow paperback edition, which was published in 1974.)

Few people--except for experts in turn-of-the century literature, horror fiction, or fantasy--are familiar with *The Lady of the Shroud*, for Bram Stoker is usually given credit for writing only one book, the supernatural thriller *Dracula*. . . . Stoker's tenth novel, *The Lady of the Shroud*, was published twelve years after *Dracula*. It is interesting in its own right, for it contains the first airplane rescue in fiction as well as a mysterious woman, a seven-foot hero, political intrigue, and an elderly woman who is gifted with second sight. *The Lady of the Shroud* is especially interesting, however, as a revised version of *Dracula*, which adapts the mythic figure of the vampire only to eliminate the uncanny and disturbing psychological characteristics so often associated with this figure. Thus, while the earlier novel raises troubling questions about individual identities and personal relationships, the later novel adapts many of the same formulas to produce merely a novel of suspense. . . .

The Lady of the Shroud includes many of the same character types that *Dracula* does, but the later novel eliminates most of the tensions associated with these characters. Teuta Vissarion, the alleged vampire in *Lady*, no longer reveals Stoker's alternative love and fear of women, for she turns out to be a woman pretending to be a vampire, not a supernatural figure with the power to destroy the male protagonist. The old generation willingly relinquishes its power to the younger; questions of personal identity are resolved mid-novel; and the rescue at the conclusion solves both political and romantic problems, so that the young lovers can live happily alongside the older generation.

One of the most obvious differences is that *The Lady of the Shroud* includes significantly less ambivalence toward women. Janet MacKelpie, Rupert's spinster aunt, is a rather fussy old lady, chronically worried about the hero's happiness and the state of his socks. Though she is credited with the ability to forsee the future, Stoker generally uses her ability to reveal her concern for her nephew rather than to suggest that women have uncanny powers. The following scene, which occurs the morning after Rupert spends the night with the supposed vampire, is typical of Aunt Janet's relationship to Rupert:

'Laddie, whativer hae ye been doin' wi' yer baith? Oh, the mess ye hae made! Tis sinful to gie sic trouble an' waste. . . .' And so she went on. I was glad to hear the tirade, which was only what a good housewife, outraged in her sentiments of order, would have made. I listened in patience--with pleasure when I thought of what she would have thought (and said) had she known the real facts. I was well pleased to have got off so easily. (58)

Such domestic tirades reveal Aunt Janet to be an uncomplicated and nurturing figure.

The other woman in the novel, Teuta Vissarion, is initially presented with greater ambivalence. The novel begins with an excerpt from *The Journal of Occultism* in which a passenger on an Italian ship observes a woman dressed in a shroud and floating along on a coffin; and even the burning eyes of the supposed vampire are likely to remind readers of the horrifying preternatural figures in *Dracula*. Other scenes in the early sections of the novel remind both Rupert and the reader that Teuta may be horrifying as well as desirable. The first time she enters Rupert's bedroom for warmth, she displays a pretty feminine helplessness. Rupert, however, is acutely aware of convention and of the impropriety of her appearing in his bedroom. In fact, her unorthodox behavior causes him to suspect that she may be a vampire.

My having to help my Lady over the threshold of my house on her first entry was in accord with Vampire tradition; so, too, her flying at cock-crow. . . . Into the same category came the facts of her constant wearing of her Shroud. . . . her lying still in the glass-covered tomb; her coming alone to the most secret places in a fortified Castle where every aperture was secured. (132)

Moreover, Teuta, who is concerned with choosing a powerful political consort reminds Rupert of the superstition so he will prove his love for her:

'But do you know what men say? Some of them, that I am dead and buried; others, that I am not only dead and buried, but that I am one of those unhappy beings that may not die the common death of man. Who live on a fearful life-in-death, whereby they are harmful to all. Those unhappy Un-dead whom men call Vampires--who live on the blood of the living, and bring eternal damnation as well as death with the poison of their dreadful kisses!' (119)

Both Teuta and Rupert allude to the vampire's horrifying capabilities. They suggest that women may be threatening as well as enticing, but there is a qualitative difference with the treatment of women here and in *Dracula*. In the earlier novel, the three women at Dracula's castle attempt to seduce Jonathan Harker and then come at him with fangs bared; and only Dracula's intervention saves Harker from death. Lucy Westenra is also both seductive and repulsive. She sucks the blood of several young children, and she attempts to suck the blood of Arthur Holmwood, formerly her fiance. In *The Lady of the Shroud*, the mysterious woman, who later will become Rupert's wife, never threatens him in any way, and her resemblance to the vampire is very indirect.

In fact, Stoker makes an even more important revelation that links Teuta with his heroines, not with his destructive women. Archbishop Steven Palealogue, one of the minor narrators of the novel (which, like *Dracula*, is told from a number of different points of view), explains that Teuta merely pretended to be vampire to protect herself from capture by enemies of her family and her people. With Palealogue's revelation, the earlier ambivalence vanishes; and Teuta begins to resemble the heroines of Stoker's other fiction. . . . Rupert often comments on her feminine behavior, noting for example: "Like a good wife, she obeyed" (182). Having abandoned her uncanny vampire disguise, she becomes a heroine to be rescued from the Turks who had kidnaped her, so that the Sultan could force a marriage on her and thereby claim the Blue Mountains or kill her and thus end the Vissarion line. . . .

The Lady of the Shroud asks the reader to consider . . . questions of identity. Rupert's first glimpse of Teuta raises important questions: Is she an innocent woman or a dreadful vampire?

There. . . stood a woman, wrapped in white graveclothes. . . . Attitude and dress and circumstance all conveyed the idea that, though she moved and spoke, she was not quick, but dead. She was young and very beautiful, but pale, like the grey pallor of death. (65)

Nonetheless, because of Teuta's non-threatening behavior, these questions do not have the urgency that they have in *Dracula*. Even though Rupert discovers her lying in her glass-covered tomb, she never threatens him or any other human being. Thus the question of whether she is a vampire remains mostly in the realm of *double entendre*, as when she informs Rupert that "Marriage with such a one as I am has its own ritual, which may not be forgone" (125). The reader may initially suspect that she is referring to her alleged vampiric condition, but she is actually referring to her political position as Voivodin.

The single biggest difference in the two novels is that power in *The Lady of the Shroud* is human, not supernatural. When Rupert and the fiercely independent mountaineers attempt to recapture her father from the Turks, Rupert notes that "her woman's quick wit was worth the reasoning of a camp full of men. . . . When she spoke, the whole plan of action, based on subtle thinking, had mapped itself out in her mind" (180). She also brandishes a sword against the Turks and dangles on a rope from Rupert's airplane to rescue her father. Nonetheless the power--whether for good or evil--that had been associated with women in *Dracula* is changed in *The Lady of the Shroud.* Janet MacKelpie and Teuta Vissarion are mortal women, and they are also willing to use their powers to support the men around them.

While Stoker's ambivalence toward women is reduced and ultimately eliminated in *The Lady of the Shroud,* so is the power associated with the Oedipal configuration of character relationships changed from *Dracula.* The Oedipus complex leads to rivalry and hostility toward the father and to the fear that the powerful father may actually castrate the boy to prevent him from attaining the mother. . . .

Parents die in *The Lady of the Shroud,* and part of the plot hinges on an inheritance left to the orphaned Rupert, but the powerful Oedipal emotions are no longer in evidence. The novel begins with Roger Melton's will, which leaves to his nephew the bulk of his fortune and a castle in the Blue Mountains, where Rupert must live for six months.

A letter addressed to Rupert by his uncle also introduces two other father-figures, the Turkish Sultan and Peter Vissarion, Voivode of the Blue Mountains, who, like Dracula and Van Helsing, are in opposition. A significant difference, however, is that the opposition in *The Lady* is political and ideological rather than emotional and personal as the following quotation reveals:

An attack by Turkey was feared. . . . and the patriotic Voivode was sacrificing his own great fortune for the public good. . . . it was always taken for granted that if the principles of the constitution should change to a more personal rule, his own family should be regarded as the Most Noble. It had ever been on the side of freedom in olden time. . . . The very name stood for freedom, for nationality, against foreign oppression; and the bold mountaineers were devoted to it, as in other free countries men follow the flag. (29)

In *The Lady,* the good father is a benevolent leader. He is willing to share his power with the mountaineers, his political children, and with his daughter and son-in-law, his literal children. The novel concludes with his ready acceptance of Rupert, presumably written in his own hand:

A man like that walks straight into my heart. . . . I put out my hand and grasped his, which seemed to leap to meet me--as only the hand of a swordsman can do. 'I am glad you are my son' I said. It was all I could say, and I meant it and all it implied. (189)

Kindly Peter Vissarion resembles Van Helsing. The bad father--the Sultan--is almost as autocratic as Dracula. Hoping to gain control of the Blue Mountains in their absence, he kidnaps both Teuta and her father; and much of the suspense of the final book depends on Rupert's rescue of them. *The Lady of the Shroud* parallels *Dracula,* but it is a watered-down version of the powerful earlier novel.

The Turk is a distant political foe who can be fought with swords and guns and airplanes rather than a sexually potent father-figure with whom it is difficult-- even impossible--to argue without altering one's relationship and one's self- identity. One possible exception occurs when the recently married Rupert, preparing to rescue his bride, contrasts Christian marriage to life in a Turkish harem:

But even if they did not kill her, to escape with her would be to condemn her to the worst fate of all--the harem of the Turk. Lifelong misery and despair. . . must be the lot of a Christian woman doomed to such a fate. . . . . that dreadful life of shameful slavery would be a misery beyond belief. (158)

Here the distant Sultan has potential power over Rupert and his young bride, a power distinctly linked with his sexual power. Despite the superficial similarity, however, the Sultan remains a distant threat rather than an immediate one. Thus the scene is a pallid reminder of the urgency associated with the sexually potent father in *Dracula*.

While the two novels reveal the same Oedipal configurations of powerful parental figures who are both loved and feared, most readers would notice a distinct difference in Stoker's handling of them. In *Dracula*, both mothers and fathers are powerful figures, capable of doing great good or great harm. Moreover, these powerful parental figures are often physically present in the novel. In *The Lady of the Shroud*, on the other hand, parental figures are either dead before the novel opens, absent during most of the novel, or powerful, but only at a great distance. Though reputed to be powerful, Peter Vissarion is in prison for most of the novel and does not appear until the conclusion, while the Sultan is seen only through his easily conquered underlings. Furthermore, while Dracula's refusal to die is a clear sign that he is unwilling to relinquish his power, Robert Melton, Peter Vissarion, and Janet MacKelpie willingly share their power with the younger generation.

Changes in Stoker's life, especially the deaths of Charlotte Stoker in 1900 and of Henry Irving, Stoker's friend and employer, in 1905, may explain the different handling of the Oedipal configuration. In 1897, when *Dracula* was published, the eighty-year old Charlotte was still alive, so much alive that she commended *Dracula* as the best thing her son had written. When she died, her son lost one of the most powerful influences in his life. The result may be that women characters in his later novels are less powerful. Likewise, Irving, who had just been knighted in 1895, was at the height of his power. With Irving's death, Stoker lost another influence in his life. His own father, fifty years old at Bram's birth, had died in 1876, right before Stoker left the civil service (the profession to which his father had dedicated his life) to become business manager for Irving's Lyceum Theatre. The change seems to have been an important symbolic gesture as well as a significant career choice. His father's death seems to have made little impact on Stoker though it may be significant that Stoker did not leave the civil service until afterwards.[1] Stoker may have transferred his feelings for his father to Irving, for Stoker had intense feelings toward Irving over twenty-nine years. At their first meeting in 1876, Irving offered to recite Hood's poem, *The Dream of Eugene Aram.* Irving collapsed on reaching the conclusion, when the murderer seems to see the ghost take shape before his eyes; and Stoker burst into hysterics.

    Dracula also suggests the intensity of their relationship. Not only does Dracula physically resemble the tall, gaunt Irving, but his aloof and haughty demeanor could also have been modeled on the autocratic Irving. [2] Frayling also notes other similarities in "the vocal tricks of the vampire Count, as well as aspects of his character and some of his physical mannerisms (particularly his melodramatic habit of holding women at arm's length and shouting at them)." Frayling concludes that "the relationship between Jonathan Harker (often Stoker's mouthpiece) and the Count may tell us as much about the business manager's relationship with his employer as does Stoker's own suggestively ambivalent *Personal Reminiscences of Henry Irving*" (75). In addition, Irving the actor was associated with the supernatural and often evoked fear in his audience when he performed one of his various demonic roles in *The Bells* and *Vanderdecken* (based on *The Flying Dutchman*).

    Stoker never again created characters as powerful as those found in *Dracula. Miss Betty* (1898) and *The Man* (1905) might be classified as sentimental novels. . . . Only *The Lair of the White Worm* (1911) and *The Jewel of Seven Stars* (1912) include any of the mystery and power of *Dracula*. The change has been explained in a variety of ways--by Stoker's age and diminished capabilities, by the greater care that he took writing *Dracula,* or by the fact that he managed to exorcise many of his Oedipal feelings by writing that novel. [3] Writing *Dracula* over a period of at least seven years--combined with the deaths of two of the most influential people in his life, his mother and his employer--seems to have reduced his intensely ambivalent feelings about parental figures. *The Lady of the Shroud*, which explains away its vampire mid-novel, is one result of the change.

    The Lady of the Shroud is a different novel in other ways. Not only is it a revision that dilutes the intense personal feelings associated with the Oedipus complex and with men's ambivalence about women's sexuality, but it diminishes the intense questions associated with the quest for personal identity; and even the repeated rescues at the conclusion are less urgent and exciting.

    In the earlier novel, the Crew of Light must traverse an entire continent to reach their opponent's lair. Moreover, they must face a more-than-human foe, as Van Helsing explains:

But to fail here, is not mere life or death. It is that we become as him . . . foul things of the night like him--without heart or conscience, preying on the bodies and the souls of those we love best. To us for ever are the gates of heaven shut. . . . We go on for all time abhorred by all. (Ch. XVIII)

Religious imagery reinforces the rescue's importance.

    In *The Lady of the Shroud*, on the other hand, Rupert suggests that he might even be able to redeem the lady from her vampiric state.

Come it from Heaven or Hell, from the Earth or the Grave, it does not matter; I shall make it my task to win her back to life and peace. If she be indeed a Vampire, the task may be hard and long; if she be not so, and if it be merely that circumstances have so gathered round her as to produce that impression, the task may be simpler and the result more sweet.(77)

Despite his promise to brave Heaven or Hell, Rupert and his band of mountaineers face a purely secular foe; and Rupert admits that, if they cannot live together, he and Teuta can at least die together. Thus, the two rescues at the conclusion (one when Rupert and his followers rescue Teuta, the other when they rescue her father) have all the intensity of a good chase scene, but they do not have the urgency of *Dracula*, where the human heroes face a formidable preternatural foe who has the power to alter their identities forever.

An essay that Stoker wrote in 1908, "The Censorship of Fiction," suggests that he may have deliberately purged certain troubling erotic elements from his fiction:

It may be taken that such works as are here spoken of deal not merely with natural misdoing based on human weakness, frailty, or passions of the senses, but with vices so flagitious, so opposed to even the decencies of nature in its crudest and lowest forms, that the poignancy of moral disgust is lost in horror. This article is no mere protest against academic faults or breaches of good taste. It is a deliberate indictment of a class of literature so vile that it is actually corrupting the nation. (*Nineteenth Century* 64 [1908], 485)

Stoker does not mention the works that he believes should be censored, but the fact that he rarely treats sexuality as openly as he does in *Dracula* and the fact that he often relies on simple formulas that come directly from the "novel of sentiment or . . . the prose or metrical romance" is consistent with a trend toward "idealizations and simplifications of his relationship with those around him" (Roth, *Bram Stoker*, p. 137). Absence of critical commentary suggests that most readers find *The Lady of the Shroud* a less intense and compelling novel than *Dracula*. Nonetheless, it is worthy of our attention. Not only does it shed light on *Dracula*, but it shows how a single writer can adapt a formula in a variety of different ways. Moreover, it is a well-executed novel of suspense. Exciting chase scenes allow readers to participate vicariously in an adventure that keeps them wondering exactly how the "heroes" will manage to elude their opponents one more time. Determining whether Teuta is a vampire or not encourages readers to ask questions about personal identity as well as about the relationship between appearance and reality. Looking at the positive relationships of Rupert with his Aunt Janet and with his wife Teuta asks readers to look at both familial and gender relationships. Finally, even though *The Lady of the Shroud* generally remains within the category of formula fiction (and the vampire was definitely a character who had appeared in much nineteenth-century formula fiction before *Dracula* had more or less altered that formula for all time), it is a work that, like Stoker's other works, deserves more critical attention than it has received so far.

NOTES

[1] Neither of Stoker's biographers suggests that Stoker's father had much influence over his son's life though both refer to his mother's significant influence.

[2] Stoker was not the first writer to use his employer as a model for a vampire. As Christopher Frayling observes: "It may be that for Stoker, as for Polidori [who modeled Lord Ruthven in "The Vampyre" on his employer, Lord Byron], the vampire as demanding employer was a crucial equation." In *The Vampire: Lord Ruthven to Count Dracula*. London: Victor Gollancz Ltd., 1978. (76).

[3] Farson suggests that Stoker's diminished capacity may have resulted from tertiary syphilis, which he contracted when his wife's frigidity caused him to seek out prostitutes as sexual partners. Thus the reason for his diminished capacity may even be linked to his aversion to sexuality.

Evidence suggests that Stoker also spent more time working on *Dracula* than he did on other novels. Joseph S. Bierman, who has studied Stoker's working papers, comments on its composition: "The earliest date on any manuscript is 8 March 1890. This date is on a manuscript in Stoker's handwriting that is an outline for a first section of the novel which differs from the final version in only a few details" ("The Genesis and Dating of *Dracula* from Bram Stoker's Working Notes," *Notes and Queries* 222 [1977], 40.) *Dracula* was not published until 1897, so Stoker apparently spent some time revising it.

Famous Impostors

"REVIEW OF *FAMOUS IMPOSTORS*," *INDEPENDENT* 70 (JANUARY 12, 1911), 102.

Bram Stoker is evidently a believer in Barnum's dictum that the people--or was it only the American people?--love to be humbugged. At least, he has written a thick volume with this title: *Famous Impostors* . . . and in his preface he writes:

"The subject of imposture is always an interesting one, and impostors in one shape or another are likely to flourish as long as human nature remains what it is."

We took it for a display of purely British humor when we remarked his offering of a portrait of "Queen Elizabeth as a Young Woman" for frontispiece, but it seems a legend has it that the Virgin Queen of history was a changeling and a male at that. Mr. Stoker's cases include examples of the faker's art as practised in many forms: by impersonators, pretenders and swindlers; by seekers after wealth, position, fame and simple adventure. The story of Perkin Warbeck carries us into English history, that of La Voisin into the France of the grand siecle. We have the Wandering Jew, and John Law, and the false Dauphins of evening, the stories being told with a certain rapidity, tho without distinction of style.

"REVIEW OF *FAMOUS IMPOSTORS*," *SPECTATOR* 106 (JANUARY 28, 1911), 153.

The term "impostor" is practically extended to swindlers and pretenders of all kinds, and even to some persons whom it might be unfair to include in these classes. There was a basis of truth, for instance, in Mesmer's claims, though his methods of enforcing them were not beyond reproach. John Law, the financier,

again, had, it is probable, some faith in his own schemes. The class of
"impostors" proper is represented by Perkin Warbeck, to whom the first place in
the volume is accorded. Mr. Bram Stoker's account is scarcely satisfactory.
There is something to be said on the other side. . . .In other chapters there is
plenty of interesting reading. We miss, however, some famous names. George
Psalmanazar, who invented a whole language and took in not a few good judges,
ought to have had a place. As for the last story, "The Boy of Bisley," a strange
legend that Queen Elizabeth was really a man, it is surely hardly worth its place.

"REVIEW OF *FAMOUS IMPOSTORS*," *DIAL* 50 (FEBRUARY 1, 1911), 97.

Entertainment of his readers appears to have been Mr. Bram Stoker's chief object
in writing his "Famous Impostors" . . . for he announces in his Preface that the
author, "whose largest experience has lain in the field of fiction, has aimed at
dealing with his material as with the material for a novel, except that all the
facts given are real and authentic"--in his opinion, at least. The book is
unquestionably of a character to interest the majority of readers, treating as it
does of a considerable number of noted impostors of various kinds, such as
pretenders to royalty, practitioners of magic, clairvoyants, so-called witches and
wizards, women playing the role of men, the authors of various hoaxes, the
famous Tichborne Claimant, and others. Of course that popular favorite,
Cagliostro, is made to perform a few of his celebrated tricks for the reader's
entertainment, nor is any hint conveyed that he was not as genuine a trickster as
the best of them. No echo from Mr. W.R.H. Trowbridge's recent attempt to
prove him an honest man is heard in Mr. Stoker's account of him. Perhaps it is
too soon to expect it. The concluding chapter of the book is the longest and
shows the most study and original research. It is a serious, an unexpectedly
serious, examination of the legend of the so-called Bisley Boy, the person
substituted, if the tradition be true, for the infant Elizabeth when that princess
had suddenly died of a fever at Bisley, and her nurse, in an agony of fear, was
momentarily expecting King Henry to pay his little daughter a visit. That Mr.
Stoker, almost against his will, was led to take a great interest in this
astonishing legend, speaks at least in favor of its plausibility. Though it was
obviously necessary to omit from his book a great many famous impostors, the
author might, with timelines, have added a chapter on notorious frauds in the
field of geographical exploration. The book is handsomely printed, and has some
well-chosen portraits.

"REVIEW OF *FAMOUS IMPOSTORS*," *ATHENAEUM*, NO. 4347 (FEBRUARY 18, 1911), 184.

Why did Queen Elizabeth never marry? The ingenuity of an historical novelist has suggested that, on accepting the well-known proposal of Sir James Melville, Elizabeth went with him to the Court of Holyrood disguised as a man, excited the jealousy of Darnley, was wounded by him in a duel, was carried to Kirk o'Field, and was there blown up by Bothwell; for Darnley had fled to England, disguised as a woman, and there, being very like his cousin the Queen, personated her for the rest of his life; of course he could not marry.

There are weak points in this theory, but it is not much feebler than Mr. Bram Stoker's tale of "the Bisley Boy" who, on the death of Elizabeth at about the age of ten, in 1543-4, personated that princess during the rest of *his* life; of course he could not marry. Mr. Stoker actually leans to a favourable view of this legend. He arranges his narrative badly. His chief source seems to be a book called 'The Girlhood of Queen Elizabeth' by Mr. Mumby, who, for his part, cites Miss Strickland. From a letter for which no reference to documents is given it appears that, in 1549, Tyrrwhit believed that there was a secret between Elizabeth, Mrs. Ashley, and Thomas Parry, faithful servants to whom their mistress was grateful. Well, there are secrets of many sorts! We are next introduced (p. 286) to a letter of Elizabeth to Seymour, the admiral "taken from Leti's 'La vie d'Elizabeth.'" Who was Leti? asks even the general reader, one hopes, and fourteen pages later it comes out that Mr. Mumby quoted a French translation (1694) of Leti's book; that Leti was born thirty years after Elizabeth's death; and that the English translation of the French translation of the late Italian original is wrong. Then why open the inquiry by quoting an erroneous English translation of a French translation of what purports to be an Italian translation of an original English letter written by Elizabeth in 1548? Where is that original? Historical mysteries cannot be cleared up by this casual method.

Mr. Stoker next describes Bisley in the Cotswold Hills, and the manor house there, with a flower-bed "set in an antique stone receptacle of oblong shape, which presents something of the appearance of a stone coffin of the earlier ages." Without ascertaining whether this setting of a flower-bed is or is not a stone coffin (and only a very minute flower-bed could be "set in" a coffin), Mr. Stoker says "of this more anon." We know what to expect: an aetiological myth is coming, but an account of the dimensions of the "stone receptacle" is not coming.

Bisley is an accommodating place. In 1544 it was "comparatively easy of access from London" (p. 290) but also far indeed from being easily accessible (pp. 293-4). The silly legend is that Elizabeth as a child, was at Bisley, that her governess (Mrs. Ashley, apparently) received news that the King was coming to visit her; that Elizabeth died; and that the governess, unable to find a convenient little girl, dressed up a convenient little boy in the raiment of the defunct princess. Neither Henry, when he came, nor any one else, detected the imposture. Only four persons "*must* have been" in the secret--the boy, Mrs. Ashley, Parry, and the boy's parent with, one supposes, the rest of the parent's family circle. Was Elizabeth, that all-important card in her father's game, left in the hands of only two attendants? She must have had a household, who, even if her death could possibly be kept secret from them, must have perceived the change, while all the village would miss and ask for the boy.

The date of the adventure, Mr. Stoker argues must be "the year ending with July, 1544." Then we have mention of an undated letter "given by Leti," from Elizabeth to Catherine Parr. Mr. Stoker fixes the date of this letter between July 12th, 1543, and July 31st, 1544, when she again writes--apparently with no address--to Queen Catherine Parr. Perhaps Mr. Stoker has not perused all the manuscripts domestic of 1543-4. As Henry's last marriage was in July, 1543, and as "ever since his last marriage he had been an invalid," while Bisley, previously so accessible, "was a long way from London," and Henry was "so heavy that he had to be lifted by machinery," one does not think it probable that he did visit Bisley, between June, 1543, and July, 1544. But the legend says that his visit, or the apprehension of it, drove the governess to substitute a living little boy for a dead little girl. Even if "Martin Hume and F.A. Mumby. . . . confess themselves puzzled by Elizabeth's attitude to men," her "attitude" was not that of a man; and a puzzling attitude of a woman to men is not so rare that we need account for it by the theory that the woman is a man. All of Elizabeth's attitudes towards men, and all of her attitudes towards women, were entirely feminine. If she had a great many wigs (p. 333), Mary Stuart--who was no man-- had also a large collection.

At last we come to what we have always expected--the fable about the hiding of Elizabeth's body in the stone coffin now occupied by a flower-bed; and the discovery, "some tens of years ago," of the bones of a young girl and the remnants of her clothes in the coffin. The whole affair is on a level with the legend that the bones of the genuine James VI. were found build up in a wall in Edinburgh Castle, while the apparent James VI. was the son of Lady Athole, Lady Mar, or any lady you please.

When we turn to Mr. Stoker's account of Cagliostro, we learn that "he called himself Comte de Saint-German [*sic*]"; that he had claimed, "as the Comte de Saint-German (*sic*) said, that he had already existed for many centuries"; and we hear of "a girl," "one Olivia," in the affair of the Diamond Necklace. This is too much, even for the general reader. He has heard of the Comte de St. Germain and of Gay d'Oliva.

"REVIEW OF *FAMOUS IMPOSTORS*," *PUNCH* 140 (FEBRUARY 22, 1911), 144.

I must confess that I always find it very fascinating to read about anyone else having his leg pulled, and Mr. BRAM STOKER'S book, *Famous Impostors*. . . . provides such delights in abundance. The subjects are treated biographically, but the author in dealing with his facts, has brought to their arrangement the skilled novelist's instinct for what is interesting. His net embraces typical impostors from the least to the greatest, from the Wandering Jew and JINNY BINGHAM (who was known as Mother Damnable) to Princess OLIVE, who cut at the throne of England, and ARTHUR ORTON, the Tichborne Colossus. We have THEODORE HOOK, who for a hoax filled Berners Street with tradesmen's carts calling at an inoffensive-looking house with a brass plate. We have JOHN LAW, who gave France a huge financial book and knocked the bottom out of it all in a few months. We have the unscrupulous quack, CAGLIOSTRO. We have PERKIN WARBECK, the pretender. And we have finally Queen ELIZABETH, whom quite a number of people believe to have been a man. Mr. STOKER puts her case judicially, but I think he is nearly convinced of the truth of the Gloucestershire tradition which tells of the Princess dying as a child and of the substitution of the Bisley boy. Personally I can seldom trust myself with such mysteries, because I find somehow that I have generally an unreasonable leaning towards the improbable and unaccepted solution. But the Maiden Queen-- Think how small RALEIGH would have felt that muddy day!

"REVIEW OF *FAMOUS IMPOSTORS*," *BOOKMAN* 40 (SUPPLEMENT SPRING 1911), 8-9.

Mr. Bram Stoker has written a book which is sure of a popular success. He has told the stories of famous pretenders, practitioners of magic, witches, and women who masqueraded as men; he has recounted divers hoaxes, and reviewed the tales of the Wandering Jew, John Law, the Tichborne Claimant, and the Chevalier d'Eon. while he has devoted a special and exhaustive section to the story of the "Bisley Boy," which "impugns the identity--and more than the identity--of Queen Elizabeth." The result is a production of varied entertainment, sometimes grim and gruesome, occasionally sensational, now and then fantastic. Mr. Stoker informs us at the outset that he has aimed at dealing with his material as with the material for a novel; and he has certainly so handled his facts that they are as interesting as fiction. It is a good book about bad people--much better, perhaps, than a book about such people ought to be.

"REVIEW OF *FAMOUS IMPOSTORS*," *LITERARY DIGEST* 42 (APRIL 1, 1911), 640-41.

Those who enjoy reading in the byways of history, or have a taste for mystery and for the tricks and tricksters by which others have been fooled, will find in this generous book much entertainment. In treating of the impostors who have become famous by a more or less harmless infamy, Mr. Stoker has gone as far afield as he chose, and hence his list includes many an interesting name and tale which a strict definition of his book title would exclude. Therefore, we find presented a wide variety of ladies and gentlemen who have taken the trouble to deceive the world for one reason or another; but there is an astonishing uniformity of credulity among the duped! In a pleasantly gossipy style Mr. Stoker writes of pretenders to the thrones of England, France, Portugal, and Russia; of women who disguised themselves as men; among them the real prototype of Gautier's *Mademoiselle de Maupin*; of impostors pretending to occult powers; of financial swindlers on the grand scale; of jocose hoaxers and morose wretches, until the reader can ask no more. Finally--the altogether the most original thing in the book--the author treats us to a most cleverly argued theory that Queen Elizabeth was not a queen, nor even herself at all, speaking *Hibernice,* but a boy brought up as a girl in place of the real little Elizabeth, who is said to have died as a child. Mr. Stoker unearthed a tradition to this effect in a remote village in the southwest of England, and discourses upon it--as upon all the rest of the subjects--most amusingly.

"REVIEW OF *FAMOUS IMPOSTORS*," *SATURDAY REVIEW* 111 (APRIL 1, 1911), 400.

Many of Mr. Bram Stoker's characters are very old friends; so old that their stories are quite stale, and can only interest very unsophisticated readers, or those readers who are sufficiently sophisticated to enjoy the humours of the writer's comically inflated style. But one of his sketches is novel enough, and Mr. Stoker deserves credit for the ingenuity he displays in it, though he has a most preposterous theme. He calls it "The Bisley Boy". It is the gem of the collection, and it has had the honour of being treated seriously in a high-class periodical, though we must say very coldly. At Bisley, in Gloucestershire, Mr. Stoker has heard an old tradition that the Princess Elizabeth, who spent her early years at Overcourt House there, in fact died suddenly on the very day when her father, Henry VIII., was expected from London to visit her. Her attendants in terror procured another child, that happened to be a boy; and this boy grew up and became the future Queen Elizabeth. Whether this was or was not the kind of scandal about Queen Elizabeth that Mr. Sneer deprecated, we have Mr. Stoker's authority that it has been believed from time immemorial by Bisley. Several persons there now accept the story, and Mr. Stoker says, "These persons are not of the ordinary class of gossipers, but men and women of light and leading, who have fixed places in the great world, and in the social life of their own neighbourhood". The strange thing is that the story has never been heard of outside Bisley until Mr. Stoker published it. Mr. Stoker's point is that there is always something in a tradition. But some fact or other in it must be proved to start with, otherwise the probability of the tradition cannot be urged by showing that it is consistent with admitted historical facts. If Mr. Stoker, for instance, had proved that a stone coffin-like vessel, alleged to have been in front of Overcourt Mansion, was actually opened and found to contain human remains with rags of finery such as would belong to a young girl, he would have put the legend into practical shape for historical argument ab extra. As it is, his copious history is all in the air, as none of the details in any version of the legend are proved. Many may think they put a poser if they ask, Did Queen Elizabeth shave? Mr. Stoker would have an answer. Many men have passed for years as women. It was quite easy for the Chevalier d'Eon, one of Mr. Stoker's well-known characters. The "Bisley Boy" story is just a mystification; but it is well worth reading, very curious and amusing, and far the best thing in the book.

The Lair of
the White Worm

"REVIEW OF *THE LAIR OF THE WHITE WORM," TIMES
LITERARY SUPPLEMENT* (NOVEMBER 16, 1911), 466.

In attempting to exceed the supernatural horrors of "Dracula" Mr. Stoker has in
his latest book degenerated into something very like nonsense. No one asks for
probability or even possibility, but coherence is a necessity. Here Mr. Stoker
has collected together some of the ingredients for a gruesome tale, a half-mad
mesmerist, a devilish negro, a dove-like girl, and, as the special feature, a cold,
passionless lady, who is being dunned for debt and is really a vast, ageless,
antediluvian worm. These ingredients are still in the melting-pot, and have not
become a story; the book is disjointed and, in fact, very silly.

HOWARD PHILLIPS LOVECRAFT, *SUPERNATURAL
HORROR IN LITERATURE.* 1939 (RPT. NEW YORK: DOVER,
1973), 78.

Better known . . . is the ingenious Bram Stoker, who created many starkly
horrific conceptions in a series of novels whose poor technique sadly impairs
their net effect. *The Lair of the White Worm*, dealing with a gigantic primitive
entity that lurks in a vault beneath an ancient castle, utterly ruins a magnificent
idea by a development almost infantile. *The Jewel of Seven Stars*, touching on a
strange Egyptian resurrection, is less crudely written. But best of all is the
famous *Dracula*, which has become almost the standard modern exploitation of
the frightful vampire myth. Count Dracula, a vampire, dwells in a horrible castle
in the Carpathians, but finally migrates to England with the design of
populating the country with fellow vampires. How an Englishman fares within

Dracula's stronghold of terrors, and how the dead fiend's plot for domination is at last defeated, are elements which unite to form a tale now justly assigned a permanent place in English letters.

LEONARD WOLF, *A DREAM OF DRACULA.* BOSTON: LITTLE, BROWN AND COMPANY, 1972, 256-59.

At this distance from the Victorian milieu in which Stoker wrote, the unacknowledged sexual detail in the narratives is sometimes only funny, but there are occasions when a raw, dangerous breeze seems to blow over the pages of the text. Nowhere is that sense of rawness and danger more chilling than in Stoker's last novel, *The Lair of the White Worm.* Coming from a young man, this record of fear and fascination might make us wonder, but we might conclude that whatever the author's misery, it would surely pass; but Stoker was sixty-four years old when the book was published, and there is no way to ignore the signs of confusion and loneliness the narrative obtrudes. . . .

Woman. The fascination, and the fear of woman. In the *Lair of the White Worm* she is the Lady Arabella March, who moves with "a quick gliding motion" among the snakes of Staffordshire. . . . She is the enemy, a huge serpent, ages old; she is also a woman who lives at the bottom of a thousand-foot hole that opens into her human habitation. To destroy her requires all the energy and devotion of Adam Salton, another of Stoker's gallant young men. Unlike the hapless Archie of *The Mystery of the Sea*, who had only a pickaxe to aid his manhood, Adam has the help of the most modern explosives. Just the same, fighting the serpent, as he learns, is not easy. Even in her woman's form, she is ferocious: she tears one mongoose to bits with her bare fingers, and shoots another dead. When Oolonga, the black servant of Edgar Caswell, a rich gentleman of unsound mind, too fervently expresses his love for the serpent-woman, she drags him, "her white arms encircling him, down . . . into the noisome depths of her hole." Adam, rushing from the scene, slips "on the steps in some sticky, acrid-smelling mass and falling forward felt his way into the inner room where the well-shaft was not."

That damned well-shaft. It has a "queer smell--yes! Like bilge or a rank swamp. It was distinctly nauseating. . . ." Stoker is insistent:

[The smell] was like nothing that Adam had ever met with. He compared it with all the noxious experiences he had ever had--the drainage of war hospitals, of slaughterhouses, the refuse of dissecting rooms. . . the sourness of chemical waste and the poisonous effluvium of the bilge of a water-logged ship whereon a multitude of rats had been drowned.

I should, perhaps, have said earlier that the hole descends into the ground at a place that used to be called Diana's Grove, where once there had been a Roman temple to that goddess of the hunt and chastity, which may explain why poor

Adam finds "that we are in an exceedingly tight place. Our first difficulty is to know where to begin. I never thought this fighting an antediluvian monster would be such a complicated job."

Adam, like the young men in *Dracula*, has an older advisor, Sir Nathaniel, who in addition to counseling young Adam, is asked by his young protege to propose to the beautiful Mimi for him, a task he performs creditably enough, though why it should have been necessary, Stoker does not make clear. In any case, Sir Nathaniel's advice to Adam is that the serpent, "being feminine, she will probably over-reach herself. Now, Adam, it strikes me that, as we have to protect ourselves and others against feminine nature our strong game will be to play our masculine against her feminine."

Lady Arabella, as a serpent, looks like this: It is so huge that its two eyes make a green light

at the summit of what seemed to be a long white pole, near the top of which were two pendent white masses, like rudimentary arms or fins. . . By degrees, as their eyes got their right focus, they saw an immense towering mass that seemed snowy white. It was tall and thin. . . the hidden mass at the base of the shaft was composed of vast coils of the great serpent's body, forming a base from which the upright mass rose.

Adam and Sir Nathaniel, when they see this thing coming toward them, hurry away.

Inexplicably, Lady Arabella sells Diana's Grove to Adam, and then confides to him that she has always wanted to know the depth of her well hole. She wonders if Adam would mind measuring it for her. "Adam," says Stoker, "was really happy to meet her wishes."

By now, my plot summary is beginning to sound ridiculous, and may already be tasteless. Let me bring the matter to an end by saying that Adam fills the hole with dynamite over which he causes many yards of sea sand to be poured. When a spark caused by lightning explodes his charges, the house at Diana's Grove, with the worm in it collapses:

From [the well hole] agonized shrieks were rising, growing ever more terrible with each second that passed. . . Once, in a sort of lull or pause, the seething contents of the hole rose . . . and Adam saw part of the thin form of Lady Arabella, forced up to the top amid a mass of slime . . .

The explosions, the destruction, go on and on, convulsion after convulsion. Stoker, less tender to his readers than I mean to be to mine, spares no mostly squirming detail that will let us know that Adam has destroyed all that stinking, slimy, nasty stuff once and for all. When the spasms have at last subsided, Adam's aged uncle, who reappears at the book's end for the occasion, says to his nephew and his young bride, "'I think it is quite time you young people departed for that honeymoon of yours!' There was a twinkle in his eye as he spoke."

"Mimi's soft shy glance at her stalwart husband, was sufficient answer."

I don't know. I don't know.

Harry Ludlam, speaking of *The Lair*, says, "The overall feeling was of some deep mystery between the lines--the mystery of the mind of the man who wrote it." Stoker, the elusive, and, I surmise, most lonely mystery maker, died in April of the year following its publication. Ludlam's remark has the ring of an epitaph.

DANIEL FARSON, *THE MAN WHO WROTE DRACULA: A BIOGRAPHY OF BRAM STOKER*. NEW YORK: ST. MARTIN'S PRESS, 1975, 217-24.

. . . by 1911 the pressures were tearing Bram apart. That year marked the publication of his last and strangest book: *The Lair of the White Worm.*

It might have been written under the influence of drugs, a 'trip', along 'the high road to mental disturbance', to use a phrase from the book. At one time I wondered if he was being treated with drugs to alleviate the painful Bright's Disease which corroded him in his last years.

At the very least, *The White Worm* is a literary curiosity. The plot is so bizarre, almost ludicrous, that it is hard to imagine anyone taking it seriously. But on a recent re-reading I became increasingly impressed by the way-out blend of Gothic surrealism; read on that level it is dazzling. Also, without a vestige of humour, it is immensely funny. Significantly, it is Stoker's most popular book after *Dracula* and has been revived in paperback over the years. It too could become a cult, with its rampant symbolism and powerful sense of hallucination.

Adam Salton, a wealthy young Australian, returns to the ancestral home in the cavernous Peak District. There is a sweet old uncle and a dear old friend, Sir Nathaniel de Salis, models of virtue. The other neighbours are downright evil: Edgar Caswall with a face 'so hard, so ruthless, so selfish, so dominant. "God help any," was the common thought "who is under the domination of such a man!"' (Could this be Irving again?) The other neighbour, anxious to ensnare Caswell as a rich husband, is Lady Arabella March, of Diana's Grove, who meets young Adam at the opening of the book when her carriage has broken down. He repairs it for her and notices several black snakes on the ground around him, but Lady Arabella, who slips from her carriage 'with a quick gliding motion' is already among them when he cries out to warn her: 'But there seemed to be no need of warning. The snakes had turned and were wriggling back to the mound as quickly as they could. He laughed to himself behind his teeth as he whispered, "No need to fear there. They seem much more afraid of her than she of them."'

He takes a good look at her, and her dress alone is enough to attract attention:

She was clad in some kind of soft white stuff, which clung close to her form, showing to the full every movement of her sinuous figure. She wore a close-fitting cap of some fine fur of dazzling white. Coiled round her white throat was a large necklace of emeralds, whose profusion of colour dazzled when the sun shone on them. Her voice was peculiar, very low and sweet, and so soft that the dominant note was of sibilation. Her hands, too, were peculiar--long, flexible, white, with a strange movement as of waving gently to and fro.

Plainly, there is something odd about Lady Arabella. At a further meeting, Adam is carrying a mongoose which he has bought to get rid of the snakes; he sees Lady Arabella walking towards him:

Hitherto the mongoose had been quiet, like a playful affectionate kitten; but when the two got close , Adam was horrified to see the mongoose, in a state of the wildest fury, with every hair standing on end, jump from his shoulder and run towards Lady Arabella. It looked so furious and so intent on attack that he called a warning.
'Look out--look out! The animal is furious and means to attack.'
Lady Arabella looked more than ever disdainful and was passing on; the mongoose jumped at her in a furious attack. Adam rushed forward with his stick, the only weapon he had. But just as he got within striking distance, the lady drew out a revolver and shot the animal, breaking his backbone. Not satisfied with this, she poured shot after shot into him till the magazine was exhausted. There was no coolness or hauteur about her now; she seemed more furious even than the animal, her face transformed with hate, and as determined to kill as he had appeared to be. Adam, not knowing exactly what to do, lifted his hat in apology and hurried on to Lesser Hill.

On another walk, Adam notices the body of a dead child by the roadside: 'She was dead, and while examining her, I noticed on her neck some marks that looked like those of teeth.'
There are many such echoes of *Dracula*. The two heroines are Lilla and Mimi, as against Lucy and Mina. Lilla is the virtuous victim; Mimi becomes Adam's wife. Over tea, Lilla has staring-matches with Caswell, apparently tests of power between good and evil. Mimi comes to Lilla's rescue with her own flow of goodliness; Lady A. sides with Caswell. After one of these bouts, immense flocks of birds are summoned, presumably in response to Lilla's dove-like qualities. They arrive in tens of thousands, attracting ornithologists bewildered by this quirk of migration. The birds decimate the land, and so Caswell from his turret flies an immense kite in the shape of a hawk and the land falls quiet. The silence spreads to all the animals:

The fear and restraint which brooded amongst the denizens of the air began to affect all life. Not only did the birds cease to sing or chirp, but the lowing of the cattle ceased in the fields and the varied sounds of life died away. In place of these things was only a soundless gloom, more dreadful, more disheartening, more soul-killing than any concourse of sounds, no matter how full of fear and dread. Pious individuals put up constant prayers for relief from the intolerable solitude. After a little there were signs of universal depression which those who ran might read. One and all, the faces of men and women seemed bereft of vitality, of interest, of thought, and most of all, of hope.

This strange though powerful theme of the birds is really irrelevant, and

Stoker soon tired of it. Adam compares notes with Sir Nathaniel, who tells him the local legend of a monster that lives underground, the great white worm. With a remarkable prophecy of the Loch Ness Monster, Stoker refers to the original plains of England with 'holes of abysmal depth, where any kind and size of antediluvian monster could find a habitat. In places which now we can see from our windows, were mudholes a hundred or more feet deep. Who can tell us when the age of the monsters which flourished in slime came to an end?' Just imagine if such a creature could assume human form! Sir Nathaniel tells Adam of an incident in Lady Arabella's childhood when she wandered into a small wood at night and was found unconscious, having received a 'poisonous bite'. To everyone surprise she makes a complete recovery, but it is noticed afterwards that she has developed 'a terrible craving for cruelty, maiming and injuring birds and small animals--even killing them'. It was hoped that her marriage to Captain March would put a stop to that, but the poor fellow was found shot through the head.

'I have always suspected suicide' [confesses Sir Nathaniel]. 'He may have discovered something--God knows what--or possibly Lady Arabella may herself have killed him. Putting together many small matters that have come to my knowledge, I have come to the conclusion that the foul White Worm obtained control of her body, just as her soul was leaving its earthly tenement--that would explain the sudden revival of energy, the strange and inexplicable craving for maiming and killing. . . God alone knows what poor Captain March discovered--it must have been something too ghastly for human endurance, if my theory is correct that the once beautiful human body of Lady Arabella is under the control of this ghastly White Worm.'

'What was the real identity of the beautiful, reptile-like Lady Arabella March?'--asks the paperback cover. *She* is the great White Worm! They see, one night in the woods, an immense tower of snowy white, tall and thin, with the green light of her eyes above the trees, and vast coils of the serpent's body below. The white colour comes from the china clay in the cavernous soil. Like Count Dracula, the Worm moves with the vital protection of darkness.

Maurice Richardson, talking to me of Dracula stressed that the mood of the manic depressive lifts as evening draws on: 'During the hours of light, the vampire is in his tomb. He's flat out. He's as near dead as can be. Evening comes on, night falls, suddenly he awakens and has magical power of every kind--he can climb down walls, he flies as a bat, and of course sexually he can have his will with anybody he wants.'

By virtue of his job at the Lyceum, Stoker himself must have been a night-animal, with discussions in the Beefsteak Room that lasted till dawn. It is wrong to press this too far, but there may have been something of the manic depressive in Stoker; certainly his night hours cannot have been conducive to regular family life.

Adam and Sir Nathaniel realise they have to destroy the White Worm:

'Such creatures may have grown down as well as up. They *may* have grown into, or something like, human beings. Lady Arabella March is of snake nature. She has committed crimes to our knowledge. She retains something of the vast strength of her primal being--can see in the dark--has the eyes of a snake. She used the nigger, and then dragged him through the snake's hold down to the swamp; she is intent on evil and hates some one we love. Result. . . '

'Yes, the result?'

'First, that Mimi Watford should be taken away at once--then--'

'Yes?'

'The monster must be destroyed.'

'Bravo!'

There is the obstacle of trespassing on private property. 'Lady Arabella, be she woman or snake or devil, owned the ground she moved in, according to British law, and the law is jealous and swift to avenge wrongs done within its ken.' Also, the monster has the unfair advantage of being a woman. 'I never thought this fighting of an antediluvian monster would be such a complicated job,' says Adam, exasperated.

This one is a woman with all a woman's wit, combined with the heartlessness of a cocotte. She has the strength and impregnability of a diplodocus [an extinct herbivorous dinosaur]. We may be sure that in the fight there is before us there will be no semblance of fair play. Also, that our unscrupulous opponent will not betray herself!'

'That is so--being feminine, she will probably over-reach herself. Now Adam, it strikes me that, as we have to protect ourselves and others against feminine nature, our strong game will be to play our masculine against her feminine. Perhaps we had better sleep on it.'

One of the delights of the book is its rampant snobbery. After a wild tea-party during which Lady Arabella first tries to suck Mimi into the well-hole and then attempts to imprison the guests, Mimi's main objection is one of etiquette--'As a social matter, she was disgusted with her for following up the rich landowner--throwing herself at his head so shamelessly.' The landowner, meanwhile, is going mad in his turret. As the climax is reached, there is another of Stoker's great storms: the lightning is attracted by the great kite he is still flying, with a wire reel found in a chest that Mesmer had left to the family. He disappears from the novel, raging against the elements: 'I am greater than any other who is, or was, or shall be. When the Master of Evil took Christ up on a high place and showed Him all the kingdoms of earth, he was doing what he thought no other could do. He was wrong--he forgot ME.'

The prevalence of sexual symbols cannot be denied. 'The dread of snakes,' wrote Freud, 'is monstrously exaggerated in neurotics--all this has a definite sexual meaning.' Chests correspond to 'the female organ, with the obvious symbolism of the lock and key to open it.' Revealingly, Mesmer's chest has no lock or key, though Caswell seems to open it in his sleep. Winding stairs 'are symbolic representations of the sexual act', and the rising kite is one of the most famous and familiar symbols of all. Finally, Stoker's disturbance over sexual intercourse can be seen in his revulsion from the snake's hole, which has to be destroyed. Adam has already laid charges of dynamite, but the whole of

Diana's Grove is consumed by fire when lightning strikes the wire of the kite which Lady Arabella has brought to her home in order to ensnare Caswell and destroy him in the hole. That hole--the smell of which was like nothing that Adam had ever met with. He compares it with all the 'noxious experiences he had ever had--the drainage of war hospitals, of slaughter-houses, the refuse of dissecting rooms. . . the sourness of chemical waste and the poisonous effluvium of the bilge of a water-logged ship whereupon a multitude of rats had been drowned.'

The lightning explodes the charge of dynamite, the house collapses, and they can look down

where the well-hole yawned a deep and narrow circular chasm. From this the agonised shrieks were rising, growing ever more terrible with each second that passed. Some of these fragments were covered with scaled skin as of a gigantic lizard or serpent. Once in a sort of lull or pause, the seething contents of the hole rose, after the manner of a bubbling spring, and Adam saw part of the thin form of Lady Arabella forced to the top amid a mass of slime, and what looked as if it had been a monster torn into shreds. Several times some masses of enormous bulk were forced up and through the well-hole with inconceivable violence, and suddenly expanding as they came into large space, disclosed sections of the White Worm. . . .

Adam, Mimi and Sir Nathaniel return the following day but the turmoil is still not over:

At short irregular intervals the hell-broth in the hole seemed as if boiling up. It rose and fell again and turned over. Showing in fresh form much of the nauseous detail which had been visible earlier. The worst parts were the great masses of the flesh of the monstrous Worm, in all its red and sickening aspect. Such fragments had been bad enough before, but now they were infinitely worse. Corruption comes with startling rapidity to beings whose destruction has been due wholly or in part to lightning--the whole mass seemed to have become all at once corrupt! The whole surface of the fragments, once alive, was covered with insects, worms and vermin of all kinds. The sight was horrible enough, but, with the awful smell added, was simply unbearable. The Worm's hole appeared to breathe forth death in its most repulsive forms.

Surely his obsession with horror and this repetition of sexual symbols indicate that Stoker was disturbed.

'Bram Stoker eludes me,' says Professor Wolf. But, 'In Stoker's own writing a *person* occasionally shows through, or, better, is exposed. Particularly in his later novels (and of course *Dracula*) there obtrudes the raw, harsh presence of a man endowed with nearly inexhaustible energy who is writing over, around, or under what he knows about loneliness and--predominantly--sexual terror.' Referring specifically to *The Lair of the White Worm*, he concludes: 'There is no way to ignore the signs of confusion and loneliness the narrative obtrudes.'

The Lair of the White Worm was published three years after Stoker had written in the *Nineteenth Century* that 'the only emotions which in the long run harm are those arising from sex impulses.'

There is no deceiver like the self-deceiver.

GREGORY A. WALLER, *THE LIVING AND THE UNDEAD: FROM STOKER'S DRACULA TO ROMERO'S DAWN OF THE DEAD.* CHAMPAIGN, ILL: UNIVERSITY OF ILLINOIS PRESS, 1985, 57-60.

Much closer in structure and ideology to *Dracula* is Stoker's last novel, *The Lair of the White Worm* (1911). [1] In both works the appearance of evil in the form of an ancient, thoroughly malevolent threat to specific individuals and by implication to all of England is once again a "blessing in disguise," [2] since it necessitates a human response that ultimately leads to the affirmation and triumph of the good. Certain details of the "bedrock struggle between good and evil" (WW, 56) in *The Lair of the White Worm* have direct analogies with *Dracula*, as the following brief synopsis suggests: Adam Salton, a young man born and raised in Australia, returns to the "heart of the old kingdom of Mercia" (WW, 11)--the ancient center of modern Britain--to meet his long-lost grand-uncle. Adam is instructed in local history, legend, and superstition by an elderly friend of the family, Sir Nathaniel di Salis, and falls in love with and then marries Mimi Watford, a beautiful young woman who combines "strength of character" with "sweetness of disposition" (WW, 129).Together these three people must combat and eventually destroy the evil of both Edgar Caswell, an irredeemably egotistical aristocrat obsessed with acquiring occult knowledge and with exercising his hypnotic power over Mimi's innocent sister, and Lady Arabella March, epitome of the predatory female, who is actually the white worm, an enormous, age-old monster with "no soul and no morals" (WW, 135) that emerges from a "mysterious orifice" in the earth to threaten the modern world (WW, 148).

Like the young men in *Dracula*, Adam Salton is a "willing and attentive pupil" (WW, 19) who is also capable of heroic, selfless action--particularly for the protection of his wife. Mimi Watford, inspired and illuminated by "divine light" (WW. 69) is quite obviously the spiritual sister of Mina Harker; both women demonstrate the necessity for faith in "God's justice" (WW, 186) yet both fully realize that faith must be accompanied by the ability and by the willingness to think and act. Like Adam (and like Stoker's vampire hunters), Mimi is motivated by an "unselfish, unchanging devotion for those she loved" (WW, 192). In their attempt to understand and destroy evil, this young couple is instructed and guided by Sir Nathaniel, the Van Helsing figure in *The Lair of the White Worm*. Sir Nathaniel is learned and experienced, his common sense matched by an overwhelming sense of duty, for he knows what all of Stoker's selfless heroes must realize: that with the gain of knowledge and experience, "our power to help others has grown--and our responsibility in equal proportion" (WW, 163). Evil must be completely destroyed to preserve Mimi and the "common weal" (WW, 74) and to this end, Sir Nathaniel insists that the hunters must "think and work patiently, fearlessly, and unselfishly" (WW, 48).

Just as similar qualities of mind and character link the defenders of the good in *Dracula* and *The Lair of the White Worm*, the embodiments of evil in both novels share the same essential characteristics and even the same purpose. Edgar Caswell, for example, is not a vampire, but his "partly hypnotic, partly mesmeric" powers are in the service of an "inflexible will"(WW, 17). He aspires toward the forbidden knowledge and dominance that Dracula has already achieved, but above all, as Stoker repeatedly emphasizes, Edgar is an aristocrat from a tainted family whose egotism and selfishness know no bounds. Lady Arabella March, motivated by similar desires, is a less sympathetic and less convincing siren than the undead Lucy Westenra. Lady Arabella, as Adam realizes, combines "the heartlessness of a *cocotte* and the want of principle of a suffragette. She has the reserved strength and impregnability of a diplodocus" (WW, 140). Edgar Caswell may represent the dangerous distortion of the "masculine," but Lady Arabella is quite literally the white worm--an antediluvian creature "without heart or consideration for anything or anyone" (WW, 153) that dwells admit the charnel house stench of dank underground caverns, ready to feed upon mankind and pollute the earth.

In the end, all three hunters contribute to the complete eradication of evil--Mimi with her faith, Sir Nathaniel with his knowledge and clear thinking, and Adam with his fearless action and military experience (dynamite is planted in the worm's lair). Yet the redemptive violence must be sparked by a tremendous, "appallingly bright" flash of lightning (WW, 213) which levels the overreaching tower on Edgar's estate and ignites the dynamite. Thus both man's selfless work and the lightning that seems to signify God's burning wrath are necessary for the 'absolute destruction" (WW, 218) of evil. As in *Dracula*, the final triumph is announced and the struggles of the living justified by the sun's "red rays," which bring "relief" and the "promise of a new order of things" (WW. 216) and even reveal that the explosions have unearthed valuable deposits of china clay on Adam's estate. The earth has been freed from the evil legacy of the past and has delivered its material treasures to the worthy. "All's well that ends well," Sir Nathaniel declares to Adam as they turn away from the rotting fragments of the white worm, now overrun with "insects, worms, and vermin of all kinds" (WW, 219-20), and head back "home" for breakfast with Mimi--domesticity and material comforts can now reign supreme. At last, the heroic survivors can, in Leonard Wolf's words, "breathe the humid air of British Decency."[3]

With its death-wielding "mysterious orifice" (the home of the feminine serpent) and its madness-inducing tower (the home of masculine egotism) *The Lair of the White Worm* suggests more than a little about Stoker's personal fears and obsessions. And the characters, narrative structure, and ideology of the novel throw certain elements of *Dracula* into high relief--the role of "God's women" and of the wise, paternal elder, for example, as well as the necessity for the violent destruction of the monster and the equation of excessive egotism with social, moral, sexual, and spiritual evil. Yet, for my purposes, the distinctions between these two novels are even more revealing. Needless to say, the King-Vampire and his brides are far more fearsome and attractive than the various embodiments of evil in *The Lair of the White Worm*. However one evaluates Stoker's literary skills, his Dracula has struck at the heartblood of the popular imagination in the twentieth century. Likewise, though the three interdependent people who constitute the force of good in the later novel share the same degree of commitment and courageous selflessness as Van Helsing, the Harkers, and Lucy's suitors, yet *The Lair of the White Worm* contains none of *Dracula's* insistence on the ritualistic, primitive basis of the community of hunters. Adam, Mimi, and Sir Nathaniel are never tempted by the evil they combat; they are never forced to undertake journeys that completely alienate them from modern society; and their wild work resembles a carefully planned military campaign more than a holy crusade of butchery and mutilation. These defenders of the good are never baptized in blood, and thus they are not rewarded with the birth of new life and with tangible proof that God is merciful as well as wrathful--Mina is redeemed, Mimi has never been tainted. When the smoke clears in *The Lair of the White Worm*, the world has been rendered comfortable, and no prayers of thanksgiving or legends of heroic struggle are necessary. Breakfast can at last be served, and the monstrous evil threat seems in retrospect no more than an irritating interruption.

It is therefore Stoker's presentation both of Dracula and of the group of vampire hunters led by Van Helsing that most clearly distinguishes *Dracula* from *The Lair of the White Worm*. . . . Dracula is not just a vampire, not just an evil predatory aristocrat, but the King-Vampire whose threat extends much further than the single family or the rural village. And for Stoker, neither a solitary hero nor a pair of brave men nor a ruling class alliance can dispose of Dracula; only a newly forged moral community can destroy the King-Vampire.

NOTES

[1] Certain details in Stoker's *The Jewel of the Seven Stars*, like the striking image of the beautiful heroine suddenly appearing in her "white nightdress stained with the blood in which she knelt" (p. 44), call to mind aspects of *Dracula*. But the quasi-detective/adventure story Stoker tells in *The Jewel of the Seven Stars* about an attempt to resurrect a mysterious, beautiful, mummified Egyptian queen shares much less with *Dracula* than does *The Lair of the White Worm* and the stories collected in *Dracula's Guest*.

[2] Bram Stoker, *The Lair of the White Worm* (1911; rpt. New York: Paperback Library, 1966), p. 142. All future references to *The Lair of the White Worm*, abbreviated WW, will be included parenthetically in my text.

[3] Leonard Wolf, *A Dream of Dracula: In Search of the Living Dead* (New York: Popular Library, 1972), p. 254.

Selected Bibliography

Adams, Norman. "Bram Stoker." *Leopard* 2 (June 22, 1976): 8.

"A Girl by the Name of Stephen." Review of *The Gates of Life. New York Times* 13 (August 15, 1908): 448.

Arata, Stephen D. "The Occidental Tourist: *Dracula* and the Anxiety of Reverse Colonization." *Victorian Studies* 33 (Summer 1990): 621-45.

Astle, Richard. "Dracula as Totemic Monster: Lacan, Freud, Oedipus and History." *Sub-Stance* 25 (1980): 98-105.

Auerbach, Nina. *Woman and the Demon: The Life of a Victorian Myth.* Cambridge: Harvard U. Press, 1982.

Barclay, Glen St. John. *Anatomy of Horror: Masters of Occult Fiction.* London: Weidenfeld and Nicolson, 1978.

Bentley, Christopher. "The Monster in the Bedroom: Sexual Symbolism in Bram Stoker's *Dracula*." *Literature and Psychology* 22 (1972): 27-34. (Carter anthology)

Bettany, F.G. "Review of *Personal Reminiscences of Sir Henry Irving*." *Bookman* 31 (November 1906): 92-94.

Bierman, Joseph S. "*Dracula*: Prolonged Childhood Illness and the Oral Triad." *American Imago* 29 (1972): 186-98.

_____. "The Genesis and Dating of *Dracula* from Bram Stoker's Working Notes." *Notes and Queries* 24 (1977): 39-41. (Carter anthology)

"Biographical Studies in Imposture." Review of *Famous Impostors. Dial* 50 (February 1, 1911): 97.

Blinderman, Charles S. "Vampurella: Darwin and Count Dracula." *Massachusetts Review* 21 (1980): 411-28.

Bonewits, Wanda. "Dracula, the Black Christ." *Gnostica* 4 (1975), No. 7.

"Bram Stoker's Book About Irving." Review of *Personal Reminiscences of Henry Irving. New York Times* 11 (October 13, 1906): 674.

"Bram Stoker's Latest Novel." Review of *The Lady of the Shroud. Bookman* 37 (January 1910): 194.

Byers, Thomas B. "Good Men and Monsters: The Defenses of *Dracula*." *Literature and Psychology* 31 (1981), No. 4: 24-31. (Carter anthology)

Carlsen, M.M. "What Stoker Saw: An Introduction to the Literary Vampire." *Folklore Forum* 10 (1977) No. 2: 26-32.

Carter, Margaret L., ed. *Dracula: The Vampire and the Critics.* Ann Arbor: UMI Research Press, 1988.

_____. *Shadow of a Shade: A Survey of Vampirism in Literature.* New York: Gordon Press, 1975.

_____. *Spectre of Delusion? The Supernatural in Gothic Fiction.* Ann Arbor: UMI Research Press, 1987.

Craft, Christopher. "'Kiss Me with Those Red Lips': Gender and Inversion in Bram Stoker's *Dracula*." *Representations* 8 (1984): 107-33. (Carter anthology)

Cranny-Francis, Anne. "Sexual Politics and Political Repression in Bram Stoker's *Dracula*." In *Nineteenth-Century Suspense: From Poe to Conan Doyle,* edited by Clive Bloom, Brian Docherty, Jane Gibb, and Keith Shand. New York: St. Martin's, 1988.

Dalby, Richard. *Bram Stoker: A Bibliography of First Editions.* London: Dracula Press, 1983.

Day, William Patrick. *In the Circles of Fear and Desire: A Study of Gothic Fantasy.* Chicago: University of Chicago Press, 1985.

Demetrakopoulos, Stephanie. "Feminism, Sex Role Exchanges, and Other Subliminal Fantasies in Bram Stoker's *Dracula*." *Frontiers* (1977), 104-13.

Dowse, Robert E. and David Palmer. "'Dracula': the Book of Blood," *Listener* 7 (March 1963).

Drummond, James. "Bram Stoker's Cruden Bay." *Scots Magazine* (April 1976): 23-38.

_____. "Dracula's Castle." *Scotsman* (June 26, 1976).

_____. "The Mistletoe and the Oak." *Scots Magazine* (October 1977).

_____. "The Scottish Play." *Scottish Review* (August 23, 1981).

Dukes, Paul. "*Dracula*: Fact, Legend and Fiction." *History Today* 32 (July 1982): 44-47.

Faig, Kenneth W. Jr. "About Bram." *Romantist* 4-5 (1980-81): 39-40.

Farson, Daniel. *The Man Who Wrote Dracula: A Biography of Bram Stoker.* New York: St. Martin's, 1975.

Fontana, Ernest. "Lombroso's Criminal Man and Stoker's *Dracula*." *Victorian Newsletter* 42 (1972): 20-22. (Carter anthology)

Frayling, Christopher. *The Vampire: Lord Ruthven to Count Dracula.* London: Gollancz, 1978.

Gattegno, Jean. "Folie, Croyance et Fantastique dans 'Dracula'," *Litterature* 8 (December 1972).

Greenway, John. "Seward's Folly: *Dracula* as a Critique of 'Normal Science'." *Stanford Literature Review* 3 (1986): 213-30.

Griffin, Gail B. "'Your Girls That You All Love are Mine': *Dracula* and the Victorian Male Sexual Imagination," *International Journal of Women's Studies* 3 (1980): 454-65. (Carter anthology)

Haining, Peter, ed. *The Dracula Scrapbook.* London: New English Library, 1976.

_____, ed. *Shades of Dracula: The Uncollected Stories of Bram Stoker.* London: Kimber, 1982.

Hatlen, Burton. "The Return of the Repressed/Oppressed in Bram Stoker's *Dracula.*" *Minnesota Review* 15 (1980): 80-97. (Carter anthology)

Hennelly, Mark M., Jr. "*Dracula*: The Gnostic Quest and the Victorian Wasteland." *English Literature in Transition* 20 (1977): 13-26. (Carter anthology)

Hollinger, Veronica. "The Vampire and the Alien: Variations of the Outsider." *Science-Fiction Studies* 16 (July 1989): 145-60.

Hood, Gwenyth. "Sauron and Dracula," *Mythlore* 52 (1987): 11-17. (Carter anthology)

Howes, Marjorie. "The Mediation of the Feminine: Bisexuality, Homoerotic Desire, and Self-Expression in Bram Stoker's *Dracula.*" *Texas Studies in Literature and Language* 30 (Spring 1988): 104-119.

"Irving as Man and Actor." Review of *Personal Reminiscences of Henry Irving. Nation* 83 (October 18, 1906): 334-35.

Irving, Laurence. *Henry Irving: The Actor and his World.* London: Faber and Faber, 1951.

Jackson, Rosemary. *Fantasy: The Literature of Subversion.* London: Methuen, 1981.

Jann, Rosemary. "Saved by Science? The Mixed Messages of Stoker's *Dracula.*" *Texas Studies in Literature and Language* 31 (Summer 1989): 273-87.

Johnson, Alan. "Bent and Broken Necks: Signs of Design in Stoker's *Dracula.*" *Victorian Newsletter* 72 (1987): 17-24. (Carter anthology)

_____. "'Dual Life': The Status of Women in Stoker's *Dracula.*" *Tennessee Studies in Literature* 27 (1984): 20-39.

Johnson, Roger. "The Bloofer Ladies." *Dracula Journals* 1 (1982), No. 4.

King, Stephen. *Danse Macabre.* New York: Berkeley, 1981.

Kirtley, Bacil F. "Dracula, the Monastic Chronicles and Slavic Folk-lore." *Midwestern Folklore* 6 (1956): 133-39. (Carter anthology)

Leatherdale, Clive. *Dracula: The Novel and the Legend.* Wellingborough, Northamptonshire: Aquarian, 1985.

Lovecraft, H.P. *Supernatural Horror in Literature.* 1939. Reprint. New York: Dover, 1973.

Ludlam, Harry. *A Biography of Dracula: The Life Story of Bram Stoker.* London: Foulsham, 1962.

Martin, Philip. "The Vampire in the Looking-Glass: Reflection and Projection in Bram Stoker's *Dracula.*" In *Nineteenth-Century Suspense: From Poe to Conan Doyle,* edited by Clive Bloom, Brian Docherty, Jane Gibb and Keith Shand. New York: St. Martin's, 1988.

MacAndrew, Elizabeth. *The Gothic Tradition in Fiction.* New York: Columbia University Press, 1979.

MacArthur, James. "Books and Bookmen." Review of *The Jewel of Seven Stars. Harper's Magazine* 48 (February 20, 1904): 276.

MacGillivray, Royce. "'Dracula': Bram Stoker's Spoiled Masterpiece." *Queen's Quarterly* 79 (1972): 518-27.

MacNally, Raymond T. and Radu Florescu. *In Search of Dracula*. Connecticut: New York Graphic Society, 1972.

_____. *The Essential Dracula*. New York: Mayflower, 1979.

MacNally, Raymond T. *Dracula was a Woman*. London: Hale, 1984.

Murphy, Brian. "The Nightmare of the Dark: The Gothic Legacy of Count Dracula." *Odyssey* 1 (1976): 9-15.

"Obituary: Mr. Bram Stoker." *Times* (April 22, 1912): 15d.

Oinas, Felix. "East European Vampires and Dracula." *Journal of Popular Culture* 16 (1982): 108-16.

Osborne, Charles, ed. *The Bram Stoker Bedside Companion*. London: Quartet, 1972.

Phillips, Robert. "The Agony and the Ecstasy: A Jungian Analysis of Two Vampire Novels, Meredith Ann Pierce's *The Darkangel* and Bram Stoker's *Dracula*." *West Virginia University Philological Papers* 31 (1986): 10-19.

Pick, Daniel. "Terrors of the Night: *Dracula* and 'Degeneration' in the Late Nineteenth Century," *Critical Quarterly* 30 (Winter 1988): 71-87.

Purvis, W.F. "Bram Stoker's Latest Novel." Review of *The Lady of the Shroud*. *The Bookman* (January 1910): 194.

Raible, Christopher Gist. "Dracula: Christian Heretic." *Christian Century* 96 (1979): 103-4. (Carter anthology)

Review of *Dracula*. *Athenaeum* 109 (June 26, 1897): 835.

Review of *Dracula*. *Bookman* 12 (August 1987): 129.

Review of *Dracula*. *Punch* (June 26, 1897).

Review of *Dracula*. *Spectator* 79 (July 31, 1897): 150.

Review of *Famous Impostors*. *Punch* 140 (February 22, 1911): 144.

Review of *Famous Impostors*. *Athenaeum* 1 (February 18, 1911): 184-85.

Review of *Famous Impostors*. *Bookman* 40 (Spring 1911): 8-9.

Review of *Famous Impostors* . *Independent* 70 (January 12, 1911): 102.

Review of *Famous Impostors*. *Literary Digest* 42 (April 1, 1911): 640-41.

Review of *Famous Impostors*. *Saturday Review* 111 (April 1911): 400.

Review of *Famous Impostors*. *Spectator* 106 (January 28, 1911): 153.

Review of *Miss Betty*. *Athenaeum* 111 (March 26, 1898): 401.

Review of *Miss Betty*. *Bookman* 14 (April 1898): 21.

Review of *Miss Betty*. *Punch* 114 (March 5, 1898): 105.

Review of *Personal Reminiscences of Sir Henry Irving*. *Academy* 71 (October 13, 1906): 369-70.

Review of *Personal Reminiscences of Sir Henry Irving*. *Blackwood's Magazine* 180 (November 1906): 613-21.

Review of *Personal Reminiscences of Sir Henry Irving*. *Putnam's* 1 (December 1906): 382.

Review of *Personal Reminiscences of Sir Henry Irving*. *Dial* 41 (November 1, 1906): 276-78.

Review of *Personal Reminiscences of Sir Henry Irving*. *Outlook* 84 (November 24, 1906): 713-16.

Review of *The Gates of Life*. *Bookman* 28 (September 1908): 69.

Review of *The Gates of Life*. *Nation* 87 (August 20, 1908): 163.

Review of *The Lair of the White Worm*. *Times Literary Supplement* (November 16, 1911): 466.

Review of *The Man*. *Bookman* 29 (October 1905): 38-39.

Review of *The Man*. *Punch* 129 (September 27, 1905): 234.

Review of *The Mystery of the Sea*. *Bookman* 23 (October 1902): 32.

Review of *The Mystery of the Sea*. *Dial* 32 (1902): 391-92.

Review of *The Mystery of the Sea*. *Punch* 123 (August 20, 1902): 110.

Review of *The Shoulder of Shasta*. *Athenaeum* 106 (November 16, 1895): 677.

Review of *The Snake's Pass*. *Athenaeum* 96 (December 20, 1890): 85.

Review of *The Snake's Pass*. *Punch* 99 (December 6, 1890): 269.

Review of *The Watter's Mou'*. *Athenaeum* (February 23, 1895).

Review of *The Watter's Mou'*. *Nation* 62 (February 27, 1896): 183.

Review of *Under the Sunset*. *Punch* (December 3, 1881).

Review of *Under the Sunset*. *Spectator* (November 12, 1881).

Review of *Under the Sunset*. *Academy* (December 10, 1881).

Richardson, Maurice. "The Psychoanalysis of Ghost Stories." *Twentieth Century* 166 (1959): 419-31.

Roberts, Bette B. "Victorian Values in the Narration of *Dracula*." *Studies in Weird Fiction* 6 (Fall 1989): 10-14.

Roth, Phyllis A. *Bram Stoker*. Boston: Twayne, 1982.

_____. "Suddenly Sexual Women in Bram Stoker's *Dracula*." *Literature and Psychology* 27 (1977): 113-21. (Carter anthology)

Seed, David. "The Narrative Method of *Dracula*." *Nineteenth-Century Fiction* 40 (1985): 61-75. (Carter anthology).

Senf, Carol A. "*Dracula*: The Unseen Face in the Mirror." *Journal of Narrative Technique* 9 (1979): 160-70. (Carter anthology)

_____. "*Dracula*: Stoker's Response to the New Woman," *Victorian Studies* 26 (1982): 33-49.

_____. "*The Lady of the Shroud*: Stoker's Successor to *Dracula*." *Essays in Arts and Sciences* (1990): 82-96.

Shuster, Seymour. "*Dracula* and Surgically Induced Trauma in Children." *British Journal of Medical Psychology* 46 (1973): 259-70.

"Sir Henry Irving and His Kingly Circle." Review of *Personal Reminiscences of Sir Henry Irving*. *Current Literature* 41 (December 1906): 659-61.

"Some Famous Impostors." Review of *Famous Impostors*. *New York Times* 16 (February 26, 1911): 107.

Stein, Gerard. "'Dracula' ou la Circulation du 'Sans'." *Litterature* 8 (December 1972).

Stevenson, John Allen. "A Vampire in the Mirror: The Sexuality of *Dracula*." *PMLA* 103 (March 1988): 139-49.

Street, Douglas Oliver. "Bram Stoker's 'Under the Sunset' with Introductory Biographical and Critical Material" Ph.D. diss., University of Nebraska--Lincoln, 1977.

Temple, Philip. "The Origins of *Dracula*." *Times Literary Supplement* 4205 (1983): 1216.

Thornburg, Thomas Ray. "The Quester and the Castle: the Gothic Novel as Myth, with Special Reference to Bram Stoker's *Dracula*." Ph.D. diss. Ball State University, 1970.

Towse, I. Ranken. "Bram Stoker's 'Irving'." Review of *Personal Reminiscences of Sir Henry Irving*. *Bookman* 24 (December 1906): 367-71.

Twitchell, James B. *Dreadful Pleasures: An Anatomy of Modern Horror*. New York: Oxford University Press, 1985.

_____. *The Living Dead: The Vampire in Romantic Literature*. Durham: Duke University Press, 1981.

_____. "The Vampire Myth." *American Imago* 31 (1980): 83-92. (Carter anthology)

Varma, Devendra P. "Dracula's Voyage: From Pontus to Hellespontus." Eighteenth National Convention, American Association of Slavic Studies, New Orleans 21 November 1986. (Carter anthology)

_____. "The Genesis of *Dracula*: A Re-Visit." In *The Vampire's Bedside Companion*, edited by Peter Underwood. London: Frewin., 1975. (Carter anthology)

Wall, Geoffrey. "'Different from Writing': *Dracula* in 1897." *Literature and History* 10 (1984): 15-23.

Waller, Gregory A. *The Living and the Undead: From Stoker's Dracula to Romero's Dawn of the Dead*. Champaign: University of Illinois Press, 1985.

Walsh, Thomas P. "Dracula: Logos and Myth." *Research Studies* 47 (1979): 229-37.

Wasson, Richard. "The Politics of *Dracula*." *English Literature in Transition* 9 (1966): 24-27. (Carter anthology)

Weissman, Judith. "Women as Vampires: *Dracula* as a Victorian Novel." *Midwest Quarterly* 18 (1977): 392-405. (Carter anthology)

Wolf, Leonard, ed. *The Annotated Dracula*. New York: Potter, 1975.

_____. *A Dream of Dracula*. Little, Brown, 1972.

Index

About the Editor

CAROL A. SENF is an Associate Professor in the School of Literature, Communication, and Culture at the Georgia Institute of Technology. She has written a book on the vampire in nineteenth-century British fiction, and her articles have appeared in *College English,* the *New Orleans Review,* and *Victorian Studies.*

ISBN 0-313-28527-6

HARDCOVER BAR CODE